Pakistan's Nuclear Policy

In May 1998, in reaction to India's nuclear weapons tests, Pakistan tested six nuclear weapons. Following this, the country opted for a policy of minimum deterrence, and within a year Pakistan had altered its policy stance by adding the modifier of minimum 'credible' deterrence. This book looks at how this seemingly innocuous shift seriously impacted on Pakistan's nuclear policy direction and whether the concept of minimum has lost its significance in the South Asian region's changed/changing strategic environment.

After providing a brief historical background exploring why and how Pakistan carried out the nuclear development program, the book questions why Pakistan could not sustain the minimum deterrence that it had conceptualized in the immediate aftermath of the 1998 test. It examines the conceptual theoretical framework of the essentials of minimum deterrence in order to question whether Pakistan's nuclear policy remained consistent with this, as well as to discover the rudimentary factors that are responsible for the inconsistencies with regard to minimum deterrence conceived in this study. The book goes on to look at the policy options that Pakistan had after acquiring the nuclear capability, and what the rationale was for selecting minimum deterrence. The book not only highlights Pakistan deterrent force building, but also analyzes closely Pakistan's doctrinal posture of first use option. Furthermore, it examines the policy towards arms control and disarmament, and discusses whether these individual policy orientations are consistent with the minimum deterrence.

Conceptually providing a deeper understanding of Pakistan's post-1998 nuclear policy, this book critically examines whether the minimum deterrence conceived could be sustained both at the theoretical and operational levels. It will be a useful contribution in the field of Nuclear Policy, Security Studies, Asian Politics, Proliferation/Non-Proliferation Studies, and Peace Studies. This book will be of interest to policy makers, scholars, and students of nuclear policy, nuclear proliferation and arms control related research.

Zafar Khan specializes in Strategic and Nuclear Studies in the Department of Politics and International Studies, University of Hull, UK. He previously lectured at the Department of International Relations University of Balochistan, Pakistan. Currently, he serves as an Assistant Professor Department of Strategic Studies, National Defense University Islamabad. His works have appeared in various academic journals such as *Contemporary Security Policy*, *Australian Journal of International Affairs*, *Cambridge Review of International Affairs*, *Korean Journal of Defense Analysis*, *Defense and Security Analysis*, *Defense Studies*, *Comparative Strategy*, *IPRI Journal*, *Strategic Analysis* and *Balochistan Review*.

Routledge Contemporary South Asia Series

1 **Pakistan**
Social and cultural transformations in a Muslim nation
Mohammad A. Qadeer

2 **Labor, Democratization and Development in India and Pakistan**
Christopher Candland

3 **China–India Relations**
Contemporary dynamics
Amardeep Athwal

4 **Madrasas in South Asia**
Teaching terror?
Jamal Malik

5 **Labor, Globalization and the State**
Workers, women and migrants confront neoliberalism
Edited by Debdas Banerjee and Michael Goldfield

6 **Indian Literature and Popular Cinema**
Recasting classics
Edited by Heidi R.M. Pauwels

7 **Islamist Militancy in Bangladesh**
A complex web
Ali Riaz

8 **Regionalism in South Asia**
Negotiating cooperation, institutional structures
Kishore C. Dash

9 **Federalism, Nationalism and Development**
India and the Punjab economy
Pritam Singh

10 **Human Development and Social Power**
Perspectives from South Asia
Ananya Mukherjee Reed

11 **The South Asian Diaspora**
Transnational networks and changing identities
Edited by Rajesh Rai and Peter Reeves

12 **Pakistan–Japan Relations**
Continuity and change in economic relations and security interests
Ahmad Rashid Malik

13 **Himalayan Frontiers of India**
Historical, geo-political and strategic perspectives
K. Warikoo

14 **India's Open-Economy Policy**
Globalism, rivalry, continuity
Jalal Alamgir

15 **The Separatist Conflict in Sri Lanka**
Terrorism, ethnicity, political economy
Asoka Bandarage

16 **India's Energy Security**
Edited by Ligia Noronha and Anant Sudarshan

17 **Globalization and the Middle Classes in India**
The social and cultural impact of neoliberal reforms
Ruchira Ganguly-Scrase and Timothy J. Scrase

18 **Water Policy Processes in India**
Discourses of power and resistance
Vandana Asthana

19 **Minority Governments in India**
The puzzle of elusive majorities
Csaba Nikolenyi

20 **The Maoist Insurgency in Nepal**
Revolution in the twenty-first century
Edited by Mahendra Lawoti and Anup K. Pahari

21 **Global Capital and Peripheral Labour**
The history and political economy of plantation workers in India
K. Ravi Raman

22 **Maoism in India**
Reincarnation of ultra-left wing extremism in the twenty-first century
Bidyut Chakrabarty and Rajat Kujur

23 **Economic and Human Development in Contemporary India**
Cronyism and fragility
Debdas Banerjee

24 **Culture and the Environment in the Himalaya**
Arjun Guneratne

25 **The Rise of Ethnic Politics in Nepal**
Democracy in the margins
Susan I. Hangen

26 **The Multiplex in India**
A cultural economy of urban leisure
Adrian Athique and Douglas Hill

27 **Tsunami Recovery in Sri Lanka**
Ethnic and regional dimensions
Dennis B. McGilvray and Michele R. Gamburd

28 **Development, Democracy and the State**
Critiquing the Kerala model of development
K. Ravi Raman

29 **Mohajir Militancy in Pakistan**
Violence and transformation in the Karachi conflict
Nichola Khan

30 **Nationbuilding, Gender and War Crimes in South Asia**
Bina D'Costa

31 **The State in India after Liberalization**
Interdisciplinary perspectives
Edited by Akhil Gupta and K. Sivaramakrishnan

32 **National Identities in Pakistan**
The 1971 war in contemporary Pakistani fiction
Cara Cilano

33 **Political Islam and Governance in Bangladesh**
Edited by Ali Riaz and C. Christine Fair

34 **Bengali Cinema**
'An other nation'
Sharmistha Gooptu

35 **NGOs in India**
The challenges of women's empowerment and accountability
Patrick Kilby

36 **The Labour Movement in the Global South**
Trade unions in Sri Lanka
S. Janaka Biyanwila

37 **Building Bangalore**
Architecture and urban transformation in India's Silicon Valley
John C. Stallmeyer

38 **Conflict and Peacebuilding in Sri Lanka**
Caught in the peace trap?
Edited by Jonathan Goodhand, Jonathan Spencer and Benedict Korf

39 **Microcredit and Women's Empowerment**
A case study of Bangladesh
Amunui Faraizi, Jim McAllister and Taskinur Rahman

40 **South Asia in the New World Order**
The role of regional cooperation
Shahid Javed Burki

41 **Explaining Pakistan's Foreign Policy**
Escaping India
Aparna Pande

42 **Development-induced Displacement, Rehabilitation and Resettlement in India**
Current issues and challenges
Edited by Sakarama Somayaji and Smrithi Talwar

43 **The Politics of Belonging in India**
Becoming Adivasi
Edited by Daniel J. Rycroft and Sangeeta Dasgupta

44 **Re-Orientalism and South Asian Identity Politics**
The oriental Other within
Edited by Lisa Lau and Ana Cristina Mendes

45 **Islamic Revival in Nepal**
Religion and a new nation
Megan Adamson Sijapati

46 **Education and Inequality in India**
A classroom view
Manabi Majumdar and Jos Mooij

47 **The Culturalization of Caste in India**
Identity and inequality in a multicultural age
Balmurli Natrajan

48 **Corporate Social Responsibility in India**
Bidyut Chakrabarty

49 **Pakistan's Stability Paradox**
Domestic, regional and international dimensions
Edited by Ashutosh Misra and Michael E. Clarke

50 **Transforming Urban Water Supplies in India**
The role of reform and partnerships in globalization
Govind Gopakumar

51 **South Asian Security**
Twenty-first century discourse
Sagarika Dutt and Alok Bansal

52 **Non-discrimination and Equality in India**
Contesting boundaries of social justice
Vidhu Verma

53 **Being Middle-class in India**
A way of life
Henrike Donner

54 **Kashmir's Right to Secede**
A critical examination of contemporary theories of secession
Matthew J. Webb

55 **Bollywood Travels**
Culture, diaspora and border crossings in popular Hindi cinema
Rajinder Dudrah

56 **Nation, Territory, and Globalization in Pakistan**
Traversing the margins
Chad Haines

57 **The Politics of Ethnicity in Pakistan**
The Baloch, Sindhi and Mohajir ethnic movements
Farhan Hanif Siddiqi

58 **Nationalism and Ethnic Conflict**
Identities and mobilization after 1990
Edited by Mahendra Lawoti and Susan Hangen

59 **Islam and Higher Education**
Concepts, challenges and opportunities
Marodsilton Muborakshoeva

60 **Religious Freedom in India**
Sovereignty and (anti) conversion
Goldie Osuri

61 **Everyday Ethnicity in Sri Lanka**
Up-country Tamil identity politics
Daniel Bass

62 **Ritual and Recovery in Post-Conflict Sri Lanka**
Eloquent bodies
Jane Derges

63 **Bollywood and Globalisation**
The global power of popular Hindi cinema
Edited by David J. Schaefer and Kavita Karan

64 **Regional Economic Integration in South Asia**
Trapped in conflict?
Amita Batra

65 **Architecture and Nationalism in Sri Lanka**
The trouser under the cloth
Anoma Pieris

66 **Civil Society and Democratization in India**
Institutions, ideologies and interests
Sarbeswar Sahoo

67 **Contemporary Pakistani Fiction in English**
Idea, nation, state
Cara N. Cilano

68 **Transitional Justice in South Asia**
A study of Afghanistan and Nepal
Tazreena Sajjad

69 **Displacement and Resettlement in India**
The human cost of development
Hari Mohan Mathur

70 **Water, Democracy and Neoliberalism in India**
The power to reform
Vicky Walters

71 **Capitalist Development in India's Informal Economy**
Elisabetta Basile

72 **Nation, Constitutionalism and Buddhism in Sri Lanka**
Roshan de Silva Wijeyeratne

73 **Counterinsurgency, Democracy, and the Politics of Identity in India**
From warfare to welfare?
Mona Bhan

74 **Enterprise Culture in Neoliberal India**
Studies in youth, class, work and media
Edited by Nandini Gooptu

75 **The Politics of Economic Restructuring in India**
Economic governance and state spatial rescaling
Loraine Kennedy

76 **The Other in South Asian Religion, Literature and Film**
Perspectives on Otherism and Otherness
Edited by Diana Dimitrova

77 **Being Bengali**
At home and in the world
Edited by Mridula Nath Chakraborty

78 **The Political Economy of Ethnic Conflict in Sri Lanka**
Nikolaos Biziouras

79 **Indian Arranged Marriages**
A social psychological perspective
Tulika Jaiswal

80 **Writing the City in British Asian Diasporas**
Edited by Seán McLoughlin, William Gould, Ananya Jahanara Kabir and Emma Tomalin

81 **Post-9/11 Espionage Fiction in the US and Pakistan**
Spies and 'terrorists'
Cara Cilano

82 **Left Radicalism in India**
Bidyut Chakrabarty

83 **'Nation-State' and Minority Rights in India**
Comparative perspectives on Muslim and Sikh identities
Tanweer Fazal

84 **Pakistan's Nuclear Policy**
A minimum credible deterrence
Zafar Khan

85 **Imagining Muslims in South Asia and the Diaspora**
Secularism, religion, representations
Claire Chambers and Caroline Herbert

86 **Indian Foreign Policy in Transition**
Relations with South Asia
Arijit Mazumdar

87 **Corporate Social Responsibility and Development in Pakistan**
Nadeem Malik

Pakistan's Nuclear Policy
A minimum credible deterrence

Zafar Khan

LONDON AND NEW YORK

First published 2015 by Routledge

2 Park Square, Milton Park, Abingdon, Oxfordshire OX14 4RN
711 Third Avenue, New York, NY 10017

Routledge is an imprint of the Taylor & Francis Group, an informa business

First issued in paperback 2017

Copyright © 2015 Zafar Khan

The right of Zafar Khan to be identified as author of this work has been asserted by him in accordance with sections 77 and 78 of the Copyright, Designs and Patents Act 1988.

All rights reserved. No part of this book may be reprinted or reproduced or utilised in any form or by any electronic, mechanical, or other means, now known or hereafter invented, including photocopying and recording, or in any information storage or retrieval system, without permission in writing from the publishers.

Notice:
Product or corporate names may be trademarks or registered trademarks, and are used only for identification and explanation without intent to infringe.

British Library Cataloguing in Publication Data
A catalogue record for this book is available from the British Library

Library of Congress Cataloging in Publication Data
Khan, Zafar, 1977- author.
  Pakistan's nuclear policy : a minimum credible deterrence / Zafar Khan. – Edition 1st.
      pages ; cm. – (Routledge contemporary South Asia series ; 84)
  1. Nuclear weapons–Pakistan. 2. Nuclear weapons–Government policy–Pakistan. 3. Deterrence (Strategy) 4. Nuclear arms control–South Asia. I. Title. II. Series: Routledge contemporary South Asia series ; 84.
  U264.5.P18K436 2015
  355.02'17095491–dc23
              2014002646

ISBN: 978-1-138-77879-5 (hbk)
ISBN: 978-1-138-47606-6 (pbk)

Typeset in Times New Roman
by Taylor & Francis Books

To Professor Bhumitra Chakma

Contents

	List of illustrations	xiv
	Acknowledgements	xv
	List of abbreviations	xviii
1	Introduction: the making of Pakistan's post-1998 nuclear policy	1
2	Historical analysis of Pakistan's nuclear development programme	19
3	Pakistan's rationale of minimum deterrence: why the minimum?	38
4	Pakistan's policy of minimum credible deterrence: why minimum is not the minimum?	54
5	Pakistan's nuclear force building	72
6	Pakistan's doctrine of nuclear first use	88
7	Pakistan's policy of arms control and disarmament: a call for an arms control regime in South Asia	113
8	Conclusion: a call for an actual minimum	130
	Bibliography	144
	Index	173

List of illustrations

Figures

3.1	The NCA	45
3.2	The SPD	46

Tables

1.1	The conceptual characters of minimum deterrence vs. deterrence via assured destruction	7
5.1	Pakistan's nuclear-capable aircraft	78
5.2	Pakistan's missile forces	79

Acknowledgements

First and the foremost, I would like to acknowledge fully the in-depth expertise and knowledge of my principal supervisor Dr Bhumitra Chakma on the subject of Pakistan's nuclear weapons programme and its policy orientation. This supported me a lot in crafting this project. Dr Chakma, who is the author of several books on South Asian nuclear studies, remained a great asset during my PhD studies. I acknowledge that without Dr Chakma's supervisory assistance and his strong conceptual and theoretical understanding on the subject of this research, this study could not possibly have reached a successful completion. Put simply, I owe Dr Chakma greatly for his intellectual support in pointing my PhD studies in the right direction, which I needed. In the pitch darkness, when I was about to falter, Dr Chakma was a beacon of light to direct my successful completion of this study. Indeed, he guided me from the basics of Pakistan's nuclear weapons programme to the higher conceptual pillars of Pakistan's post-1998 nuclear policy via his strong intellectual horizon. This was an asset in my contribution to the field of Pakistan's nuclear weapons programme in general, and nuclear policy of other nuclear weapon states in particular.

My thanks also to the Higher Education Commission (HEC) Pakistan for providing me with a scholarship for my MSc and PhD studies in the UK. In addition, there are several policy institutes both in Pakistan and the UK and many individuals whose time and support cannot be ignored. I thank the key policy institutes in Pakistan such as the Islamabad Policy Research Institute (IPRI), the Institute of Policy Studies (IPS), Jinnah Academy Islamabad, the Institute of Strategic Studies Islamabad (ISSI), the Institute of Regional Studies (IRS), the South Asian Strategic Stability Institute (SASSI), and the Centre for International Strategic Studies (CISS). All these institutes allowed me access to the data and enabled me to meet key respondents in relation to my project. My thanks also to the Strategic Plans Division (SPD) in Rawalpindi, Pakistan, which gave me the time to interact with key officials, including Khalid Banuri, Adil Sultan and Zafar Ali, who clarified my conceptual understanding of Pakistan's post-1998 nuclear policy. Their intellectual and academic interaction and contribution on the subject were more fruitful than I could have expected. My thanks also go to key officials within

Pakistan's Foreign Ministry, Ambassador Tariq Osman Hyder, Usman Iqbal Jadoon and Dr Aman Rahid, whose expertise on arms control and disarmament, including Pakistan's policy of minimum deterrence, were immensely beneficial to my understanding of Pakistan's nuclear policy.

I also acknowledge both in-service and retired Pakistani officials who served Pakistan in key positions. The opportunity to interview them enabled me to gain a better understanding of Pakistan's post-1998 nuclear policy: posturing for a minimum credible deterrence. Amongst these are Feroz Hassan Khan, a former director within SPD now teaching in the USA, who is the author of a recent book on Pakistan's nuclear weapons programme, *Eating Grass: The Making of the Pakistani Bomb*; a former Pakistani foreign minister, Abdul Sattar, whose key and often-cited article "Securing the Nuclear Peace" has become the starting point for any scholarship on Pakistan's nuclear policy; retired Ambassador Ali Sarwar Naqvi; and many other officials who wished to remain anonymous and contributed towards my project. I also thank Dr Zulfqar Khan, a nuclear policy analyst working within Pakistan's Ministry of Defence, interaction with whom I found useful in various aspects of my research.

I extend my thanks to the International Institute for Strategic Studies (IISS), London, which allowed me to meet senior research fellows and provided me with the opportunity to access documents on military/nuclear forces of the world in relation to Pakistan's force building. Also, I thank the IISS for allowing me to attend an important and valuable presentation by Pakistani Ambassador Zamir Akram, a permanent representative of Pakistan to the United Nations office in Geneva. It was thought provoking and beneficial to my research.

Moreover, my deepest gratitude goes to Professor Masoom Yasinzai, vice-chancellor, and his administration at Quaid-i-Azam University, Islamabad, who provided me with comfortable accommodation when I was worried about financial hardship. I also thank a number of leading academicians and nuclear policy experts, such as Dr Riffat Hussein, former Foreign Secretary Shamshad Ahmed, retired General Talat Masood, Professor Zafar Iqbal Cheema, Professor Pervez Iqbal Cheema, Dr Zafar Nawaz Jaspal, Dr Rizwana Abbasi, Dr Noman Sattar, Dr Mansoor Ahmed, retired Brigadier Ghulam Mujadidd, retired Ambassador Tariq Fatemi, Dr Maria Sultan, Dr Shireen M. Mizari and Dr Meleeha Lodi – just a few amongst others in connection to Pakistan's nuclear weapons programme and policy. Unfortunately, some of them were unable to meet me because of abrupt changes in schedule. I acknowledge the support of the National Defence University, Islamabad, which allowed me to attend the library and meet key respondents within the NDU.

I thank my family members and friends who supported me both morally and financially in the successful completion of this project. I also thank the University of Hull, which provided me with a comfortable study environment and research facilities in which to complete this project. I thank Dr Thomas Kane, Professor Rudiger Wurzel, Justin Morris (HoD), the Department of

Politics and International Studies, the Graduate School, and the University of Hull Student Support Services for their support of my PhD studies.

Finally, I extend my special and heartfelt gratitude to both my wife, Aisha Naz, and my daughter, Maryam Khan, who supported and strengthened me throughout my PhD studies. They remained patient with me amidst my critical hours of study and financial hardship. My future belongs to them.

List of abbreviations

ABM	anti-ballistic missiles
ACR	arms control regime
AEC	Atomic Energy Council
ALCM	air-launched cruise missile
ARC	Atomic Research Committee
BJP	Bharatiya Janata Party
BMD	ballistic missile defence
CBMs	confidence-building measures
C4ISR	command, control, communications, computers, intelligence, surveillance and reconnaissance
CCCCIISR	Computer, Command, Control, Communications, Information, Intelligence, Surveillance and Reconaissance
CD	Conference on Disarmament
CENTO	Central Treaty Organization
CIA	Central Intelligence Agency
CSD	cold start doctrine
CTBT	Comprehensive Test Ban Treaty
DCC	Development Control Committee
ECC	Employment Control Committee
EU	European Union
FAS	Federation of American Scientists
FMCT	Fissile Material Cut-off Treaty
FU	first use
GZ	Global Zero
HEU	highly enriched uranium
IAEA	International Atomic Energy Agency
ICBM	intercontinental ballistic missiles
IISS	International Institute for Strategic Studies
IOR	Indian Ocean Region
IPFM	International Panel on Fissile Materials
ISPR	Inter-Services Public Relations
KANUPP	Karachi Nuclear Power Project
LOC	line of control

List of abbreviations xix

MCD	minimum credible deterrence
MD	minimum deterrence
MTCR	Missile Technology Control Regime
MW	megawatt
NATO	North Atlantic Treaty Organization
NCA	National Command Authority
NDMD	non-deployed minimum deterrence
NFU	no first use
NPR	nuclear posture review
NPT	Treaty on the Non-Proliferation of Nuclear Weapons, Non-Proliferation Treaty
NSG	Nuclear Suppliers Group
PAEC	Pakistan Atomic Energy Commission
PAF	Pakistan Air Force
PAROS	Prevention of an Arms Race in Outer Space
PINSTECH	Pakistan Institute of Nuclear Science and Technology
PN	Pakistan Navy
PNE	peaceful nuclear explosion
PPP	Pakistan People's Party
PTBT	Partial Test Ban Treaty
R&D	research and development
SAARC	South Asian Association for Regional Cooperation
SASSI	South Asian Strategic Studies Institute
SEATO	Southeast Asia Treaty Organization
SFC	Strategic Forces Command
SLBM	submarine-launched ballistic missile
SPD	Strategic Plans Division
TNW	tactical nuclear weapons
UK	United Kingdom
UN	United Nations
UNGA	United Nations General Assembly
UNIDR	United Nations Institute for Disarmament Research
UNSC	United Nations Security Council
US	United States
USSR	Union of Soviet Socialist Republics

1 Introduction
The making of Pakistan's post-1998 nuclear policy

Introduction

Pakistan tested six nuclear weapons on 28 and 30 May 1998 in reaction to India's nuclear tests on 11 and 13 May. Immediately after the nuclear tests, Pakistan adopted a nuclear policy of minimum deterrence. However, it could not sustain this policy in subsequent years.[1] In making this policy shift, Islamabad added the term 'credible' within its original stance of 'minimum deterrence'.[2] The question, therefore, is: why Pakistan gradually shifted from minimum deterrence it initially conceptualized to a broader policy orientation; that is, minimum credible deterrence? This book explains the puzzle in Pakistan's nuclear policy in light of theoretical framework of essentials of minimum deterrence.

Prior to becoming an overt nuclear weapon state, Pakistan's covert nuclear weapons programme was conceptualized as a 'non-weaponized', 'recessed', 'opaque' and 'existential' deterrent.[3] During the period of nuclear opacity, Pakistan, unlike the established nuclear weapon states,[4] lacked a coherent nuclear structure and doctrinal posture that would guide its nuclear stewardship. Stephen Cohen, an eminent specialist on South Asian affairs, stated that 'a wide range of nuclear and missile programs has been authorised, started, and allowed to slowly mature, without a clear policy decision about their consequences'.[5] During the pre-test era, it is not clear how Pakistani security planners formulated Pakistan's nuclear policy, nor was it absolutely obvious that Pakistan was following a policy of minimum deterrence. Given the nuclear opacity and subsequent revelation of Pakistani military chiefs, it can, however, be presumed that Pakistan might have been following the principle of minimum deterrence even in the pre-test period. Pakistan's then chief of army staff, General Aslam Beg, stated in an interview: 'In the case of weapons of mass destruction it is not the numbers that matter, but the destruction that can be caused by even a few … The fear of retaliation lessens the likelihood of full-fledged war between India and Pakistan.'[6] Hence, an emphasis on minimum deterrence was present in the pre-test era, although it was not clearly elaborated.

Evidence suggests that the Pakistani elite initially thought that a few nuclear weapons could sustain the minimum deterrence, which would be credible enough to deter the adversary. For example, Samar Mubarakmand, one of the leading Pakistani nuclear scientists who headed Pakistan nuclear weapon tests in 1998, stated that 60–70 nuclear weapons would be enough to deter the adversary.[7] Zafar Iqbal Cheema, a leading Pakistani nuclear strategist, stated that 45–60 nuclear weapons would be enough to constitute a credible 'minimum nuclear deterrence' to deter the adversary.[8] In a similar vein, Naeem Salik, the then director within Pakistan's nuclear Strategic Plans Division (SPD), believed 68–70 nuclear warheads would suffice to achieve 'minimum' nuclear deterrent capability.[9] It is evident that a low number was the dominant thinking for a Pakistani nuclear deterrent in the wake of the 1998 nuclear tests. However, the dominant perception within the Pakistani elite treated minimum differently in the later stages of Pakistan's nuclear policy orientation. The Pakistani prime minister, Nawaz Sharif, declared after one year of Pakistan's nuclear weapon tests on 20 May 1999 that, 'In maintaining the nuclear deterrence, we remain acutely conscious of the risk and responsibilities arising from the possession of nuclear weapons ... Nuclear restraint, stabilisation and *minimum credible deterrence* constitute the basic elements of Pakistan's nuclear policy'.[10] Abdul Sattar, the then Pakistani foreign minister, similarly asserted that credibility is crucial: 'The minimum cannot be quantified in static numbers. The Indian build up will necessitate review and reassessment in order to ensure the survivability and *credibility* of the deterrent. Pakistan will have to maintain, preserve, and upgrade its capability'.[11]

The addition of *credibility* indicated Pakistan's changing nuclear perception that the minimum might not remain fixed to a specific number of nuclear warheads. It meant that Islamabad would continue to upgrade and maintain the credibility of its nuclear forces in view of the changes in the South Asian strategic environment. It also showed that Pakistan desired both to maintain a small number of nuclear warheads to avert the arms competition, as well as preserve the viability and credibility of its deterrent capability vis-à-vis India. However, the two objectives of Pakistan's nuclear policy were contradictory. On the one hand, Pakistan declared that it would pursue a policy of minimum deterrence, meaning it wanted to keep its nuclear forces at a minimum level, but on the other hand credibility demanded modernization and, if necessary, an increase in the number of nuclear warheads, which led it to expand its nuclear forces. This book explores this growing contradiction and explains why, when and how a departure occurred in Pakistan's post-1998 minimum deterrent policy, and why Pakistan could not sustain the policy of minimum deterrence it initially conceptualized and formulated. To facilitate that discussion in greater detail, it is first necessary to examine the issue of minimum deterrence conceptually and see what alternative options Pakistan had.

Various forms of deterrence policy[12]

There are various forms of deterrence policy options a state may adopt. The adoption of certain deterrence policy options may vary from one state to another given the strategic and security milieu in which it lives. Conceptually, they are highlighted in this section.

Deterrence via assured destruction

This policy includes large, expensive and sophisticated conventional and nuclear forces, with the capability to inflict greater damage vis-à-vis the adversary. Only two major nuclear weapon states – the USA and the former Soviet Union – adopted the policy of assured destruction during the Cold War period. Their arsenals include a triad of air-, land- and sea-based nuclear forces capable of destroying each other. As this type of deterrence includes both counter-value and counter-force targeting, it seems highly destructive and dangerous. This policy goes against the conceptual understanding of minimum deterrence conceived here. Minor nuclear weapon states simply cannot afford the policy of assured destruction because of their economic constraints and lack of technological wherewithal. However, the US and Soviet/Russian example and their drive to modernize their nuclear forces provide incentive to minor nuclear weapon states to upgrade their triad of nuclear forces. Technological breakthroughs, accessibility and growing economic capability increase the propensity of minor nuclear weapon states to reconsider their nuclear policy options.

Limited deterrence

This type of deterrence is considered an 'affordable' and restricted version of assured destruction. The fundamental characteristics of limited deterrence somewhat match assured destruction, but differ in terms of limited resources allocation in contrast to assured destruction. In other words, in limited deterrence a state's strategic desire to acquire the capability of assured destruction is restricted by a lack of resources. China is considered a case in practice of limited deterrence.[13] There are varying perceptions of China, whether or not it practises the low scale of minimum deterrence when it confronts the two giants – the USA and Russia – and keeps its forces limited at the theatre level. Others also think China's limited deterrence is more aspirational than actual.[14]

Virtual deterrence

This type of deterrence informs us of a state's acquisition of nuclear weapons-building capability, but without actually constructing one. This type of deterrence may also be called a 'non-weaponized' and 'recessed' deterrence, terms coined later in the 1990s. That is, a state possesses the technical capability, but does not build nuclear weapons. Waltz argues that virtual deterrence remains *unstable* because it does not address the issue of second-strike capability essential for deterrence success.[15] Both the South Asian nuclear adversaries – India and Pakistan – belonged to this category when they achieved the technical capability of crossing the nuclear threshold in the 1980s, but did not do so. India acquired this capability in 1974 by testing its first nuclear weapon, which at that time it called a peaceful nuclear explosion (PNE). Both India and Pakistan have had virtual nuclear deterrence since the mid-1980s, but were unwilling to test their nuclear weapons openly until May 1998. Japan is a classic example of this type of deterrence and is in possession of technical capability to translate its nuclear technology into actual nuclear weapons. Other examples include Germany and Sweden, which both have vast peaceful nuclear programmes which could be translated into military projects if they so desired.

Opaque deterrence

Opaque deterrence includes states that do not necessarily declare officially that they possess and deploy nuclear weapons, even though they have the capability to come out of self-proclaimed opacity. Both India and Pakistan fell into this category in the late 1980s and 1990s. Israel is still under nuclear opacity.[16] Opaque nuclear deterrence includes the features of absence of nuclear testing, denial of possession, avoidance of nuclear threats and non-deployment. Opacity is adopted as a policy option to avoid the Non-Proliferation Treaty (NPT) obligations, international sanctions and preventive war. On the other hand, states are pressurized to come out of opacity because it increases crisis instability and the possibility of war due to weak command and control structure.[17]

Minimum deterrence

Minimum deterrence is a concept that developed in the context of the Cold War. On the one hand, the USA and the Soviet Union expanded their conventional and nuclear forces to inflict unacceptable damage because they largely believed that the size of their deterrent forces really mattered when deterring the adversary. On the other hand, critics opposed these options as unnecessary because the matching and overmatching interactive process caused an arms race, crisis instability and danger of military escalation to the nuclear level. To critics, the deterrent size of nuclear forces did not really matter. This school of thought developed a concept in which a small number of nuclear forces could deter the adversary and cause unacceptable damage.[18] Minimum deterrence in its true sense is considered cost effective and does not necessarily burden the state's economy to a great extent. France and the UK are cases of minimum deterrence. The USA, which provides these states with a security umbrella, allows them to pursue a policy of minimum deterrence. Minimum deterrence suits the smaller/minor nuclear weapon states such as Pakistan because of its lack of economic and technological bases, although it can also be applicable to the established nuclear weapon states.

The above discussion highlights that Islamabad had a number of options to choose from in the aftermath of its nuclear tests in May 1998. It could opt for a policy of assured destruction, but for a state like Pakistan it remained both expansive and expensive given its limited economic resources and lack of technological advancement. It could opt for a nuclear policy of *non-weaponized deterrence* or *existential deterrence* without testing nuclear weapons in the aftermath of India's nuclear tests, simply maintaining its previous nuclear policy. It is noteworthy that Pakistan deterred India by its non-weaponized deterrence posture in the 1980s and 1990s. However, this policy became redundant as Pakistan conducted open nuclear tests in view of domestic pressure as well as credibility of its nuclear forces. Theoretically, Pakistan could also opt for an offensive deterrence posture, but it would have needed to build a tough, large, complex command and control system. Such an option was impracticable. Leaving aside these options, the Pakistani leadership declared that Islamabad would pursue a policy of minimum deterrence.

Minimum deterrence became the pragmatic nuclear policy option for Pakistan after the nuclear tests. The Pakistani policy elite viewed that the country did not need 'parity' vis-à-vis India. A few survivable nuclear weapons could 'inflict unacceptable damage'. Chakma observes that Pakistan's option of minimum deterrence is practical for three reasons: 1 given Pakistan's limited resource base and financial constraints, minimum deterrence is the most cost-effective and pragmatic option; 2 it is apparent that only a minimum deterrent posture can help avoid a ruinous nuclear arms race with India, and Islamabad is well aware that if a nuclear arms race were to eventuate, it would hurt Pakistan more than its larger neighbour; and 3 it is easier to build a command and control system if the nuclear arsenal is small.[19]

The Pakistani concept of minimum deterrence includes that it would not indulge in an acute arms competition; it would not respond to its adversary's weapon-to-weapon tests; it would upgrade and maintain the credibility of deterrence forces; and these weapons are security oriented and not for fighting purposes.[20] Yet, many questions still remain unanswered in the view of Pakistan's nuclear behaviour. It is also noteworthy that conceptually minimum deterrence remains indeterminate, as Rajesh Basrur points out:

> While the development of capabilities in technology and organization proceeds apace, nobody is quite clear about what minimum deterrence means. How many weapons are adequate, and of what kind? Might deployments become necessary at some point of time, and if so, under what circumstances? Is war still possible, and if so, how? What kind of arms control is feasible?[21]

Pakistan confronted an obvious dilemma – whether to continue to limit its nuclear forces or to increase them as the changing strategic environment demanded. Pakistan, it is now clear, emphasized credibility over the minimum. To understand Pakistan's policy shift or adjustment, it is essential to understand the basics of minimum deterrence. What follows is a discussion on the essentials of minimum deterrence.

The essentials of minimum deterrence

The essentials of minimum deterrence elaborate how a nuclear weapon state manages its nuclear weapons both at the minimum operational and declaratory level; what its nuclear force structure will be; whether it will prioritize nuclear weapons militarily or politically; how nuclear weapons might conceptually be understood as non-military weapons; whether or not the minimum requires reinforced shelters and sophisticated technology; what framework is required for a robust command and control system; and why nuclear weapon states incline towards arms control and the disarmament process.

Force structure

Minimum deterrence requires a low number of nuclear forces which are kept in a non-deployed position. Nuclear weapon states that pursue a policy of minimum deterrence need to determine their force structure, declaratory and operational policy choices in order to manage their nuclear forces efficiently.[22] First, *force structure* policy depicts states' intention of keeping force levels that cover nuclear as well as conventional forces. As part of this nuclear policy, states elaborate on how large and penetrating the forces should be; if the first strike should be effective, and if so, how much so; if there is a need for nuclear superiority and parity in relation to the adversary; if it should include a sophisticated and invulnerable delivery system; and what type of missile systems the force structure requires. Second, the *operational policy* includes the nuclear alert and targeting policy options. Nuclear weapon states calculate when to use nuclear weapons if they are needed (positive control), and not use them when absolutely not needed (negative control). The alert policy level requires nuclear weapon states to measure carefully the risks of unauthorized and accidental use of nuclear weapons associated with both positive and negative control of nuclear weapons.[23] Operational policy also embodies the targeting plans. These include counter-value and counter-force targeting. Third, *declaratory policy* covers the kinds of attacks a nuclear weapon state constructs. It includes how these declaratory policy options are conveyed and communicated; whether it would include nuclear deterrence against nuclear weapons or conventional forces, or include deterring both types of the adversary's forces. This also includes the discussion of how deterrence could be extended to other states both at the strategic and tactical levels (see Table 1.1). With the management of nuclear forces at the declaratory and operational levels, nuclear forces require either to be used militarily or politically.

Table 1.1 The conceptual characters of minimum deterrence vs. deterrence via assured destruction

	Nuclear essentials/variants	Minimum deterrence	Deterrence via assured destruction
1	Nuclear parity and superiority	Not needed	Yes
2	Number game	Conceptually minimum emphasizes for small numbers, but may be ambiguous	Ambiguity is practised. It goes for a high number
3	Triad	It does not necessarily require a triad. Few survivable deterrent forces can replace a triad	Yes
4	No first use (NFU)	States with weak conventional forces may not sustain the no-first use option	NFU can be a clear possibility/option
5	Nuclear ambiguity	Yes	Yes, but less required
6	Credibility/survivability	Yes, but not expansive and expensive	Highly expansive and expensive
7	Targeting options	Counter-value and counter-force options	Counter-value and counter-force options
8	Targeting plans	Ambiguous	Ambiguous
9	Command and control system	Small and simple with little or no possibility of decentralization	Enlarged and sophisticated with higher chance of decentralization
10	Extended deterrence	No	Yes, nuclear weapons can be stationed in allied countries
11	Deployment options	Little or no possibility	High possibility
12	Bigger sizes and high alerts	No	Yes
13	Arms control and disarmament	Possible, but contingent	Difficult to achieve

The military and political priority of nuclear weapons

The leadership of nuclear weapon states must decide whether to prioritize military or political aspect of the arsenals. Of course, the relationship between these two aspects is hard to disentangle. The military aspect encourages the nuclear weapon states to include these weapons as *regular weapons* to achieve certain strategic objectives. The political aspect prioritizes deterrent forces politically and discourages the use of nuclear weapons in an offensive manner. It means that nuclear weapons are primarily used to gain political objectives.

Rationally, nuclear weapons should be considered political weapons rather than military ones as they are generally viewed as unusable weapons. Considering this aspect, US President Harry S. Truman advocated the non-use of nuclear weapons. He told David Lilienthal that: 'You have got to understand this isn't a military weapon. It is used to wipe out women, children and unarmed people, and not for military use.'[24] In addition, US President Dwight Eisenhower, who was initially inspired by Secretary of State F.J. Dulles's policy of *massive retaliation*,[25] later stated that: 'Gain such a victory and what would you do about it? I ask you, what would the civilized world do about it? I repeat that there is no victory in any war except through imaginations, through our dedication and through our work to avoid it.'[26]

Knowing their destructive nature, these statements urge a political priority for nuclear weapons. The political aspect of nuclear weapons reflects a minimalist approach of minimum deterrence. The less the deterrence forces, and the less we rely on them, the better. If the deterrence forces increase, then it would require maximum state responsibility and a maximum number of people within the command and control system. This in turn leads a nuclear weapon state to a maximalist approach which underlines that 'the bigger and more sophisticated the arsenal, the better'. There is a discomfort between the maximalist approach that encourages the military aspect of nuclear weapons, and the minimalist prospect that embraces the political aspect of nuclear weapons. Ironically, the two deterrent aspects are used interchangeably without going for a complete and proper grasp on a minimalist approach. Whilst describing the discomfort between the political and military strategic approaches of nuclear weapons, Basrur points out: 'It is vital that minimum deterrence be underscored by a clear understanding of the dual character of nuclear weapons, and that *the political be prioritised*.'[27] Why is the need for a political priority of nuclear weapons at its minimalist approach emphasized for deterrence purposes? This is largely linked with the fear and risk of nuclear weapons use in the event of military escalation.

Centrality of risk, uncertainty and unacceptable damage

The military aspect of nuclear weapons embodies fear, risk and uncertainty. This becomes a key factor in our understanding of minimum deterrence. The risk factor becomes the focal point of minimum deterrence. The use of even only one nuclear weapon against the enemy state can be considered unacceptable because of its destructive characteristics. McGeorge Bundy stated:

> A decision that would bring even one hydrogen bomb on one city of one's own country would be recognized in advance as a catastrophic blunder; ten bombs on ten cities would be a disaster beyond history; and a hundred bombs on a hundred cities are unthinkable.[28]

Introduction 9

This does not only suggest the minimalist approach of nuclear policy, but also largely highlights the centrality of fear and risk associated with the use of nuclear weapons. The minimalist approach in this sense is close to 'existential deterrence' in that it is not the number of nuclear weapons that matter, nor the strategies based on the relative damage these nuclear forces embody; what is more crucial is the mere existence of a couple of nuclear weapons with potential survivability and penetrability. Bundy, who developed the concept of existential deterrence, stated: 'As long as each side has thermonuclear weapons that could be used against the opponent, even after the strongest possible pre-emptive attack, *existential deterrence* is strong and *it rests on uncertainty about what could happen.*'[29] Given the risk, uncertainty and unacceptable damage factor, it can be postulated that more is not better. Nuclear weapon states can achieve their politico-strategic goals through minimum deterrence.

Fewer are better

Fewer are better because with more, the risks of nuclear escalation increase and may emerge out of conventional, sub-conventional and limited war. Military escalations increase the chances of risk of nuclear use especially when the two states are in possession of nuclear weapons and follow the maximalist approach.[30] The central point to make is that nuclear weapons, particularly at maximalist mode, maximize greater fear and risk of the use of nuclear weapons. Minimum deterrence with smaller nuclear forces can reduce, if not completely diminish, the centrality of fear, risk and uncertainty associated with nuclear weapons. It is considered that smaller nuclear forces embodied with the principle of minimum deterrence make the margin of error thinner than that of having larger nuclear weapons.[31] In other words, the deterring objectives can be attained with a *smaller nuclear force* and *smaller threat of punishment*. Fewer are risk reducers. An Indian nuclear strategist, K. Subrahmanyam, starkly pointed out that 'deterrence is not to be measured in terms of any equation of damages each side inflict on the other' and 'one bomb on one city is unacceptable'.[32] This reflects the notion that the minimum can deter. As Basrur states, 'The implication is clear. Minimum deterrence does not require a calculation of the balance of capabilities in a nuclear relationship. Whether one side has more and/or "better" weapons does not matter'.[33] However, minimum deterrence forces should be survivable.

Survivability and credibility

Survivability, credibility and the ability to communicate the right message at the right time are important ingredients of deterrence. Nuclear weapon states ensure the survivability and credibility of nuclear weapons they possess. The established nuclear weapon states took greater pains to ensure that their nuclear forces were credible and survivable. Reinforced shelters, mobile missiles, sophisticated accuracy and submarine-launched ballistic missiles (SLBM) are considered for the credibility of deterrence. Influenced by the Cold War nuclear concepts, even the nuclear strategists of smaller nuclear weapon states do not neglect the concept of nuclear forces' accuracy, assured second-strike capability, accurate penetrability, survivability, reinforced protection, dispersal and mobile basing.[34]

Does minimum deterrence require all these deterrent variables in terms of their survivability and credibility? Although a policy of the minimum does not rule out these variables, it discourages expensive and expansive measures (see Table 1.1). For minimum deterrence, the mere existence of nuclear weapons induces credibility. The deadly characteristics of nuclear weapons emphasize that even a small survivable number of nuclear forces could cause dreadful damage. The Cuban Missile Crisis in 1962, during the peak of the Cold War between the USA and the former Soviet Union, reflects that even a small number of nuclear weapons could inhibit the use of larger forces. In this context, then US Secretary of State Henry Kissinger stated: 'The Soviet Union had only 60–70 truly strategic weapons while we had something like 2,000 missiles and bombs ... with some proportion of Soviet delivery vehicles surviving, the Soviet Union could do horrendous damage to the United States.'[35] The Waltzian account on the 'possibility of annihilation' by nuclear weapons that induce credibility[36] and Kissinger's critique on the Cuban Missile Crisis indicate a clear reflection of minimum deterrence that can deter. That is, a few survivable nuclear weapons are enough to deter, given the destructive characteristics of nuclear forces. This reflects minimum deterrence. The few survivable nuclear forces may not include higher numbers, larger sizes or more expensive technological wherewithal (see Table 1.1).

Size, number and technological sophistication

Deterrent forces of a larger size, higher number and technological sophistication attract both the established and minor nuclear weapon states. Technological sophistication and a variety of nuclear forces are considered part of deterrence requirements. Notwithstanding, this affects the sustainability of minimum nuclear deterrence both at operational and political levels. That is, if a nuclear weapon state increases its force size beyond the minimum level conceived here, then it will have strategic implications for other nuclear weapon states, resulting in an arms race. One is urged to contemplate *why the minimum is not the minimum*. It is important to question if the minimum really requires a greater number, bigger size and expensive technological sophistication. Can the minor nuclear weapon states, whilst maintaining minimum deterrence, afford expansive and expensive Cold War-style deterrence? Basrur asserts that 'minimum deterrence does not require any of this unless one contemplates *actually fighting and winning a nuclear war*'.[37] If nuclear weapons are not considered for the purpose of fighting and winning wars, then the minimalist approach is the optimum choice.

Targeting, escalation, usability and deployment

On targeting, nuclear planners choose from two basic options. The first is counter-value targeting which means city busting, and the second is counter-force targeting which includes targeting military installations and military forces of the adversary. Counter-value targeting requires strategic nuclear forces and counter-force requires miniaturization of nuclear weapons – that is, tactical nuclear weapons (TNWs). Contextualizing the Cold War, many posit today that TNWs can be stabilizing and these weapons can be used to fight limited wars for limited objectives. However, critics argue that any use of TNWs could escalate to a strategic level. It remains uncertain whether or not TNWs can be stabilizing for the South Asian region. Although these types of weapons were not used during the Cold War, they confronted force-protection, pre-delegation, and command and control issues. They induce risk of escalation from a tactical to a strategic level. To be sure, the risk of escalation rules out the feasibility of limited war and counter-force targeting. The risk of escalation entails minimum deterrence. Minimum deterrence with a centralized command and control system negates these worries. Nuclear weapon states behave rationally in terms of conceptually dealing with nuclear policy options. Minimum deterrence encourages nuclear weapon states in non-deployment and non-use of nuclear weapons in the event of a crisis. For effective command and control, the minimum highlights that nuclear weapons are non-military weapons and should, therefore, be treated differently. In other words, nuclear weapons are for deterrence, not for war-fighting purposes.

Command and control

Nuclear weapon states confront challenges in making nuclear weapons *safe, reliable, and secure*.[38] On top of this, nuclear weapons need to be protected against the twin threats of *decapitation* and *unwanted use*.[39] With minimum deterrence the command and control system remains more effective. The making of nuclear policy is a complex and demanding enterprise. Given the past experiences of the use of nuclear weapons, nuclear weapon states are much more cautious about avoiding use of these deadly weapons militarily. Nuclear optimists are of the view that minor nuclear weapon states would have no problem in organizing, managing and safeguarding their nuclear weapons. They are also of the opinion that minor nuclear weapon states need small, simple and manageable nuclear weapons that do not require sophisticated, strengthened technology, and a large organizational set-up to command and control their deterrent forces. Therefore, small and simple nuclear weapons, coupled with the advantages of manageable organizational set-up and nuclear policy of concealment would not create any major worries for minor nuclear weapon states.[40] Conceptually and rationally, the more the minor nuclear weapon states expand their nuclear arsenals,[41] the more complex and sophisticated technology and management manpower they require, and the command and control of these weapons becomes more difficult (see Chapter 6).[42]

Hypothetically, more nuclear weapons for minor nuclear weapon states bring more worries and more pressure on a centralized command and control system. The smaller the number of nuclear weapons, the smaller the pressure and the better and easier the command and control will be.[43] Effective command and control systems always take care of the nuclear leadership, deterrence forces and personnel working within the system. A non-deployed posture reduces the worries of accidental and unauthorized use of nuclear weapons. An effective command and control system and non-deployed posturing of a small number of nuclear forces entails minimum deterrence. In this context, one of the solutions to these emerging nuclear-related issues is the adoption of a true *non-deployed defensive minimum deterrence* (NDMD) (the cost-effective option). It is important to observe how this NDMD approach can best persuade nuclear weapon states in the initiation of arms control and the disarmament process. If states are discouraged from fighting and winning nuclear wars and if nuclear weapons cannot be eliminated, then at least efforts can be made to control and reduce the deterrent forces to a minimum.

Arms control and disarmament

The process of arms control and disarmament facilitates minimum deterrence. It is considered that amidst the presence of nuclear weapons, the possibility of war is not completely diminished. It is also thought that nuclear weapons have rather protracted conflicts between the nuclear weapon states. Leading US nuclear strategists who once favoured the upgradation and expansion of nuclear forces now call for arms control and disarmament both to strengthen the process of non-proliferation and meet the desired objective of Global Zero (GZ). This was reinstated by US President Barack Obama's Prague speech in April 2009; however, in fact the significance of and reliance on nuclear weapons has not changed. The logic of disarmament is not considered to lessen the proliferation process. Fear of cheating and the lack of a concrete inspection system are obstacles the arms control and disarmament regime may confront (see Chapter 7). In this context, Waltz argues:

> Arms agreements are difficult to reach because their provisions may bear directly on the prospects for victory or defeat ... in a nuclear world peace is maintained by the presence of deterrence forces, strategic arms agreements do not have militarily but economic and political, significance ... Agreements that reduce one category of conventional weapons may shift competition to other types of weapons and lead to increase in their numbers and capabilities.[44]

Nevertheless, non-deployed minimum deterrence is the first step in acknowledging the process of arms control and disarmament without compromising a state's security. Nuclear weapon states informed by the non-deployed minimum concept do not ignore the arms control and disarmament regime. Minimum deterrence discourages nuclear parity, large sizes and high numbers. It encourages arms control and reduction, if not the complete elimination of nuclear weapons. Even the staunch nuclear advocates of nuclear weapons consider that numbers are not important and the minimum can deter.[45] Waltz states: 'if they are right, then unilateral reduction of weapons to small numbers is possible without further ado.'[46]

The above discussion highlights that the essentials of minimum deterrence can be applied to both the established and minor nuclear weapon states pursuing minimum deterrence. In this study, these essentials are applied to examine the changing contour of Pakistan's nuclear policy in the post-test era.

The study: objectives and structure

This study aims to provide an in-depth analysis of the evolution of Pakistan's post-1998 nuclear policy: posturing for minimum credible deterrence. It explores the question of why Pakistan could not sustain the policy of minimum deterrence which it adopted in the immediate aftermath of the May 1998 nuclear tests. It explains why Pakistan moved from a 'minimum deterrence' posture to 'minimum credible deterrence', and the factors that pushed Islamabad to shift to such a policy. In order to answer these questions, the study looks at the rationale of Pakistan's minimum deterrence, the sustainability of minimum deterrence, nuclear force building, utility of nuclear forces, and policy of arms control and disarmament. The aim is to find out how minimum is treated and played out in the politics of nuclear weapons in South Asia. It explores whether the minimum can be sustained both at the theoretical and operational levels.

In this chapter the essentials of minimum deterrence have already been illuminated. These essentials can be applied universally. Pakistan's minimum deterrence policy will be judged in light of those essentials. The essentials of minimum deterrence highlight that a small number of nuclear weapons can deter; survivability is essential for minimum deterrence, but sophisticated technology and expensive reinforced shelters are not always required; a triad can be achieved through smaller, survivable nuclear weapons; larger weapon sizes, higher numbers of weapons and complicated command and control systems are not necessary; the minimum emphasizes the political priority or political aspects of nuclear weapons, the mere secure existence of which would suffice to deter; and the minimum discourages nuclear weapon states from thinking of using nuclear weapons for military purposes. Also, minimum deterrence does not impede arms control and disarmament processes. Thus, the aim of this study is to locate Pakistan within the essentials of minimum deterrence and analyse its policy pursuit. In addition, the study analyses whether minimum deterrence encourages nuclear weapon states to establish an arms control regime.

This book comprises of eight chapters including this Introduction and the Conclusion. This chapter elaborated the conceptual dimensions of Pakistan's post-1998 nuclear policy in light of the essentials of minimum deterrence and discussed the objectives, structure and significance of the study.

Chapter 2 looks back to the development of Pakistan's nuclear weapons programme and its policy evolution. It discusses the origins of the Pakistani nuclear programme and explains how it evolved, why it came to the decision to test nuclear weapons in 1998, and what external and internal pressures it confronted prior to nuclear weapon tests. The historical analysis of Pakistan's nuclear weapons programme sets the backdrop for analysing Pakistan's post-test nuclear policy.

Chapter 3 discusses Pakistan's option of minimum deterrence in the post-1998 era. It elaborates the rationale of adopting this policy option. It asks why Pakistan adopted minimum deterrence and discusses how Pakistan subsequently added the modifier 'credible' to its policy of minimum deterrence.

Chapter 4 focuses on why the minimum in reality is not the minimum. It examines in what sense 'minimum deterrence' is an idea in the context of Pakistan. It elaborates why Pakistan's minimum deterrence did not remain the minimum.

Chapter 5 looks at Pakistan's nuclear force-building approach. It elaborates how Pakistan's nuclear force-building policy changed in the vortex of South Asian strategic dynamics. It analyses why Pakistan is building up its nuclear forces (e.g. missile system, air force, nuclear submarine and plutonium enrichment), and whether this arms build-up meets the criterion of minimum deterrence.

Chapter 6 examines how Pakistan strategizes its nuclear forces for deterrence purposes. It discusses Pakistan's nuclear policy of first use under the banner of minimum credible deterrence and analyses why, how and under what circumstances Pakistan plans to use nuclear forces. This chapter briefly brings the Cold War debate between first use and no first use in order to focus on Pakistan's policy of first use.

Chapter 7 explores Pakistan's role in global arms control and disarmament, and evaluates whether it conforms to Pakistan's policy of minimum deterrence. It discusses how Pakistan supported the international disarmament process and why it later shifted its perception. It mainly focuses on why Pakistan remains defiant to the NPT, the Comprehensive Test Ban Treaty (CTBT) and the Fissile Material Cut-off Treaty (FMCT) post-1998 tests, and whether it conforms to the basics of minimum deterrence. Also, it broadly analyses the challenges in relation to arms control and the disarmament process which hamper the creation of an arms control regime (ACR) in the South Asian region.

The findings of this study are summarized in Chapter 8, which examines the key points of the study and identifies areas of future research.

Notes

1 Hans M. Kristensen and Robert S. Norris, 'Nuclear Notebook: Pakistan's Nuclear Forces, 2011', *Bulletin of the Atomic Scientists* 67(4), 2011: 91–99; Zia

Mian, 'Pakistan', 2012, www.princeton.edu/sgs/faculty-staff/zia-mian/Pakistan-nuclear-modernization-2012.pdf (accessed 27 June 2012), 58; David Albright and Robert Avagyan, 'Construction Progressing Rapidly on the Fourth Heavy Water Reactor at the Khushab Nuclear Site', Institute for Science and International Security, 2012, isis-online.org/isis-reports/detail/construction-progressing-rapidly-on-the-fourth-heavy-water-reactor-at-the-k/ (accessed 22 June 2012).
2 There is a difference between the terms 'minimum deterrence' and 'minimum credible deterrence'. Although the element of *minimum* (representing small and a low number) exists within both types of deterrence and both require survivability and credibility in terms of deterrence, minimum *credible* deterrence, as conceived in this study, is more ambiguous, remains dynamic, and changes in accordance with the region's altered strategic environment.
3 Jasjit Singh 'Prospects for Nuclear Proliferation', in Serge Sur (ed.) *Nuclear Deterrence: Problems and Perspectives in the 1990s*, New York: United Nations Institute for Disarmament Research, 1993; George Perkovich, 'A Nuclear Third Way in South Asia', *Foreign Policy* 91, 1993: 84–104; Devin Hagerty, 'Nuclear Deterrence in South Asia: The 1990 Indo-Pakistani Crisis', *International Security* 20(3), 1995: 79–114.
4 The USA, the Soviet Union/Russian Federation, UK, France and China are established/major nuclear weapon states, and are also the recognized nuclear weapon states under the Nuclear Non-Proliferation Treaty (NPT); Pakistan, India and Israel are minor/smaller nuclear weapon states.
5 Perkovich, 'A Nuclear Third Way in South Asia', 88.
6 Ibid., 88–89.
7 Quoted in *Dawn* International (News), 1998.
8 Zafar Iqbal Cheema, 'Pakistan's Nuclear Use Doctrine and Command and Control', in S.D. Sagan, J.J. Wirtz and P.R. Lavoy (eds) *Planning the Unthinkable: How New Powers Will Use Nuclear, Biological, and Chemical Weapons*, New York: Cornell University, 2000, 179.
9 Naeem Salik, 'Minimum Deterrence and India-Pakistan Nuclear Dialogue: Case Study on Pakistan', 2006, www.centrovolta.it/landau/content/binary/01.%20Naeem%20Salik-Minimum%20deterrence%20and%20India%20Pakistan%20dialogie,%20PAKISTAN.%20Case%20Study%202006.pdf (accessed 18 June 2012), 15.
10 The former Pakistani Prime Minister Nawaz Sharif's declaratory statement in relation to Pakistan's nuclear policy on 20 May 1999 at the National Defence University, Islamabad, quoted in Rodney W. Jones, 'Pakistan's Nuclear Posture: Quest for Assured Nuclear Deterrence – A Conjecture', *Spotlight* (Regional Studies Islamabad) XIX(1), 2000: 27, emphasis added.
11 Abdul Sattar, 'Pakistan's Nuclear Strategy', inaugural address at a seminar on Council for Foreign Affairs and Institute of Strategic Studies, Islamabad, 25 November 1999, printed in 'The Nuclear Debate', *Strategic Issues*, Islamabad Strategic Studies Institute, March 2000, 3, emphasis added. See also, Abdul Sattar, Zulfiqar Ali Khan and Agha Shahi, 'Securing the Nuclear Peace', *The News*, 5 October 1999.
12 This section borrows heavily from Rajesh Basrur, *Minimum Deterrence and India's Nuclear Security*, California: Stanford University Press, 2006.
13 Alastair Ian Johnston, 'China's New "Old Thinking": The Concept of Limited Deterrence', *International Security* 20(3), 1995: 5–42.
14 Ibid.
15 Kenneth Waltz, 'Thoughts about Virtual Nuclear Arsenals', *Washington Quarterly* 20(3), 1997: 153–61.
16 Zeev Maoz, 'The Mixed Blessing of Israel's Nuclear Policy', *International Security* 28(2), 2003: 44–77; Avner Cohen, *Israel and the Bomb*, New York: Columbia University Press, 1998.

16 *Introduction*

17 For an interesting account on this perspective, see Bradley A. Thayer, 'The Causes of Nuclear Proliferation and the Utility of the Nuclear Non-Proliferation Regime', *Security Studies* 4(3), 1995: 463–519; for other useful studies on *state opacity*, see Peter D. Feaver, 'Proliferation Optimism and Theories of Nuclear Operations', *Security Studies* 2(3/4), 1993: 172–73; H.G. Quester, 'Knowing and Believing about Nuclear Proliferation', *Security Studies* 1(2), 1991: 270–82.
18 P.M.S. Blackett, 'A Critique of Defence Thinking', *Survival* 3(3), April 1961: 126–34; P.M.S. Blackett, *Studies of War: Nuclear and Conventional*, London: Oliver & Boyd Publications, 1962; Anthony Buzzard, 'Massive Retaliation and Graduated Deterrence', *World Politics* 8(2), 1956: 228–37; Anthony Buzzard, 'Defence, Disarmament and Christian Decision', *Survival* 3(5), 1961: 207–19; Anthony Buzzard, John Slessor and Richard Lowenthal, 'The H-Bomb: Massive Retaliation or Graduated Deterrence', *International Affairs* 32(2), 1956: 148–65.
19 Bhumitra Chakma, *Pakistan's Nuclear Weapons*, London: Routledge, 2009.
20 These views are developed based on the author's field work in Pakistan in meeting with senior officials and analysts from various government agencies such as Pakistan's SPD, Foreign Ministry and Defence Ministry.
21 Basrur, *Minimum Deterrence*, 1.
22 For excellent elaboration of these sub-policy options in relation to minimum deterrence, see Tom Sauer, *Nuclear Inertia. US Nuclear Weapons Policy after the Cold War*, London: I.B. Tauris, 2005; Tom Sauer, 'A Second Nuclear Revolution: From Nuclear Primacy to Post-Existential Deterrence', *Strategic Studies* 32(5), 2009: 745–67; Basrur, *Minimum Deterrence*.
23 Bruce Blair, *Strategic Command and Control: Redefining the Nuclear Threat*, Washington: The Brookings Institution, 1985; Paul Bracken, *The Command and Control of Nuclear Forces*, New Haven: Yale University Press, 1983; Peter D. Feaver, *Guarding the Guardians: Civilian Control of Nuclear Weapons in United States*, Ithaca: Cornell University Press, 1992; Scott D. Sagan, 'The Perils of Proliferation: Organization Theory, Deterrence Theory, and the Spread of Nuclear Weapons', *Security Studies* 18(4), 1994: 66–107; Scott D. Sagan, 'Proliferation Optimism and Theories of Nuclear Operations', *Security Studies* 2(3/4), 1993: 172–73.
24 Quoted in Lawrence Freedman, *The Evolution of Nuclear Strategy*, New York: Palgrave Macmillan 2003, 49.
25 Zafar Khan, 'Makers of the US Nuclear Strategy: From Policy of Massive Retaliation to Nuclear Stability', *IPRI Journal* X(2), 2010: 72–73.
26 John Lewis Gaddis, *Strategies of Containment: A Critical Appraisal of Post-war American National Security Policy*, London: Oxford University Press, 1982, 135.
27 Basrur, *Minimum Deterrence*, 36, emphasis added.
28 McGeorge Bundy, 'To Cap the Volcano', *Foreign Affairs* 48(1), 1969: 9–10.
29 McGeorge Bundy, 'The Bishops and the Bomb', *The New York Review of Books*, 16 June 1983, emphasis added; McGeorge Bundy, 'Existential Deterrence and its Consequences', in Douglas MacLean (ed.) *The Security Gamble: Deterrence Dilemmas in a Nuclear Age*, Totowa, NJ: Rowman & Allanheld, 1984, 9–10.
30 James E. King, 'Nuclear Plenty and Limited War', *Foreign Affairs* 34(1/4), 1956: 238–56; Thomas Schelling, 'Nuclear Strategy in Europe', *World Politics* 14(3), 1962: 421–32; Blackett, *Studies of War*; Andrew Phillips, 'Horsemen of the Apocalypse? Jihadist Strategy and Nuclear Instability in South Asia', *International Politics* 49(3), 2012: 297–317.
31 Rodney W. Jones, 'Pakistan's Nuclear Option', in Hafeez Malik (ed.) *Soviet-American Relations with Pakistan, Iran, and Afghanistan*, New York: St Martin Press, 1987.
32 K. Subrahmanyam, 'Nuclear Force Design and Minimum Deterrence Strategy for India', in Bharat Karnad (ed.) *Future Imperilled*, New Delhi: Viking, 1994, n.p.; K. Subrahmanyam, 'A Credible Deterrent: Logic of the Nuclear Doctrine', *Times of India*, 1999.

33 Basrur, *Minimum Deterrence*, 39.
34 Gurmeet Kanwal, *Nuclear Defence – Shaping the Arsenal*, New Delhi: IDSA, 2001, 110–11; Kapil Kak, 'Command and Control of Small Nuclear Arsenals', in Jasjit Singh (ed.) *Nuclear India*, New Delhi: Institute for Defence Studies and Analysis, 1999; K. Sundarji, *Blind Men of Hindustan: India-Pak Nuclear War*, New Delhi: UBS Publishers, 1993; K. Sundarji, 'Proliferation of Weapons of Mass Destruction and the Security Dimensions in South Asia: An Indian View', in W.H. Lewis and S.E. Johnson (eds) *Weapons of Mass Destruction: New Perspectives on Counter Proliferation, National Defence*, Washington, DC: University Press, 1995; Zafar Ali, 'Pakistan's Nuclear Assets and Threats of Terrorism: How Grave is the Danger?' 2007, www.stimson.org/books-reports/pakistans-nuclear-assets-and-threats-of-terrorism-how-grave-is-the-danger/ (accessed 28 June 2011); Adil Sultan, 'Pakistan's Emerging Nuclear Posture: Impact of Drivers and Technology on Nuclear Doctrine', *Strategic Studies*, 2012, www.issi.org.pk/publication-files/1340000409_86108059.pdf (accessed 28 June 2012); Cheema, 'Pakistan's Nuclear Use Doctrine'; Zafar Iqbal Cheema, 'The Role of Nuclear Weapons in Pakistan's Defence Strategy', *IPRI* 4(2), 2004: 72–87; Zafar Iqbal Cheema, 'The Role of Nuclear Weapons in Pakistan's Defence Strategy', in Muhammad B. Alam (ed.) *Constructing Nuclear Strategic Discourse: The South Asian Scene*, New Delhi: India Research Press, 2007; Zafar Iqbal Cheema, 'Pakistan's Posture of Minimum Credible Deterrence: Current Challenges and Future Efficacy', in Zulfqar Khan (ed.) *Nuclear Pakistan: Strategic Dimensions*, London: Oxford University Press, 2011, 43–84.
35 Henry Kissinger, 'Kissinger's Critique', *The Economist*, 3 February 1979: 18.
36 Kenneth Waltz, 'Nuclear Myths and Political Realities', *The American Political Science Review* 84(3), 1990: 731–45.
37 Basrur, *Minimum Deterrence*, 43, emphasis added.
38 I have borrowed the words: *reliable*, *safe* and *secure* from an article by Peter D. Feaver, who presents a theoretical framework under the taxonomy of nuclear weapons, *the always/never dilemma*, and states that nuclear weapons must be '*reliable*: unlikely to fail at the moment when leaders want to use them; *safe*: unlikely to detonate accidently; and *secure*: resistant to efforts by unauthorized people to detonate them' (emphasis added): Peter D. Feaver, 'Command and Control in Emerging Nuclear Nations', *International Security* 17(3), 1992: 163; also see Feaver, *Guarding the Guardians*.
39 For detailed elaboration of this theoretical framework, see Feaver, *Guarding the Guardians*.
40 Nuclear optimists, who consider that the adoption of robust and effective nuclear strategy for minor proliferators would not be a major issue, see Kenneth Waltz, *The Spread of Nuclear Weapons: More May Be Better*, Adelphi Paper No. 171, London: International Institute for Strategic Studies, 1981; Scott D. Sagan and Kenneth Waltz, *The Spread of Nuclear Weapons: A Debate Renewed*, New York: W.W Norton & Company, 2003; B.B. Mesquita and William H. Riker, 'An Assessment of the Merits of Selective Proliferation', *Journal of Conflict Resolution* 26(2), 1982: 283–306; Peter R. Lavoy, 'Civil-Military Relations, Strategic Conduct, and the Stability of Nuclear Deterrence in South Asia', in Scott D. Sagan (ed.) *Civil-Military Relations and Nuclear Weapons*, Stanford: Center for International Security and Arms Control, 1994, 79–109; Peter R. Lavoy, 'The Strategic Consequences of Nuclear Proliferation: A Review Essay', *Security Studies* 4(4), 1995: 695–753; Hagerty, 'Nuclear Deterrence in South Asia'; Perkovich, 'A Nuclear Third Way in South Asia'; Sumit Ganguly and T.D. Hagerty, *Fearful of Symmetry: India-Pakistan Crises in the Shadow of Nuclear Weapons*, New Delhi: Oxford University Press, 2005.

41 In this case, Pakistan (a minor nuclear weapon state) tends to increase its nuclear weapons capability against its adversary in the South Asian region. See Kristensen and Norris, 'Nuclear Notebook'.
42 Author's interview with Feroz Hassan Khan, former director of arms control and disarmament affairs within Pakistan's SPD, September 2012.
43 Bracken, *The Command and Control of Nuclear Forces*, 180–92.
44 Waltz, 'Nuclear Myths and Political Realities', 741.
45 See Bernard Brodie, Robert S. McNamara, Kenneth Waltz and still many others who do not deny the minimalist approach of nuclear forces, cited in Sagan and Waltz, *The Spread of Nuclear Weapons: A Debate Renewed*, 141–43.
46 Waltz, 'Thoughts about Virtual Nuclear Arsenals', 154.

2 Historical analysis of Pakistan's nuclear development programme

Introduction

Before the birth of Pakistan, 'Pakistan' was just an idea, not a state.[1] Before and after the partition of the subcontinent in 1947 and the creation of Pakistan, no one realized that an insecure and weaker Pakistan would emerge, and decades later would acquire nuclear weapons. Pakistanis have always considered the country to be an insecure state since its inception. When Pakistan emerged on the world map as an independent state, its top priority was security and survival. Vincent Sheean stated: 'I shall never forget that when I first visited the new establishment [Karachi, 1947], there was only one typewriter in the whole Foreign Office.'[2] With this one typewriter, the enormous difficulties of Pakistan can well be imagined. In the west was Afghanistan, with which it had unsettled territorial issues.[3] With its eastern neighbour, India, it had various disputes, including Kashmir. In addition, Pakistan faced a communist threat from the Soviet Union. Analysing the position of the would-be-Pakistan in the security context, a renowned member of the Indian National Congress argued that Pakistan would have insufficient resources to defend itself *without outside help*, for it would face three conflicts involving two fronts. In the west there was a potential threat from both the Soviet Union and Afghanistan, in the east from Japan and China, and in both the east and west from India.[4]

Therefore, for its security and defence, Pakistan had to forge alliances with the major powers such as the USA and China. Conventionally weak, Pakistan thought that these security pacts, the Southeast Asia Treaty Organization (SEATO) and Central Treaty Organization (CENTO) in 1954–55, would provide a 'security guarantee' to the emerging threats. However, Pakistan's conventional capabilities, coupled with its alliances, did not ensure security. Pakistani security elites adopted drastic new measures in order to bolster the security of the state: the acquisition of nuclear capability.

Although Pakistan pursued a peaceful nuclear energy programme in the 1950s, a favourable perception of acquiring nuclear weapons emerged in the 1960s. There was a shift in that perception in the 1970s following the dismemberment of the state in 1971, and India's nuclear testing in 1974.

Pakistan went through various phases between the political decision to acquire nuclear weapons being taken in the 1970s, until it conducted nuclear tests in May 1998. Pakistan, in reaction to Indian nuclear tests, tested six nuclear devices on 28 and 30 May 1998. After the tests, Prime Minister Nawaz Sharif declared: 'No matter we are recognised as a nuclear weapon state or not, we are a nuclear power.'[5] The Pakistani nuclear weapon tests marked a major turning point in the country's long history of nuclear development. There were domestic, regional and international variables that affected Pakistan's nuclear journey. The West failed to dissuade Pakistan from acquiring nuclear weapons because it did not understand Pakistan's pursuit of a nuclear weapons programme.[6]

This chapter explores the determinants of Pakistan's nuclear weapons development and explains them in order to understand Pakistan's nuclear evolution. The first part of the chapter explores Pakistan's nascent nuclear programme. It discusses the setting up of Pakistan's peaceful nuclear programme in the 1950s. The second part looks at how the programme evolved in the 1960s under the Ayub military regime. The third section elaborates the shift of Pakistan's nuclear development from a peaceful to a military programme when Zulfiqar Ali Bhutto came to power in December 1971. The dismemberment of Pakistan in 1971, the secret meeting of Multan in 1972, the Indian nuclear test in 1974 and Bhutto's charismatic personality all influenced Bhutto's decision expeditiously to acquire nuclear weapons capability. Section four evaluates the Zia military regime, its approaches and actions to develop the Pakistani nuclear weapons programme. The entire nuclear programme was ambiguous to avoid external pressure and internal public debate. The final section examines how Pakistan took the decision to test nuclear weapons in 1998 after facing both internal and external pressures.

The initial years of Pakistan's nuclear programme

Pakistan's nuclear development programme in its initial years started with the aim of using the atom for peaceful purposes. Pakistan did not commence its nuclear programme immediately after independence; rather, it took several years to embark finally on a peaceful nuclear development programme. There is little evidence that Pakistan aspired to build nuclear weapons in its initial years of nuclear development.[7] The initial impetus to build a peaceful nuclear programme came from the US 'Atoms for Peace' initiative. In 1954, Pakistan's Industry Ministry announced the establishment of an atomic research body that would promote peaceful use of nuclear facilities around the country. The body comprised 12 members headed by Dr Nazir Ahmed, who was later to become the chairman of the Pakistan Atomic Energy Commission (PAEC).

The atomic research body was named the Atomic Research Committee (ARC), and was assigned to estimate the requirements of an atomic organization, identify the personnel needed, devise a plan to survey and assess radioactive materials in the country, and advise the Pakistani government on their peaceful uses.⁸ The ARC was converted into the Atomic Energy Council (AEC) in 1956, and into the PAEC in 1957. In 1954, the visit of the US Atoms for Peace mission raised interest among Pakistanis about the benefits of the peaceful uses of nuclear technology for national development.⁹ The PAEC sent Pakistani scientists and technicians to the West to acquire knowledge on nuclear technology. Soon it also set up a nuclear research reactor for its indigenous nuclear development programme.¹⁰ The PAEC planned to develop, as Nazir Ahmed stated:

> ... peaceful uses of atomic energy with special reference to survey, procurement and disposal in radioactive materials, planning and establishment of Atomic Energy and Nuclear Research Institute, installation of Research and Power Reactors, negotiations with international Atomic Energy bodies, selection and training of personnel, application of radio-isotopes to agriculture, health, industry etc.¹¹

Although Nazir Ahmed achieved international cooperation in terms of training the team and drawing other benefits in advancing the nuclear programme, he confronted certain bureaucratic and financial constraints due to which he was unable to provide Pakistan with its first nuclear reactor. Ahmed complained:

> This work [the technical evaluation of a research reactor] was, more or less, completed last year (1957) and the commission's proposal for the acquisition of a research reactor was finalised. This choice was made purely on technical grounds, taking into consideration the good of the country as a whole. Unfortunately, at this critical stage, other considerations of a non-technical nature were allowed to creep in and cloud the issue with the result that approval of the reactor project has been held up for over a year for which the commission cannot be held responsible.¹²

Pakistan was slow in its nuclear development. The reasons were: 1 the Pakistani domestic socio-political environment, compared with India, was not conducive to launching a nuclear programme in its initial years of independence; 2 there was a lack of awareness of the use of nuclear technology in the fields of medicine, agriculture and energy; 3 Pakistan lacked a well-trained scientist and nuclear enthusiast political leader; and 4 Pakistan's rudimentary industrial infrastructure restrained the development of a nuclear programme.¹³

This short phase of Pakistan's nuclear development programme indicates the introduction of nuclear facilities for peaceful purposes. The period witnessed the formation of the PAEC and the benefits of international cooperation in setting up Pakistan's nuclear programme. At this stage the programme suffered from bureaucratic and financial constraints and there was no clear political commitment. However, the following period of the Ayub military regime saw considerable changes in Pakistan's nuclear development programme. Usmani replaced Nazir Ahmed as the chairman of the PAEC. Usmani provided a new rigour to the PAEC and its activities, although the programme remained peaceful.

Pakistan's nuclear development programme under the Ayub military regime

In 1958, attempts were made to operationalize Pakistan's first nuclear research plant, but the PAEC failed in its first attempt. At the same time, General Ayub Khan took over state power in a military coup. The General was not very enthusiastic about the nuclear development programme and he believed that conventional weapons were sufficient to safeguard Pakistan's security quest in relation to India. In fact, Ayub was the main architect of Pakistan's entry into the US-sponsored alliances, SEATO and CENTO. Ayub had the confidence that in a time of crisis, the USA would come forward in Pakistan's defence. Therefore, there was no need to acquire nuclear weapons. When pressed by Bhutto, his foreign minister, to develop a nuclear weapons programme to meet Pakistan's security needs, Ayub rejected the idea and replied that if he needed one, he would buy a nuclear weapon 'off the shelf', obviously referring to the USA.[14] In addition to this, Ayub Khan stated: 'What do we need a bomb for? Pakistan is a poor country ... we cannot afford it ... We should put money into schools, maybe hospitals and industry.'[15]

However, during Ayub's time, some progress was made in developing Pakistan's nuclear programme. As the new chairman, Usmani brought greater leadership dynamism and vigour into the PAEC, making it an autonomous statutory body, which induced inspiration to speed up the nuclear activities. The PAEC established eight medical and agriculture centres as part of its nuclear development activities, and trained some 350 nuclear scientists and engineers under the stewardship of Usmani.[16] The Pakistani government also sent scores of its scientists and technicians to the USA, France, Canada, Great Britain, the Soviet Union and to the International Atomic Energy Agency (IAEA) headquarters in Austria for training purposes. Of course, many of those scientists did not return to Pakistan, which hampered the development of Pakistan's nuclear programme. The Pakistani military government under Ayub Khan additionally allocated Rs/400 million for the construction of the Karachi Nuclear Power Project (KANUPP) and the establishment of the Pakistan Institute of Nuclear Science and Technology (PINSTECH). The KANUPP signed an agreement with Canada to purchase a 137-megawatt (MW) heavy-water reactor, which was placed under the IAEA safeguard mechanism.[17] The KANUPP was not built until 1972.[18]

The 1965 Indo–Pakistan war: lessons for Pakistan

Military tension between India and Pakistan grew high when the countries fought a second war in 1965. The 1965 war with India had significant implications for Pakistan. First, Kashmir would continue to be an issue between the two arch rivals. Second, it had shown that Pakistan was not able to deter India conventionally. Third, both SEATO and CENTO were of no potential use for the security of Pakistan. The USA not only refused to assist Pakistan in the hour of crisis, but also imposed an arms embargo. Having little or no reliance on the USA as a security guarantor, Pakistan slowly disassociated itself and finally withdrew from SEATO in 1972.[19] Disillusioned with the USA, Bhutto stated that 'With its [Pakistan's] alliance torn to shreds, the country was compelled to explore new avenues to safeguard its national security and territorial integrity'.[20] Bhutto was referring to cultivating good relationships with China and at the same time with the former Soviet Union. Bhutto argued in Ayub's Cabinet in 1960 that Pakistan needed to shift towards the Soviet Union and China.[21] By the mid-1960s, Pakistan had a good relationship with China, which became a greater source for Pakistan of conventional weapons.

The aftermath of the 1965 war also hardened Pakistan's choice not to sign the NPT, even though it remained a strong proponent of the NPT's formation (this issue is further discussed in Chapter 7). When Pakistan observed India's unwillingness to join the NPT and its motive for going nuclear, it became a cause of concern and a reason not to sign the treaty but to keep its nuclear options open. Former US Senator Robert Kennedy presumed in the US Senate on 23 June 1965: 'If India acquires nuclear weapons, Pakistan will not be far behind.'[22] Agha Shahi, a Pakistani representative to the United Nations (UN) who would later become foreign minister during the Zia military rule, was not in favour of signing the NPT because he assumed that India would soon acquire nuclear capability.[23] Shahi, then the Pakistani envoy to the UN General Assembly (UNGA), criticized India on 29 October 1965 for its refusal to open its nuclear facilities to international inspection, and stated that India could become a sixth nuclear power.[24] Whilst refusing to sign the final document on the NPT formation, Shahi maintained: 'In the final analysis, the position of Pakistan with regard to signing the treaty will turn on consideration of its own enlightened national interest and national security in the geo-political context of the region in which Pakistan is situated.'[25] The implications for not signing the NPT were clear: if India would not sign, Pakistan was to keep its nuclear options open. Islamabad's nuclear diplomacy turned Indian-centric. Chakma stated two principal reasons that turned Pakistan away from the NPT: 'First, it was a clear manifestation of Islamabad's growing concern over India's nuclear potential which ushered in a new era of India-oriented nuclear policy. Second, it confirmed that Pakistan has a policy of "nuclear option", which meant that it would retain the option to develop nuclear weapons if circumstances demanded it.'[26]

The Indian-centricity was obvious in Bhutto's statements on various occasions just before his emergence as president of Pakistan. In the wake of the Indo-Pakistan war in 1965, Bhutto declared while addressing the UNGA in 1965 that 'Pakistan is a small country facing a greater monster ... that is determined to annihilate Pakistan'.[27] Bhutto portrayed India as a monstrous country with a desire to build its hegemony on the subcontinent and obliterate Pakistan. Bhutto later called this a 'principal objective of India'.[28] For Bhutto, Pakistan's security and territorial integrity were more important than economic development. He realized that the conventional weakness of Pakistan's armed forces would not ensure the security of Pakistan and his country needed nuclear weapons to thwart India's security threat.

Munir Ahmed Khan, working in the IAEA in the 1960s, influenced Bhutto's perception of acquiring nuclear weapons capability, as depicted by Khan's speech after the 1998 nuclear test:

> After the 1965 war, our vulnerability increased. Mr. Bhutto visited Vienna, where I was working at the IAEA, and I briefed him about what I knew of India's nuclear program and the facilities that I had seen myself during a visit to Trombay in 1964, consisting of a plutonium production reactor, a reprocessing plant, and all the associated facilities, which added up to one thing, bomb making capability. I told him that a nuclear India would further undermine and threaten our security, and for our survival, we needed a nuclear deterrent.[29]

Elaborating on the nuclear deterrence, Bhutto stated that, 'All wars of our age have become total wars; all European strategy is based on the concept of total war; and it will have to be assumed that a war waged against Pakistan is capable of becoming a total war … our plan, therefore, should include the nuclear deterrent'.[30] This indicates Bhutto's strong determination to build nuclear weapons. For Bhutto, given the weakness of conventional forces in respect of India, the acquisition of nuclear weapons became the first national objective: 'If Pakistan restricts or suspends her nuclear program, it would not only enable India to blackmail Pakistan with her nuclear advantage, but would impose a crippling limitation on the development of Pakistan's science and technology … Pakistan must therefore embark on a similar program.'[31] Bhutto believed that India soon would acquire nuclear weapons to blackmail Pakistan and threaten its existence. He declared in 1966 that, 'Pakistan will always find it difficult to quantitatively keep pace with India … I warned that nation sometime back if India acquires nuclear status, Pakistan will have to follow suit even *if it entails eating grass*'.[32] The 'India factor' was developed in Bhutto's statements when he became a foreign minister during the Ayub military rule. The 'India factor' became official in Pakistan's nuclear policy option. It indicated the basic rationale of Pakistan's nuclear weapons programme which was to be pursued in practice after Bhutto came to power in December 1971.

The rise of Bhutto: a shift to go nuclear

Pakistan sensed that India was on the move to test its nuclear weapons either for peaceful or military purposes. Pakistani perceptions of its adversary's nuclear testing were clear when the country submitted a Working Paper to the Conference of the Committee on Disarmament, in which it argued that 'there is no difference between nuclear weapons and the so-called peaceful nuclear explosive devices'.[33] Once in power, the first thing Bhutto did was call a secret meeting, often called the 'Multan Meeting', in 1972. Khalid Hassan, Bhutto's former press secretary, stated:

> He [Bhutto] spoke of Pakistan's defeat and humiliation in the war with India, and vowed that he would vindicate the country's honour. He said that he had always wanted Pakistan to take the nuclear road, but nobody had listened to him. Now fate had placed him in a position where he could make the decision, he had the people of Pakistan behind him, and he wanted to go ahead. Pakistan was going to have the bomb, and the scientists sitting under the *Shamiana* [tent shelter] at Multan were going to make it for him.[34]

Bhutto asked the scientists if they could give him the bomb. Khalid Hassan recalled Bhutto's sentences during that historic meeting with the scientists: that 'this is a very serious political decision, which Pakistan must make, and perhaps all third world countries must make one day, because it is coming. So can you do it?' The enthusiastic group of scientists replied, 'Yes, we can do it, given the resources and given the facilities'. Bhutto's answer was simple: 'I shall find you the resources, and I shall find you the facilities.'[35]

Three events influenced Pakistani leaders to begin a nuclear project: 1 the bloody civil war in 1971 when India's direct military intervention caused the dismemberment of Pakistan, giving birth to an independent Bangladesh; 2 India's nuclear test in 1974, which encouraged Pakistan to rethink its security policy and expedite the process of acquiring nuclear weapons at the earliest date; and 3 the rise of Bhutto as a civilian leader. Multiple crises in the early 1970s facilitated the rise of Bhutto as a populist leader. Once he became president of Pakistan, he took the decision to build nuclear weapons. Before this decision, he had long aspired to build a Pakistani bomb, going back to the late 1950s. He claimed:

> I have been actively associated with the nuclear program of Pakistan from October 1958 to July 1977, a span of nineteen years. I was concerned directly with the subject as Foreign Minister, as Minister for Fuel, Power and Natural Resources and as Minister in Charge of Atomic Energy. When I took charge of Pakistan's Atomic Energy Commission, it was no more than a signboard of an office. It was only a name. Assiduously and with granite determination, I put my entire vitality behind the task of acquiring nuclear capability for my country ... I negotiated the agreement for the 5-MW research reactor located in PINSTECH ... I negotiated with success to obtain from Canada the 137-MW Karachi nuclear power plant and performed its opening ceremony ... I gave the highest priority

to train thousands of nuclear scientists in foreign countries. Now we have the brainpower, we have the nuclear power plant in Karachi. All, we needed, was the nuclear reprocessing plant.[36]

He undertook several critical decisions after taking over as the president of Pakistan. First, he took upon himself the responsibility of Pakistan's atomic energy affairs. Second, Bhutto provided impetus to the PAEC, turned its affairs secret, and made it answerable only to him. Aware of the red tape of the bureaucratic establishment, Bhutto also avoided the bureaucratic intervention that would hamper the activities of the PAEC. Third, Dr Usmani was replaced by Munir Ahmed Khan (the third chairman of PAEC), who was a strong advocate of Pakistani nuclear force. Fourth, Bhutto called a meeting in 1972 in which he asked the country's scientists if they could build the bomb.[37]

Bhutto hurries for the bomb

Bhutto's assumption about India acquiring nuclear weapons proved correct when India tested its first nuclear device, Buddha Smile, in 1974. The Bhutto government reacted sharply when India exploded the device. New Delhi stated that it was a PNE with no military, political or foreign policy implications. Bhutto was sceptical of India's assurances and replied

> it is well established that the testing of a nuclear device is no different from the detonation of a nuclear weapon. Given this indisputable fact, how is it possible for our fears to be assuaged by mere assurances which may in any case be ignored in subsequent years? Governments change, as do national attitudes, but the acquisition of a capability, which has direct and immediate military consequences, becomes a permanent factor to be reckoned with.[38]

Islamabad perceived the explosion to be a grave threat to Pakistan's security. The Buddha Smile provided further impetus to Pakistan's nuclear weapons programme. Abdul Qadeer Khan, a Dutch-trained scientist who was later to be called the father of Pakistan's nuclear weapons, emerged at this time to support Pakistan's nuclear development programme. Bhutto assigned Khan the task of enriching uranium to weapons grade. Khan is believed to have transferred the technology and blueprints for uranium enrichment while working at the Almelo ultracentrifuge uranium plant in the Netherlands.[39] At the same time, the civil bureaucracy and military intelligence set up a clandestine network to acquire the essentials of nuclear technology.[40]

Pakistan signed a nuclear deal with Paris in 1976 for setting up a plutonium reprocessing plant. The Franco-Pakistan nuclear agreement created a serious controversy between Islamabad and Washington. The USA feared that this would lead to horizontal nuclear proliferation, hence applying pressure to scrap the agreement.[41] Despite US pressure on both Pakistan and

France to cancel the nuclear deal, Pakistan remained committed and launched a diplomatic campaign to make the world understand Pakistan's reasons for acquiring the reprocessing plant, which was for peaceful purposes.[42] Despite this, the deal eventually had to be cancelled in 1979. According to one of the declassified reports released in 2010 by the US State Department, Pakistan would not be able to acquire nuclear weapons capability perhaps for the next decade or even longer because of 'difficulty of producing usable plutonium, domestic financial problems, fear of an active major Indian response, and concern over the adverse foreign powers, and continued uncertain political atmosphere'.[43] However, Pakistan remained determined to move ahead with its nuclear programme. This can be understood when Agha Shahi stated that, 'Pakistan has the unfettered right to do what it wishes and will retain all its options'.[44]

Zia military rule: the nuclear programme becomes ambiguous

In July 1977, Bhutto was removed from power by General Zia ul-Haq in a military coup. The new military regime, however, continued Bhutto's policy of clandestinely building nuclear weapons. This could be gauged from the fact that Dr A.Q. Khan (the head of the uranium enrichment programme at Kahuta) and Munir Ahmed Khan (the head of the PAEC) were not removed from their positions.[45] The West failed to dissuade Pakistan from acquiring nuclear technology.[46]

So, even though Zia ended Bhutto's rule by staging a military coup, he continued Bhutto's goal with some modifications for acquiring nuclear capability.[47] Zia declared on 30 August 1979 that, 'The acquisition of nuclear energy has become the matter of life and death ... the Pakistani nation is convinced that the acquisition of atomic technology is its basic right, which cannot be denied by any foreign power nor can any government in Pakistan surrender it'.[48] This made 'many in the US Congress deeply suspicious'.[49] Zia skilfully manipulated the covert nuclear programme, neither admitting nor denying the existence of a military nuclear programme. To avoid external pressures and strengthen Pakistan's stand on a peaceful nuclear programme, the Zia regime proposed a score of regional non-proliferation initiatives including the proposal for joint Indo-Pakistan adherence to the NPT and accepting the IAEA's safeguards. As expected, this was opposed by New Delhi, because it did not include China.[50]

The Zia regime faced two difficulties in pursuing the nuclear weapons programme. First, there were severe pressures from the West to abandon it. The USA also imposed arms and economic sanctions on Pakistan in 1976 by applying the Glenn-Symington Amendment.[51] Second, it became far more difficult for Pakistan to acquire the nuclear technology because of the formation of an international nuclear export cartel, known as the Nuclear Suppliers Group (NSG), or 'London Group', which imposed certain restrictions on the export of nuclear technology to the non-NPT states.[52] Yet Pakistan did not deviate from pursuing its nuclear weapons programme. This is evidenced by recently declassified documents released by the US State Department which show that the USA remained unable to dissuade Pakistan from acquiring nuclear weapons despite the establishment of the NSG and other punitive measures.[53]

Pakistan was looking for an immediate shift not only to avoid external pressures, but also to maintain the nuclear option. The country pursued nuclear ambiguity to avoid both internal and external pressures. Arguably, there was no public discussion during the Zia military regime. Nuclear ambiguity was at the root of Zia's tenure. As Wirsing stated, the '[p]olicy of acquiring nuclear weapons capability [was] *rarely* to be encountered in the media, in public seminars and conferences focused on regional security, or in public pronouncement of major opposition political leaders'.[54] Despite severe odds, Zia demonstrated astuteness is carrying forward the nuclear programme. Ashok Kapur maintains:

> The foundation of Pakistan's nuclear infrastructure belongs to Bhutto but the credit for taking Bhutto's nuclear ambitious to their logical conclusion – by developing Pakistan's nuclear weapons potential and by developing Pakistan's nuclear presence in regional and international affairs – belongs to Zia.[55]

Zia exploits opportunity

The Soviet Union's intervention in Afghanistan and the Iranian revolution in 1979 proved to be classic episodes of international affairs which later shaped the nuclear policy of Pakistan. The external pressures to dissuade Pakistan from building nuclear weapons capability eased and ultimately disappeared when the USA found that Pakistan was a key frontline state for containing the Soviet Union in Afghanistan. Soon the USA lifted the non-proliferation sanctions against Pakistan and began to provide military and economic assistance. As the USA seemed almost to be ignoring Pakistan's nuclear ambitions, Zia skilfully and diplomatically exploited this opportunity, although the nuclear development programme remained clandestine. At that point in time, the USA had only one goal, which was the containment of the Soviet Union in Afghanistan. The USA even ignored its intelligence reports in 1983 and 1984 that China had assisted Pakistan by providing the low-yield uranium device.[56] Economic and military aid from the USA started to pour into Pakistan. Zia dismissed President Jimmy Carter's initial economic package amounting to US$400 million, describing it as 'peanuts', as he knew that a new US Administration was taking over soon and could provide a bigger share of military and economic assistance to Pakistan. The Ronald Reagan Administration announced a $3.2 billion aid package to induce Pakistan to contain the further spread of Soviet military forces in Afghanistan.[57] Thus, the geopolitical catalyst provided by the Soviet intervention in Afghanistan proved a blessing in disguise for Pakistan to advance its nuclear ambitions. The USA also consistently claimed from the mid- to late 1980s that Pakistan was not pursuing a nuclear enrichment programme, despite intelligence reports and other evidence that suggested otherwise.

In the early 1980s, India reportedly planned a pre-emptive strike on Kahuta nuclear facility, upon which Pakistan threatened India by saying that it would undertake punitive retaliation. Subsequently, Dr A.Q. Khan claimed that, 'for the sake of existence, integrity, independence, and security, the President of Pakistan makes the decision [to make a nuclear bomb] ... We are fully capable of carrying out the job'.[58] However, Khan's proclamation was considered an exaggeration as Pakistan was still facing technical barriers hampering it from crossing the nuclear threshold.[59] Khan was a restless character. He wanted to make a name for himself. He gave an interview to a prominent journalist, Kuldip Nayar, on 28 January 1987:

> What the CIA has been saying about our possessing the bomb is correct and so is the speculation of some foreign newspapers ... They told us that Pakistan could never produce the bomb and they doubted my capabilities, but they know now we have done it. Nobody can undo Pakistan or take us for granted. We are here to stay and let it be clear that we shall use the bomb if our existence is threatened.[60]

This interview was given during the peak of the Brasstacks Crisis in 1986–87 between India and Pakistan. This crisis was the result of a huge Indian military exercise along the Indo–Pakistani border, which Islamabad perceived as a military threat to Pakistan's sovereignty and territorial integrity.

By the time the Soviets decided to withdraw from Afghanistan and the death of General Zia in a mysterious plane crash, Pakistan had already acquired nuclear weapons capability. However, the country was still pursuing the policy of 'nuclear ambiguity' without openly declaring its nuclear status. Once again Pakistan became isolated when the USA cut off all its aid under the Pressler Amendment.[61] This was a reminder to Pakistanis of how they were left alone in the 1971 Indo–Pakistan crisis, despite being an ally of the USA.

Restoration of democracy: the genie out of the bottle

After the demise of Zia and the subsequent restoration of democracy in Pakistan, the military remained in charge of its nuclear development programme. Benazir Bhutto became prime minister. In exchange for military and economic assistance, the new prime minister assured the USA that Pakistan would no longer pursue the enrichment programme.[62] However, the chief of army General Aslam Beg maintained that Pakistan had already acquired enough enrichment for deterrence purposes.[63] With mounting tension between

India and Pakistan over Kashmir in 1990, Beg accelerated Pakistan's nuclear weapons programme, keeping the civilian government in the dark. This was exposed when US intelligence officials showed evidence of the nuclear development activities to Prime Minister Benazir Bhutto.[64] It came as a shock to the civilian leader, which led to an episode of tension between the civilian leadership and the army, and impacted on the prospect of democracy.[65] Soon Benazir was ousted from office. The Kashmir Crisis in 1990 had provided a further boost to Pakistan's nuclear programme when Pakistan realized that the presence of and threat to use a nuclear weapon could deter its adversary. Many claimed that India was deterred in the 1990 Kashmir Crisis because of Pakistan's possession of nuclear weapons.[66]

Pakistanis considered the stabilizing impact of nuclear weapons on the South Asian region and believed that nuclear ambiguity deterred and suited Pakistan's nuclear policy. Nuclear ambiguity remained the centrepiece of Pakistan's nuclear policy prior to the May 1998 nuclear tests. Pakistan remained committed to its nuclear development programme in the 1990s, despite several dismissals and restorations of civilian governments (both Benazir Bhutto and Nawaz Sharif were twice elected and dismissed by the military). After the Soviet withdrawal from Afghanistan and the end of the Cold War, Pakistan felt vulnerable. Its defence posture largely hinged upon the nuclear weapons programme. To offset this vulnerability, Islamabad hinted on various occasions that it had acquired nuclear capability. In February 1992, the foreign secretary admitted that Pakistan had the capability to assemble at least one nuclear device, but it had refrained from doing so. In other interesting revelations, former Prime Minister Sharif stated: 'I confirm Pakistan possesses atomic bomb.'[67] These revelations about Pakistan's possession of nuclear weapons indicate that: 1 Pakistan wanted to offset its conventional vulnerabilities by relying on nuclear diplomacy; 2 Pakistan realized that it would soon be under US pressure on non-proliferation initiatives, and being a non-NPT state it could be pressurised by the USA to 'cap, reduce, and roll back' its nuclear capability; and 3 it was to avert India's possible alteration at the line of control (LOC) in Kashmir.

Islamabad, in fact, did not come under US pressure to roll back its nuclear weapons programme, nor did it accept a US offer of delivery of 38 F-16 aircraft in exchange for Pakistan's acceptance of the US non-proliferation objectives in the South Asian region. The Pakistani parliament rejected the US proposals of economic and military assistance, and concluded with an agreement that Pakistan would not roll back, but continue with its nuclear option.[68] The Pakistani Army did not agree to the US proposal of military aid in exchange for its nuclear roll back.[69] Generally, public option remained supportive of the country keeping its nuclear options open. In 1996, a public opinion survey indicated that 61 per cent supported Pakistan's nuclear policy option, whilst 32 per cent favoured the overt acquisition of nuclear weapons capability.[70]

In April 1995, the NPT was extended for an indefinite period of time at the NPT Extension and Renewal Conference in New York. To date, Pakistan has remained outside the NPT since its formation. With the NPT's extension, its non-proliferation initiatives loomed large in the South Asian region, persuading Pakistan to become a part. It is interesting to note that Pakistan was ready to sign the NPT if India did so.[71] Put simply, it remained obvious that Pakistan would not join the NPT until India became part of it. Its nuclear weapons programme remained Indian-centric to offset Pakistan's conventional vulnerabilities.

In the mid-1990s, there was a debate in Pakistan on whether or not it should join the NPT. The Pakistani strategic community emerged in support of its nuclear weapons tests. The strategic community insisted that Pakistan needed to unveil its nuclear ambiguity to test nuclear weapons. Tariq Jan's edited volume stated that to deter India, a nuclear weapons option was important for Pakistan. The volume considered that the acquisition of nuclear weapons was both to protect the ideology and territorial integrity of Pakistan. The volume condemned the NPT nuclear discrimination and urged Pakistani nuclear leadership to be self-reliant in connection with the acquisition of nuclear weapons.[72] Agha Shahi stated: 'In the South Asian context, nuclear weapons are instruments of military and political powers that could be turned to advantage in the pursuit of regional hegemony.'[73] Abdul Sattar emphasized: 'Not until 1971, when Pakistan's conventional defence capacity proved inadequate to safeguard its territorial integrity, and East Pakistan was militarily separated by India to create Bangladesh, did Pakistan embark upon efforts to acquire nuclear weapons option as a means of deterring the persistent Indian threat.'[74] Besides Shahi and Sattar, others from within the Pakistani strategic community, like retired army General K.M. Arif and former Air Marshal Zulfiqar Ali Khan, remained equally influential in urging Pakistani nuclear leadership to keep the nuclear option open. Arif stated that Pakistan faced a strong Indian conventional might and this could be deterred neither by conventional means nor by the external security guarantee,[75] and Zulfiqar Ali Khan contended that:

> The threat faced by Pakistan from its adversary is not a dream but a 'harsh reality' ... Pakistan should have an option for acquiring nuclear weapons in order to offset India's conventional power. The acquisition of nuclear weapons will provide Pakistan a strong deterring force vis-à-vis India, improve its status as a major power in the region even though it is smaller in size than its adversary, and would ensure Pakistan's security and territorial integrity.[76]

The proponents were of the view that Pakistan should not sign the NPT, but retain the nuclear option.

In a similar vein, Pakistan retained its position on the CTBT in relation to India in 1996. That is, it would be suicidal for Pakistan to sign the CTBT, compromising its security. Pakistan could not sign the CTBT because it had become aware through intelligence sources that India planned to conduct nuclear tests in 1995. This was confirmed when the US intelligence agency observed India's plan for a nuclear test at the Pokhran test site.[77] India's defiance on both the NPT and the CTBT and opting for a nuclear test had a strategic impact on Pakistan's nuclear policy. Given the 'test scare', Pakistan also started preparing for overt nuclear tests. US satellite photos reportedly revealed that Pakistan was getting ready for nuclear tests at the Chagai test site.[78] Although Islamabad dismissed these reports as 'speculation', Pakistani Foreign Minister Asif Ahmed Ali maintained that, 'If India wants to prove its manhood by conducting nuclear tests, then we have the capability to prove our manhood'.[79] Eventually, when India abandoned its plan for a nuclear test in 1995, Pakistan followed suit.

The 'tit-for-tat' scenario

Pakistan did not unveil its nuclear ambiguity by going for the overt nuclear weapon tests until India did so. The Bharatiya Janata Party (BJP), a Hindu nationalist political party, won India's general election in early 1998 and formed the government in New Delhi. The BJP-led government reversed India's longstanding policy of ambiguity and conducted nuclear tests on 11 and 13 May 1998. After the Indian nuclear tests, there were intense external and internal pressures on Pakistan on whether or not to react to its adversary. The international community called on Pakistan to show restraint. The USA offered military and economic assistance to dissuade Pakistan from nuclear weapon tests. It is interesting to note that between 12 May and 27 May, US President Bill Clinton phoned Pakistani Prime Minister Nawaz Sharif four times to influence Pakistan's decision on conducting nuclear tests. In addition to this, Deputy Secretary of State Strobe Talbott, Commander of the US Central Command General Anthony Zinni and Assistant Secretary of State for South Asia Karl Inderfurth visited Pakistan four days after India conducted their tests in order to offer Pakistan economic and military support for not doing likewise. The military offer included F-16 aircrafts which Pakistan claimed that they had already been given in the 1980s. The US ambassador to Pakistan, Thomas Simons, stated that these kinds of offers had never been put forward before to 'a non-ally like Pakistan'.[80] Internally, some Pakistani officials also urged the leadership to acquire the international military and economic benefits for not conducting nuclear tests. They urged the then civilian and nuclear leadership that Pakistan had already acquired nuclear capability and there was no need to demonstrate it. They pinpointed it as an opportunity not be missed.[81]

However, after India tested its nuclear devices, it issued threatening rhetoric against Pakistan, aimed at dissuading the country from conducting nuclear weapons tests. The Indian minister of state for science and technology, Murali Manohar Joshi, declared that 'India's missiles would be armed and deployed with the country's new nuclear weapons', and the Indian home minister, L.K. Advani, explicitly threatened Pakistan if it supported Kashmir in waging a proxy war against India.[82] India's nuclear tests put strategic pressure on Pakistan to test its nuclear capability in order to exhibit its deterrent capability. The nuclear tests became important for Pakistan for its security and survival in the South Asian region. Pakistan blamed India for initiating a nuclear arms race. Gohar Ayub stated on 11 May 1998: 'Pakistan strongly condemns this Indian act and the entire world should condemn it. It has sucked Pakistan into an arms race.'[83]

Pakistan observed that France, Germany and the UK at the G8 Summit failed to take a united stand to put sanctions on India for conducting nuclear tests, and that the European Union (EU) avoided taking practical measures against Indian nuclear tests – except expressing concerns about the emitted dangers in the South Asian region – and that the EU should put sanctions on India if it did not join the NPT. Amid domestic and international pressure, Pakistan ultimately reacted by demonstrating its nuclear weapons capability on 28 and 30 May 1998. In the wake of the May 1998 nuclear tests, Nawaz Sharif stated: 'we have settled scores with India ... We have paid them back.'[84]

Conclusion

Pakistan's quest to acquire nuclear weapons capability was neither a miracle nor an overnight development. There were internal constraints and external pressures, but strategic factors prevailed which eventually led Pakistan towards the Chagai tests in May 1998. Pakistan initially pursued a peaceful nuclear programme, but things started to change when India began to flirt with nuclear weapons in the 1960s and eventually conducted its first test in 1974. Bhutto realized that its conventional weakness would not protect Pakistan, so he advised the Ayub military regime to develop nuclear weapons for deterrence purposes. However, Ayub chose to rely on the US-led alliances and their security guarantees instead of building a Pakistani nuclear deterrence. Subsequently, Bhutto initiated a clandestine nuclear weapons programme against the backdrop of the break-up of Pakistan in 1971. The process of seeking nuclear capability was expedited following the Indian 1974 nuclear test.

Even though Bhutto was ousted from the government, his nuclear policy was followed by the Zia military regime in the late 1970s and throughout the 1980s. The Pakistani civilian governments following the military rule in the 1990s also followed the basic line of Pakistan's longstanding nuclear policy pursuit. Eventually, the long pursuit of nuclear weapons culminated into the May 1998 nuclear tests.

In the aftermath of its nuclear weapon tests, Pakistan confronted several challenges. As an overt nuclear weapon state, it needed to build various nuclear structures to manage its deterrent. It was uncertain which nuclear policy option Pakistan would pursue. There were several options before Islamabad, but it opted for a policy of minimum deterrence. However, Pakistan soon added the notion of credibility to its policy of minimum deterrence. The question that arises is why did Pakistan choose the policy of minimum deterrence? The next chapter addresses this question.

Notes

1 The idea for the name of a would-be-new nation 'Pakistan' was provided by a young Pakistani Cambridge University student, Rehmat Ali, who wrote a piece in 1933 entitled, 'Now or Never: Are We to Live or Perish Forever'. The central point of the piece stated: 'At this solemn hour in the history of India, when British and Indian statesmen are laying the foundations of a Federal Constitution for that land, we address this appeal to you, in the name of our common heritage, on behalf of our *thirty million Muslim* brethren who live in *PAKISTAN* – by which we mean the five Northern units of India, Viz: Punjab, North-West Frontier Province (Afghan Province), Kashmir, Sind and Baluchis*tan*'. See Choudhary Rehmat Ali, *Complete Works of Rehmat Ali*, Pakistan: National Commission on Historical and Cultural Research, 1978; Khurshed Kamal Aziz, *Rehmat Ali: A Biography*, Lahore: Vanguard, 1987, quote on p.495.
2 Vincent Sheean, *Nehru: The Years of Power*, London: Gollancz, 1960, 93.
3 The border between Afghanistan and British India was demarcated in 1893 by Sir Mortimer Durand, the British foreign secretary to the government of India and Afghan ruler Amir Abdur Rehman Khan. This boundary artificially split Pashtoon. The Pashtoon did not accept this artificial border including the Taliban. For useful studies on Pakistan-Afghanistan relations, see Ahmed Rashid, *Taliban. Islam, Oil and the New Great Game in Central Asia*, London: I.B. Taurus, 2000; Frederic Grare, 'Pakistan-Afghanistan Relations in the Post 9/11 Era', *Carnegie Endowment for International Peace*, South Asia Project No. 72, 2006; Ali Zaman, 'India's Increased Involvement in Afghanistan and Central Asian: Implications for Pakistan', *IPRI Journal* III(2), 2003: 1–20; Cyprus Hodes and Mark Sedra, *The Search for Security in Post-Taliban Afghanistan*, Adelphi Paper, No. 391, London: Routledge, 2007; Christine Fair, 'Pakistan's Relations with Central Asia', in R. Jelty (ed.) *Pakistan in Regional and Global Politics*, London: Routledge, 2009, 125–49; Christine Fair, 'The Militants Challenge in Pakistan', *Asia Policy* 11, Washington, 2011; Fazal Rahman, 'Pakistan's Evolving Relations with China, Russia, and Central Asia', in I. Akihiro (ed.) *Eager Eyes Fixed on Eurasia: Russia and its Neighbours in Crisis*, Report No. 16-1, 2007, The Salvic Research Centre; Syed Farooq Hasnat, 'Pakistan's Strategic Interests, Afghanistan and the Fluctuating US Strategy', *Journal of International Affairs* 63(1), 2009: 141–55; Sumit Ganguly and Nicholas Howenstein, 'India-Pakistan Rivalry in Afghanistan', *Journal of International Affairs* 63(1), 2009: 127–40; Z.A. Hilali, *US-Pakistan Relationship: Soviet Invasion of Afghanistan*, London: Ashgate, 2005.
4 Shaukatullah Ansari, *Pakistan: The Problem of India*, Lahore: Minerva Books Shop, 1944.
5 Nawaz Sharif, Declaration to the Nation 1998, cited in Samina Ahmed, 'Pakistan Nuclear Weapons Program: Turning Points and Nuclear Choices', *International Security* 23(4), 1999: 178–204.
6 Feroz Hassan Khan, 'Nuclear Proliferation Motivations', *The Non-Proliferation Review* 13(3), 2006: 501–17.
7 Zafar Iqbal Cheema, 'Pakistan's Nuclear Policies: Attitudes and Posture', in P.R. Chari, P.I. Cheema and Iftekharuzzaman (eds) *Nuclear Non-Proliferation in India and Pakistan: South Asian Perspective*, New Delhi: Manohar Publications, 1996, 104.
8 Ashok Kapur, *Pakistan's Nuclear Development*, New York: Croom Helm, 1987, 35.
9 Naeem Salik, *The Genesis of South Asian Nuclear Deterrence: Pakistan's Perspective*, London: Oxford University Press, 2009, 93.

10 Ahmed, 'Pakistan Nuclear Weapons Program', 181.
11 Nazir Ahmed, 'The Pakistan Atomic Energy Commission', *Pakistan Quarterly* 8 (3), 1958: 14.
12 Ibid., 50–53.
13 Bhumitra Chakma, 'Road to Chagai: Pakistan's Nuclear Programme: Its Sources and Motivations', *Modern Asian Studies* 36(4), 2000: 874; Bhumitra Chakma, *Pakistan's Nuclear Weapons*, London: Routledge, 2009, 10–11.
14 Samina Ahmed and David Cortright (eds), *Pakistan and the Bomb: Public Opinion and Nuclear Option*, Indiana: Notre Dame Publications, 1998, 90.
15 Steve Weissman and Herbert Krosney, *The Islamic Bomb: The Nuclear Threat to Israel and the Middle East*, New York: Times Books, 1981, 49.
16 Ziba Moshaver, *Nuclear Weapons Proliferation in the Indian Subcontinent*, London: Macmillan, 1991, 100.
17 Chakma, 'Road to Chagai', 877.
18 Yousuf Saeed, 'Motivation of Nuclear Proliferation in Pakistan: The India Factor', *Journal of South Asia and Middle Eastern Studies* XXVII(4), 2004: 35–36.
19 Chakma, *Pakistan's Nuclear Weapons*, 16.
20 Zulfiqar Ali Bhutto, *The Myth of Independence*, London: Oxford University Press, 1969, 86.
21 S. Wolpert, *Zulfi Bhutto of Pakistan: His Life and Times*, London: Oxford University Press, 1993, 66.
22 Congressional Record III: 14566, 23 June 1965.
23 Agha Shahi, 'Nuclear Non-Proliferation Treaty and the Security Dilemma', in Tariq Jan (ed.) *Pakistan's Security and the Nuclear Option*, Islamabad: Institute of Policy Studies, 1995, 51–52.
24 UN General Assembly, First Committee, 20th Session, 22 September–2 December 1965, *Political and Security Questions: Summary Records of Meetings*, 96–97.
25 UNGA Official Records, 22nd Session, First Committee, 1580th Meeting, 13 May 1968, 9.
26 Chakma, *Pakistan's Nuclear Weapons*, 16–17.
27 Zulfiqar Ali Bhutto, 'Bhutto's Declaration to the UN General Assembly', in A. Jalal and H. Khan (eds) *Reshaping Foreign Policy: Articles, Statements, and Speeches, Vol. 1 1948–66*, Karachi: Pakistan Publications, 1965, 221.
28 Bhutto, *The Myth of Independence*, 173.
29 Munir Ahmed Khan, 'Speech on Pakistan's Nuclear Weapons', 20 March 1999, www.pakdef.info/nuclear&missile/speech_munirahmed.html (accessed 28 January 2013).
30 Bhutto, *The Myth of Independence*, 153.
31 Ibid., 153.
32 'Bhutto's Larkana Declaration December 29, 1966 on Pakistan and Nuclear Proliferation', in Wolpert, *Zulfi Bhutto of Pakistan*, 113, emphasis added.
33 *Documents on Disarmament, 1971*, Washington, DC: United States Arms Control and Disarmament Agency, 1970, 489–90.
34 Weissman and Krosney, *The Islamic Bomb*, 44–45.
35 Ibid., 45–46.
36 Zulfiqar Ali Bhutto, *If I am Assassinated …* , New Delhi: Vikas Publishers, 1979, 137–38.
37 Chakma, 'Road to Chagai', 887.
38 'The Prime Minister of Pakistan Z.A. Bhutto's Reply', 5 June 1974, printed in *Pakistan Horizon* XXVII(3) (Third Quarterly 1974): 198–200.
39 L.S. Spector, *Nuclear Proliferation Today*, Cambridge: Mass Ballinger, 1984, 75–76.
40 Ahmed, 'Pakistan Nuclear Weapons Program', 184.
41 Spector, *Nuclear Proliferation Today*, 79.
42 Ahmed, 'Pakistan Nuclear Weapons Program', 185.

43 See a declassified report from the Central Intelligence Agency, 'Pakistan Nuclear Study', 26 April 1978, excised copy www.gwu.edu/~nsarchiv/nukevault/ebb333/index.htm#1 (accessed 1 January 2012).
44 See the declassified report released in 2010, State Department cable 205550 to Embassy Islamabad, 'Discussion between Under Secretary Newsom and Pakistan's Minister of State for Foreign Affairs Agha Shahi on the Reprocessing Issue', 14 August 1978, www.gwu.edu/~nsarchiv/nukevault/ebb333/index.htm#1 (accessed 1 January 2012).
45 R.G Wirsing, *Pakistan's Security under Zia, 1977–1988: The Policy Imperative of a Peripheral Asian State*, New York: St Martin's Press, 1991, 113.
46 Khan, 'Nuclear Proliferation Motivations'; Zafar Khan, 'Pakistan's Nuclear Weapons Testing May 1998: External and Internal Pressures', *IPRI Journal* 12(1), 2012: 28–45.
47 Wirsing, *Pakistan's Security under Zia*.
48 Zia's 1979 public statement, quoted in Haider Khan Nizamani, 'Rewriting Third World Security', 1999, circle.ubc.ca/bitstream/handle/2429/10213/ubc_1998-272184.pdf (accessed 11 December 2013).
49 See the declassified State Department cable 204785 to Embassy Islamabad, 'Pakistan Reprocessing', 12 August 1978, www.gwu.edu/~nsarchiv/nukevault/ebb333/index.htm#1 (accessed 1 January 2012).
50 Ahmed, 'Pakistan Nuclear Weapons Program', 186.
51 This amendment was enacted as part of US efforts to strengthen its position on non-proliferation. It meant to ban the US economic and military assistance to countries that deliver or receive, acquire or transfer nuclear enrichment technology when they do not comply with the IAEA regulations and inspections.
52 Chakma, 'Road to Chagai', 893.
53 For details, see a number of declassified documents on Pakistan's nuclear weapons development programme: www.gwu.edu/~nsarchiv/nukevault/ebb333/index.htm#1. These inform us how the Carter Administration in the late 1970s remained unsuccessful in dissuading Pakistan from acquiring nuclear weapons rather than that the USA remained deeply suspicious and shocked when it came to know that Pakistan continued to build nuclear weapons capability despite the cancellation of the Pakistan-France uranium enrichment deal and the US sanctions on Pakistan. See State Department cable to US Embassy, Austria, 'Pakistan Nuclear Issue: Briefing of IAEA Director General Eklund', 9 July 1979, www.gwu.edu/~nsarchiv/nukevault/ebb333/index.htm#1 (accessed 1 January 2012).
54 Wirsing, *Pakistan's Security under Zia*, 117.
55 Kapur, *Pakistan's Nuclear Development*, 183.
56 Spector, *Nuclear Proliferation Today*, 101.
57 Kapur, *Pakistan's Nuclear Development*, 192; Wirsing, *Pakistan's Security under Zia*, 101.
58 Abdul Qadeer Khan, 'Interview', *Nawa-i-Waqt* (in Urdu); an English version was reprinted in *Defence Journal* X(4), 1984.
59 Chakma, 'Road to Chagai', 898.
60 Abdul Qadeer Khan, *The Tribune*, 1 March; reprinted in *Strategic Digest* (New Delhi) XVII(5), May 1987. This indicates the nuclear legitimization of the state either as an established or minor nuclear weapon state – that is, once a state is in possession of nuclear weapons, it becomes difficult for the international community to reverse such an acquisition. This can be observed in all the established and minor nuclear weapon states, whereby having acquired nuclear weapons, none has lost these, although there are nuclear talks to reduce the growing number of nuclear weapons in order to avoid their inadvertent and unwanted use.
61 This amendment, named after US Senator Larry Pressler, was adopted in August 1985 to ban most military and economic assistance to Pakistan unless the USA

certified on an annual basis that Pakistan did not possess a nuclear device, and the proposed US assistance programme would reduce significantly the risk of possessing such a device.
62 D. Kux, *The United States and Pakistan, 1947–2000: Disenchanted Allies*, Washington: Woodrow Wilson Center Press, 2001.
63 Muhammad Aslam Beg, *Development and Security: Thoughts and Reflections*, Rawalpindi: Foundation for Research on National Development and Security Press, 1994.
64 Kux, *The United States and Pakistan*.
65 Talat Syed Hussein, 'Pakistan Hedged on Obvious Bet', *The Nation*, 29 May 1998.
66 Devin Hagerty, 'Nuclear Deterrence in South Asia: The 1990 Indo-Pakistani Crisis', *International Security* 20(3), 1995: 79–114; Sumit Ganguly and D.T. Hagerty, *Fearful of Symmetry: India-Pakistan Crises in the Shadow of Nuclear Weapons*, New Delhi: Oxford University Press, 2005; K.M. Arif, 'Retaining the Nuclear Option', in T. Jan (ed.) *Pakistan's Security and the Nuclear Option*, Islamabad: Institute of Policy Studies, 1995, 121–29; Beg, *Development and Security*; Mushahid Hussain, 'The Nuclear Issue and South Asia: Security via Deterrence', *The News*, 14 April 1994.
67 Nawaz Sharif's public statement, quoted in Chakma, *Pakistan's Nuclear Weapons*, 35.
68 Chakma, *Pakistan's Nuclear Weapons*, 35.
69 Hussain, 'The Nuclear Issue and South Asia'.
70 Ahmed and Cortright, *Pakistan and the Bomb*, 17.
71 Chakma, *Pakistan's Nuclear Weapons*, 35.
72 Tariq Jan (ed.), *Pakistan's Security and the Nuclear Option*, Islamabad: Institute of Policy Studies, 95.
73 Agha Shahi, 'Nuclear Non-Proliferation Treaty and the Security Dilemma', in Tariq Jan (ed.) *Pakistan's Security and the Nuclear Option*, Islamabad: Institute of Policy Studies, 1995, 53.
74 Abdul Sattar, 'Nuclear Issue in South Asia: A Pakistani Perspective', in Tariq Jan (ed.) *Pakistan's Security and the Nuclear Option*, Islamabad: Institute of Policy Studies, 1995, 59.
75 K.M. Arif, 'Retaining the Nuclear Option', in Tariq Jan (ed.) *Pakistan's Security and the Nuclear Option*, Islamabad: Institute of Policy Studies, 1995, 122.
76 Zulfiqar Ali Khan, 'Pakistan's Security and Nuclear Option', in Tariq Jan (ed.) *Pakistan's Security and the Nuclear Option*, Islamabad: Institute of Policy Studies, 1995, 140–44.
77 Rodney W. Jones and Mark McDonough, *Tracking Nuclear Proliferation: A Guide in Maps and Charts*, Washington: Carnegie Endowment for International Peace, 1998.
78 Jeffrey Smith, 'Pakistan's Plans Tit for Tat Test of Nuclear Blast, Officials Say', *The Washington Post*, 1996.
79 Quoted in Chakma, *Pakistan's Nuclear Weapons*, 35.
80 Hassan Askari Rizvi, 'Pakistan's Nuclear Testing', *Asian Survey* 41(6), 2001: 941.
81 Hassan Askari Rizvi, 'Pakistan in 1998: The Polity under Pressure', *Asian Survey* 39(1), 1998: 177–84; Samina Yasmeen, 'Pakistan's Nuclear Tests: Domestic Debate and International Determinants', *Australian Journal of International Affairs* 53(1), 1999: 43–56.
82 For these statements, see www.washingtonpost.com/wp-srv/inatl/longterm/southasia/timeline.htm (accessed 14 July 2011).
83 For the Pakistani foreign minister's statement in response to India's 11 May 1998 nuclear test, see www.fas.org/news/pakistan/1998/05/index.html (accessed 14 June 2011); other Pakistani officials' statements against the Indian nuclear weapon tests can also be seen at www.fas.org/news/pakistan/1998/05/index.html; see also, Pakistani Foreign Minister Gohar Ayub Khan, *The News International*, 12 May 1998.
84 Nawaz Sharif, Declaration to the Nation 1998.

3 Pakistan's rationale of minimum deterrence
Why the minimum?

Introduction

Each state adopts certain policies in order to meet its security objectives. The basic principles of these policy options are more or less the same for all states, although the parameters upon which the policy is chosen could vary from one state to another depending on the geography, threat perception, history, strategic culture, emerging technologies and type of government. Whilst defining the tasks for adopting certain policy options, Henry Kissinger stated that the aim of choosing certain policy options is to 'translate the power into policy', so that states know 'what objectives are worth contending for and determine the degree of force appropriate for achieving them'.[1]

The rationale behind shaping a particular nuclear policy option is 'to achieve intended political, military or other objectives' and 'guide procurement, deployment and employment of the country's nuclear assets', which results in the structure, force building, use and sustainability of the adopted policy options.[2] Scott Sagan has conceptually identified three different perspectives which elaborate the understanding of a state's adoption of certain doctrinal postures. First, stemming from the argument of a realist theoretical explanation, a state adopts certain policy options for security reasons. Second, organizational interests and biases of military institutions determine the nature of a country's nuclear policy. Third, the national strategic culture comprising the country's unique history, religion, the development of the perception of a state's ideology and identity have significant influence on a state's determination of nuclear policy.[3] Chakma adds a fourth perspective on a state's adoption of nuclear policy: 'global strategic culture', nuclear learning of minor nuclear weapon states from the experiences of the established nuclear weapon states. Chakma observes that the realist and organizational perspectives best explain Pakistan's adoption of nuclear policies.[4]

The rudimentary conceptual development of the Pakistani nuclear deterrence occurred decades ago when Pakistan started to contemplate the acquisition of nuclear weapons in the 1960s and 1970s. It is unknown whether at that time Pakistan developed any definitive doctrinal posture except that it was pursuing a policy of nuclear ambiguity. Following the nuclear tests,

Pakistan disclosed that it would pursue a policy of minimum deterrence. However, Islamabad did not elaborate on the specifics of the policy.

The specifics of this policy only began to emerge later in the evolution of Pakistan's nuclear policy. A Pakistani security analyst stated that, 'The minimum deterrence has got two connotations, that is, minimum is a time-specific whilst deterrence is non-time specific. The minimum of 10 years ago may be different from today's minimum. Minimum deterrence is not an inevitable'.[5] As the Pakistani policy of minimum deterrence evolved, terms like *credible*, *defensive* and *offensive* began to act as qualifiers, starting to modify the nature of Pakistan's policy of minimum deterrence. Being a minor nuclear weapon state of the second atomic age, Pakistan's security planners use the term *minimum* for acquisition of and dependence on smaller nuclear weapons which can better be commanded and controlled, concealed, dispersed, employed and deployed during both war and peace. The minimum minimizes the dangers of inadvertence and misuse of nuclear weapons.

It is intriguing that although Pakistan acquired nuclear weapons capability in the 1980s, it only started to contemplate a nuclear policy seriously after the May 1998 nuclear tests. The Pakistani policy elites gradually began to define aspects of the country's nuclear policy: 1 deterrence of all forms of external aggression that could endanger Pakistan's national security; 2 deterrence will be achieved through the development and maintenance of an effective combination of conventional and strategic forces, at adequate levels within the country's resources constraints; 3 deterrence against Pakistan's adversaries attempting a counter-force strategy against the country's strategic assets; and 4 the stabilization of strategic deterrence in the South Asia region.[6] Pakistani security planners, scholars and nuclear analysts alike consider minimum deterrence a suitable nuclear policy option for Pakistan, given the country's conditions. At the same time, Pakistani officials view that the minimum deterrence is not a static phenomenon. They consider this policy option dynamic. It evolves and can be revisited in accordance with changing and/or changed strategic realities.[7]

This chapter discusses Pakistan's option of minimum deterrence. It will both examine the rudimentary rationale and explore Pakistan's adoption of minimum deterrence in the initial phase of its nuclear policy. It aims to look at why and how minimum deterrence is sufficient to deter, cost effective and suitable for an effective command and control system.

The rationale of minimum deterrence

The concept of minimum deterrence was developed during the Cold War period. As the USA and the former Soviet Union rapidly expanded their nuclear arsenals, many argued that it was unnecessary because a small arsenal could deter the aggression of the adversary. According to critics, the size of nuclear forces did not really matter. Instead, they argued, a few survivable nuclear weapons that could cause unacceptable damage were enough to deter the adversary. They further argued that minimum deterrence is cost effective and does not burden the state's economy. France and the UK were attracted by the idea of minimum deterrence.[8] Minimum nuclear deterrence suits the smaller nuclear weapon states such as India and Pakistan because of their lack of resources. Also, they learn from their nuclear predecessors that small is better and reduces risk.

Against this backdrop, when Pakistan tested its nuclear weapons in 1998, it initially followed minimum deterrence, rationalizing that it would not indulge in an arms race against its nuclear rival and a few weapons would suffice to deter. Minimum deterrence became the central feature of Pakistan's nuclear policy. The basic question that arises is why the minimum? To answer this, the following section elaborates the rudimentary rationale of Pakistan's minimum deterrence informed by the essentials of the minimum.

State survivability

Although there is no official document on Pakistan's minimum deterrence, Pakistani nuclear leadership maintains that minimum deterrence is realistic, safe and favourable to the security of Pakistan. After the nuclear weapon tests in 1998, Pakistan declared that it would follow a policy of minimum deterrence. According to a Pakistani military official, Mahmud Ali Durrani, the central themes of Pakistan's nuclear policy are:

1 Pakistan's nuclear capability is solely for the purposes of deterrence and the defence of sovereignty;
2 Pakistan will not use or threaten to use nuclear weapons against any state that does not possess nuclear weapons;
3 the maintenance of *minimum deterrence* is the guiding principle of Pakistan's security policy;
4 Pakistan will refrain from entering into an arms race;
5 Pakistan will not transfer nuclear weapons or weapons-related material or technology to any other entity or state;
6 Pakistan will continue to support international arms control and disarmament initiatives that are universal and non-discriminatory in character; and
7 command and control of nuclear forces will be vested in the president and will be exercised through a National Command Authority (NCA) assisted by the SPD as its secretariat and strategic command within the armed forces.[9]

This indicates that Pakistan does not consider nuclear weapons for warfighting purposes, but instead only to deter its adversary's conventional and nuclear threats.[10] The aim of Pakistan going nuclear was to safeguard its territorial integrity, sovereignty and independence against its adversary. This perception was reflected in the authoritative statement made by three

Pakistani officials, Abdul Sattar, Agha Shahi and Zulfiqar Ali Khan, after the procurement of nuclear weapons:

> Deterrence was the sole aim and a *small arsenal was considered adequate*. At no time did Pakistan contemplate the use of nuclear weapons for war fighting or seek to develop capability for a pre-emptive attack. Apart from the obvious constraint resources, it was not so unrealistic as to entertain such thoughts. India is too large and too well armed to be vulnerable to a disabling strike. Besides, any such attempt would provoke retaliation with disastrous consequences.[11]

The officials were convinced to maintain *minimum deterrence* after thoughtful consideration that: 1 it would strengthen its deterrent capability; 2 Pakistan might not be pulled into an extreme arms race; and 3 it would remain cost-effective given Pakistan's fragile economy. However, in due course it was proven that minimum deterrence was an indeterminate idea and might need adjustment from time to time. Nuclear ambiguity became the centrepiece of Pakistan's policy of minimum deterrence.

The centrality of ambiguity

Since Pakistani officials did not provide the specifics, minimum deterrence becomes subject to interpretation. Calculated ambiguity, therefore, emerged as a key aspect of the country's minimum deterrence policy, remaining vague to the adversary as well. Perhaps this was intentional and indeed helped to maintain security in the region. Although ambiguity also has destabilizing effects,[12] many Pakistani security managers think ambiguity suits Pakistan's nuclear deterrent capability. In this context, the senior officials working within the SPD consider that ambiguity suits smaller nuclear weapon states. Ambiguity, given the strategic environment of South Asia, suits Pakistan's deterrence capability. 'Ambiguity has both operational and political advantage. Pakistan keeps nuclear ambiguity at the declaratory level, but it is less ambiguous at the operational level.'[13] Pakistan's Foreign Ministry also views ambiguity as working towards the credibility of nuclear weapons and meeting and satisfying Pakistan's deterrence purposes.[14] Tariq Osman Hyder stated: 'We are a smaller nuclear weapon state. Therefore, we keep our nuclear weapons program ambiguous. We cannot afford to go open. The openness would make Pakistan vulnerable to external threats.'[15] In contrast, Zafar Iqbal Cheema stated that, 'ambiguity can skilfully be written like the US and other major nuclear weapon states that, despite having written nuclear policy, still practice ambiguity both at the strategic and operational level'.[16]

It can be assumed that: 1 ambiguity has a central role in Pakistan's nuclear weapons programme, which may not easily be eradicated even if Pakistan maintains minimum deterrence; 2 Pakistani nuclear leadership believes that ambiguity has worked in the past and will possibly work in the future to deter the adversary; and 3 although the term minimum remains undefined, it appears that nuclear ambiguity will remain a centrepiece of Pakistan's nuclear policy. Rodney W. Jones stated that:

> The term minimum rapidly became a fixture of the public nuclear discourse in South Asia. Neither India nor Pakistan officially clarified what the term minimum means, leaving this open to speculation. Does minimum imply the sufficiency of small numbers of nuclear weapons; Nuclear weapons held in reserve; Low readiness or alert rates of a nuclear force; Renunciation of nuclear war fighting or mainly counter-value targeting? Or does the term minimum merely make a virtue of today's facts of life in the subcontinent – limited resources, scarce weapons material, unproved delivery systems, and still undeveloped technical military capabilities?[17]

It means that the word minimum as a term is not fully defined by the Pakistani nuclear policy makers, which has created confusion and vagueness. Pakistani officials maintain that the 'Minimum is open for debate. It has got an open interpretation. It remains flexible. There is no number game. It, thus, remains a non-fixed entity',[18] and 'Minimum nuclear deterrence will remain the guiding principle of our [Pakistan's] nuclear strategy. The *minimum cannot be qualified in static numbers*'.[19]

The contradiction in Pakistan's policy of minimum deterrence is obvious. On the one hand, it says Pakistan would 'maintain, preserve and upgrade' its weapons capability, but on the other hand, it insists that Pakistan would 'not to engage in an arms race'. The process of maintenance, perseveration and upgradation is a step to go beyond minimum as conceptualized before, say, 'sufficiency' and/or 'offensive deterrent force capability', thus increasing the chances of an arms race. Therefore, ambiguity will remain a key feature of Pakistan's nuclear policy with all its consequences. This might pull Pakistan into a vicious cycle of arms competition with the adversary. However, Pakistan understands that with rapid expansion, there would be pressure on its command and control system. It also understands that minimum deterrence with a smaller number of arms makes command and control effective.

An effective command and control system

A key rationale of Pakistan's adoption of minimum nuclear deterrence is that it would be easier to build a less complex but effective command and control system. It is interesting to note that Pakistan was able to build a sophisticated command and control mechanism in a relatively short period of time after it tested nuclear weapons. Prior to its overt nuclear tests, it was not certain if Pakistan had developed a fully fledged command and control system, but following the tests, it acted quickly on this front.

One of the advantages of minimum deterrence is that if the number of nuclear warheads is smaller, it is easier to guard and conceal. Validating this argument, Pakistan apparently has built an effective command and control structure to manage its nuclear forces. Although the international community has concerns about Pakistan's nuclear forces falling into the hands of extremists and terrorists given its poor law and order situation and the rise of extremism and terrorism across the country, 'there is no evidence that Pakistan has lost control of its nuclear weapons'.[20]

A.Q. Khan, who is largely held responsible for transferring nuclear technology and nuclear-related materials to Libya, Iran and North Korea, has put a question mark on Pakistan's nuclear command and control system, and particularly on the safety and security of its nuclear weapons and nuclear facilities. Many questions on this aspect are yet to be answered. However, Pakistan's Foreign Ministry considers that A.Q. Khan's file is closed and Pakistan has brought about systemic changes in its export-import system.[21] Apparently, there is a general view in Pakistan that the world community does not blame Pakistan directly as a state actor for this incident. The world blames A.Q. Khan for his alleged illegal nuclear activities.[22] This remains uncertain at the regional and international levels. In the meantime, the Pakistani government has established a formal structure to manage its nuclear forces as well as to alleviate any misgivings about the safety and security of its nuclear weapons.

Pakistan has established a formal nuclear command structure (see Figure 3.1). The military regime of General Pervaiz Musharraf took the initiative of forming the NCA to oversee Pakistan's nuclear command and control system. Although the NCA became operational in March 1999, it was not formally announced until February 2000. The former Pakistani military leader stated:

> When I took the helm of the ship of the state on October 12, 1999, I was solely in charge of all our strategic programs. I soon realised that I could not devote as much time to them as they required. I decided to implement the system that I had proposed earlier. In February 2000, our strategic weapons program came under formalised institutional control and thorough oversight, duly approved by my government.[23]

For the effective handling of Pakistan's nuclear forces and their related facilities, the NCA was instituted in three tiers: the Employment Control Committee (ECC) and the Development Control Committee (DCC) make one tier; the SPD, whose directorates (i.e. Operations and Planning Directorate, Armament and Disarmament Affairs Directorate, Strategic Weapons Development Directorate, and Computer, Command, Control, Communications, Information, Intelligence, Surveillance and Reconaissance directorate, or CCCCIISR), run by the three armed forces of Pakistan (see Figure 3.2), function as a secretariat to the NCA constitute the second tier; and the three services strategic forces command, that is, the Army, Navy and Air Force of Pakistan make up the third tier of the institutionalized command and control of the country's nuclear infrastructure.[24] The NCA and its tiers comprise the amalgamation of both Pakistani armed forces and civilian leadership. After the overt nuclear tests in 1998, it became essential for Pakistan formally to institutionalize its command and control system to oversee its small nuclear weapons effectively, both for setting up its nuclear weapon policy and providing a credible strategic deterrence.[25] Effective command and control helps nuclear weapon states determine how and why nuclear forces and the related facilities should be dispersed and concealed.

Dispersal and concealment

There is a running debate between nuclear optimists and pessimists on the issue of whether minor nuclear weapon states can manage their nuclear forces properly and effectively. The debate will probably continue as long as pessimists argue that the lack of appropriate technology, strategic vulnerability, civilian-military tension, and vulnerability of nuclear weapons security against theft make it difficult for smaller nuclear weapon states to build effective command and control systems.[26] In contrast, optimists argue that due to experience and learning from their predecessors and less complexity due to the smaller size of their nuclear forces, it is easier for smaller nuclear states to build effective command and control systems. Minor nuclear weapon states with their small number of nuclear weapons are in a better position to control their nuclear weapons, despite the concerns.[27]

The size of the Pakistani nuclear forces, despite reported expansion, can still be considered small unlike its nuclear predecessors who possessed up to 70,000 nuclear warheads at the peak of the Cold War. Presently, the minimum maintained by the established nuclear weapon states may not be applicable to minor nuclear weapon states. It is important to note that the concept of minimum *credible* deterrence is different from the concept of minimum deterrence. The rationale behind keeping a minimum deterrence is to avoid an overkill strategy like that of the USA and the former USSR during the peak of the Cold War in the 1960s. Although there has been arms competition between the two nuclear rivals of South Asia, it is not akin to the Cold War era. Pakistan has the added advantage that its minimum nuclear forces can be better dispersed and concealed.

There is no official declaration on the exact number and locations of Pakistan's nuclear weapons and this is for obvious reasons. It is assumed that Pakistan's nuclear arsenal is small and is dispersed, concealed, fenced off and non-deployed. If these practices are set, then Pakistan's nuclear policy conforms to the basics of minimum deterrence. As Luongo and Salik stated, 'The weapons are believed to be kept separate from the delivery systems, with the nuclear cores removed from the detonators. Some estimates claim that the weapons themselves be scattered at up to six separate locations ... nuclear weapons certainly would be dispersed at multiple sites'.[28] The dispersal and concealment of Pakistan's deterrent forces may meet the essentials of minimum deterrence.

Minor nuclear weapon states would prefer to have small, simple nuclear arsenals which can better be concealed and dispersed, rather than to opt for large, complex forces like their predecessors did which could invite certain vulnerabilities. According to Seng, 'minor states will have small arsenals that can be controlled with small control organisation, and they can achieve second-strike capability through simple concealment strategies ... Minor proliferators, however, do not need advanced technologies if their arsenals are small, simple, and concealed'.[29] The smaller size of the arsenal allows states to adopt the policy of minimum deterrence and this increases the survivability of nuclear weapons.[30] A former Pakistani foreign minister articulated: 'Purely deterrence forces can be relatively modest *provided their survivability can be assured against a surprise attack*, continued build-up of nuclear weapons should be unnecessary. Nor does a strategic arsenal have to match the adversary's arsenal'.[31]

One rationale of Pakistan's adoption of minimum deterrence is to keep its arsenal small and simple so that it can be kept safe and secure from

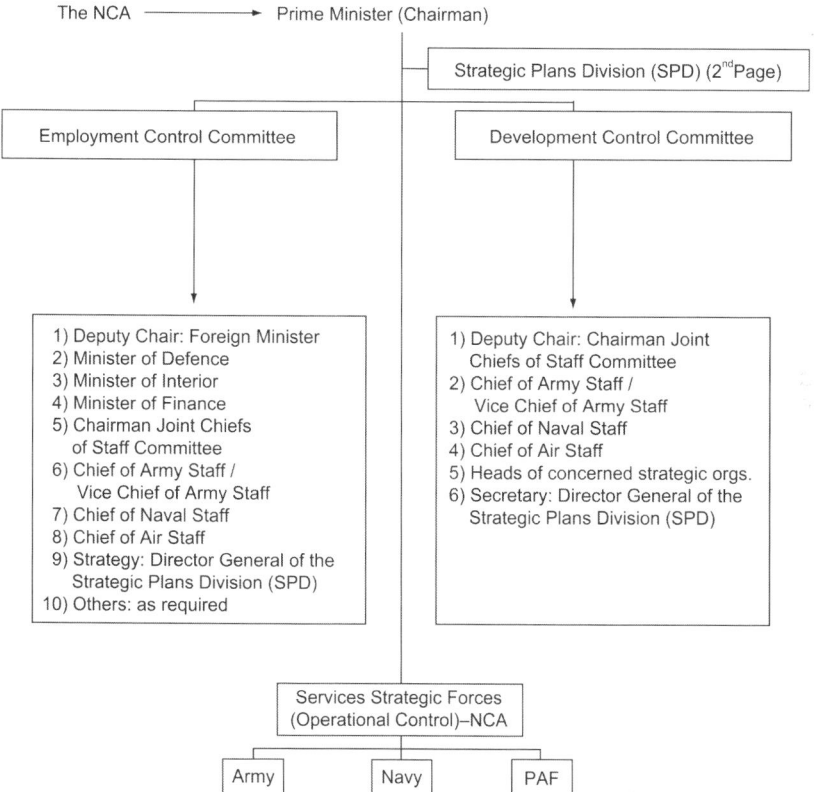

Figure 3.1 The NCA
Source: IISS Dossier on A.Q. Khan, www.iiss.org/publications/strategic-dossiers/nbm/ (accessed 18 February 2013)

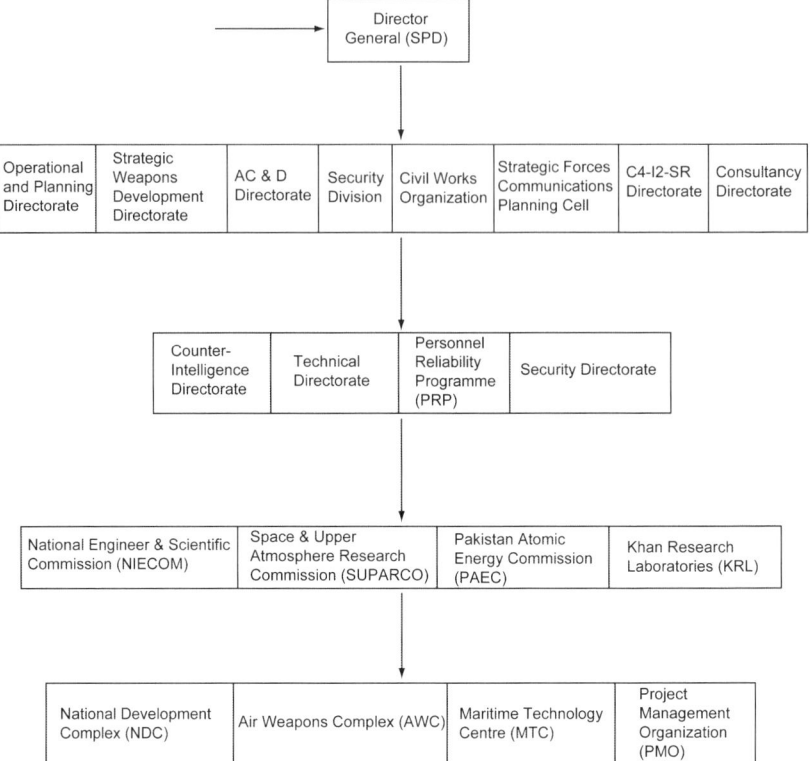

Figure 3.2 The SPD
Source: IISS Dossier on A.Q. Khan, www.iiss.org/publications/strategic-dossiers/nbm/ (accessed 18 February 2013)

vulnerabilities, which enhances the credibility of deterrent forces.[32] Pakistan's nuclear weapons are not on hair-trigger alert. They are small and kept in a disassembled form. Each of their components is reportedly stored separately.[33] Zafar Ali, an officer in the Pakistan Army and SPD, has stated that 'The smaller size of Pakistan's nuclear assets and facilities decrease the chances of theft as these could be easily secured and guarded. In contrast, a larger nuclear establishment and the possession of nuclear materials would correspondingly present more targets and thus more vulnerability'.[34] Ali believes that Pakistan's arsenals are better concealed, dispersed and disassembled. However, Pakistan does not ignore technical improvements given the challenges to strategic stability.[35] These observations indicate that small nuclear forces can have effective dispersal and concealment tactics. They will have less vulnerability if they are kept small, dispersed and secure. Besides this, another strategic advantage of a small force can be its cost effectiveness, considering the precarious economic condition of Pakistan.

Cost effectiveness

The initial conceptualization of minimum deterrence provided a 'minimum-cost deterrent' to Pakistan without indulging in an arms race with its rival India. It did not induce a great economic burden on Pakistan. After overt nuclear tests, the adversaries became less secure militarily and economically.[36] Munir Ahmed Khan, a former chairman of the PAEC, predicted that the overt nuclear weapon tests would suck India and Pakistan into an unending arms race to build expensive delivery and command, control and communication systems. According to Khan, 'Pakistan with a smaller economic base may suffer more economically than India'.[37] Against the backdrop of such a possibility, Islamabad adopted a policy of minimum deterrence so that it would keep its nuclear arsenal cost effective. More importantly, it would not be sucked into a vicious arms race with India.

These factors in the realm of nuclear forces have greater strategic and economic implications for Pakistan. The statement referred to earlier, by Samar Mubarakmand, Naeem Salik and Zafar Iqbal Cheema, that 60–70 nuclear weapons would define Pakistan's minimum deterrence contradicts the current estimate that Pakistan could be in possession of more than 100 nuclear warheads.[38] However, Pakistani officials deny that Pakistan is expanding its nuclear forces. For example, Tariq Osman Hyder stated that 'there is no concrete evidence to this that Pakistan is expanding'. He pointed out that 'it is Pakistan's nuclear adversary who is expanding its nuclear forces and looking for a triad in the South Asian region. Pakistan follows a policy of *minimum deterrence which is cost-effective*'.[39] In a similar vein, the SPD officials stated: 'When deterrence stabilizes, the minimum deterrence accentuates in accordance with that nuclear stability. It does not mean that we are expanding.'[40] The Pakistani officials' statements reflect the pursuit of minimum deterrence that is cost effective. However, it is difficult to figure out whether or not Pakistan is spending much on its nuclear forces, given the secretive and sensitive nature of Pakistan's nuclear weapons programme. Various sources indicate that Pakistan has recently increased its spending on its nuclear weapons programme.[41]

Little is made public about the economics of Pakistan's nuclear weapon spending. Zia Mian contended that 'The secrecy about the history and scale of the nuclear weapons and missile programs, the extent of external technical and material support, and the effect of indirect support through military and economic aid means the full cost of Pakistan's nuclear weapons program cannot be estimated with any reliability'.[42] In 2008, Pakistan debated the annual military budget in parliament for the first time since 1965,[43] revealing from the views of General Pervaiz Musharraf, that Pakistan had started to spend more on the military than in the previous 30 years of its history.[44] Pakistan's estimated annual military expenditure is about US$6 billion, but its adversary's spend is seven times larger, at $40–42 billion.[45] This reflects that Pakistan still spends a minimum on its nuclear weapons programme. Given the poor economy and poor allocation of economic resources, Pakistan may not spend much more than its adversary currently does. Larger nuclear forces require a larger economy and for this, Pakistan requires a peaceful and secure domestic environment. This will not only bring domestic stability to Pakistan, but also ease the international pressure on Pakistan's nuclear forces.

Easing external pressure

Pakistan historically confronted severe external pressure to pursue its nuclear weapons programme. In the 1980s, the Zia regime neutralized external pressure through the policy of calculated ambiguity. The same approach was followed in the 1990s. After the nuclear tests, Islamabad adopted a minimum deterrence policy, calculating, amongst others factors, that a small nuclear force would help to ease external pressure. The International Institute for Strategic Studies (IISS) observed that 'one of the aims of Pakistan's minimum deterrence is not only to pacify external pressure with regard to Pakistan's nuclear weapons, but also to justify Pakistan's stance on its proliferation for maintaining minimum deterrence'.[46]

To do so, Pakistan draws the attention of the international community towards the loopholes and discriminatory approaches within the NPT, the CTBT and the FMCT. It also justifies Pakistan's pursuit of a policy of minimum deterrence by pinpointing the existence of nuclear weapons in the world. Moreover, it holds the international community, including the USA, responsible, for their armed support to its rival India, which Pakistan thinks has security implications for the South Asian region.[47]

Given this, Pakistan is apparently not ready to become part of the NPT. It maintains minimum deterrence by keeping nuclear forces for security reasons although it was an enthusiast of arms control and disarmament and often proposed recommendations to the would-be NPT establishment. The rationale behind Pakistan not signing the NPT and the CTBT, including its differences with the FMCT, is based on its security concerns in the South Asian region. In addition, Pakistan also pinpoints the existence of discrimination within the NPT, the disenchanted and unsatisfactory role of the established nuclear weapon states, its demands for nuclear legitimacy, and nuclear leverage over its adversary by the NPT members (see Chapter 7).[48] Pakistan maintains minimum deterrence capability in the absence of security guarantees and the existence of a security threat from its rival India. Although Pakistan understands that this is against the NPT regime, it requires a minimum number of nuclear forces for its security, survival and the easing of external pressure.

Conclusion

In the aftermath of nuclear weapons tests in 1998, Pakistan adopted a policy of minimum deterrence which became a centrepiece of its nuclear policy. This chapter traced out Pakistan's rationale of minimum deterrence – that is, the Pakistani nuclear planners conceptualized that the adoption of a minimum deterrence would ensure Pakistan's security and survival; minimum deterrence forces can quickly be dispersed and concealed to avert the adversary's threat of pre-emption; smaller nuclear forces can better be protected and disaggregated; the command and control system remains effective in terms of handling minimum deterrence, which in turn reduces the possibility of unwanted and accidental use of nuclear weapons; given the country's economic fragility, the nuclear leadership understands that minimum deterrence remains cost effective without necessarily spending much on nuclear forces; and minimum deterrence helps avert international pressure.

It was considered that Pakistan's policy of minimum deterrence would suffice to deter. However, the Pakistani nuclear leadership left a chasm within minimum deterrence that is a 'calculated ambiguity'. Nuclear ambiguity remains the central part of Pakistan's nuclear weapons programme, retained by maintaining that the minimum cannot be quantified. In doing so, Pakistan adds credibility as a modifier within its policy of minimum deterrence. The minimum deterrence becomes minimum *credible* deterrence. So why has Pakistan added 'credibility' within the minimum, and why is the minimum not minimal? This is discussed next.

Notes

1 Henry Kissinger, *Nuclear Weapons and Foreign Policy*, New York: Harpers and Brothers, 1957, 7–8.
2 Bhumitra Chakma, 'Pakistan's Post-Test Nuclear Use Doctrine', in Bhumitra Chakma (ed.) *The Politics of Nuclear Weapons in South Asia*, London: Ashgate, 2011, 75.
3 For useful discussion on this perspective, see Scott D. Sagan, 'The Origins of Military Doctrine and Command and Control System', in S.D. Sagan, J.J. Wirtz and P.R. Lavoy (eds) *Planning the Unthinkable: How New Powers Will Use Nuclear, Biological, and Chemical Weapons*, London: Cornell University, 2000, 16–46.
4 Chakma, 'Pakistan's Post-Test Nuclear Use Doctrine', 75.
5 Author's interview with Khalid Rehman, director-general of the Institute of Policy Studies, Pakistan, September 2012.
6 Mahmud Ali Durrani, 'Pakistan's Strategic Thinking and the Role of Nuclear Weapons', 2004, www.cmc.sandia.gov/cmc-papers/sand2004-3375p.pdf (accessed 18 June 2012), 23.
7 Author interviews with Khalid Banuri, director-general of arms control and disarmament, Adil Sultan, and Zafar Ali within SPD, September 2012.
8 Although the critics during the Cold War era criticized the US nuclear policy of 'massive retaliation' and high spending on nuclear forces rather than on conventional ones, these accounts also reflect the minimal treatment of strategic forces. For interesting accounts, see P.M.S. Blackett, 'A Critique of Defence Thinking', *Survival* 3(3), April 1961: 126–34; P.M.S. Blackett, *Studies of War: Nuclear and Conventional*, London: Oliver & Boyd, 1962; Anthony Buzzard, 'Massive Retaliation and Graduated Deterrence', *World Politics* 8(2), 1956: 228–37; Anthony Buzzard, 'Defence, Disarmament and Christian Decision', *Survival* 3(5), 1961: 207–19; Anthony Buzzard, John Slessor and Richard Lowenthal, 'The H-Bomb: Massive Retaliation or Graduated Deterrence', *International Affairs* 32(2), 1956: 148–65. For a fresh, contemporary account of minimum deterrence, see Peter Gizewski,

Minimum Nuclear Deterrence in a New World Order, Aurora Papers 24, Ottawa: Canadian Centre for Global Security, 1994; Avery Goldstein, *Deterrence and Security in the 21st Century: China, Britain, France, and the Enduring Legacy of the Nuclear Revolution*, California: Stanford University Press, 2000; M.R. Basrur, *Minimum Deterrence and India's Nuclear Security*, California: Stanford University Press, 2006; James Wood Forsyth Jr, B. Chance Saltzman and Gary Schaub Jr, 'Minimum Deterrence and its Critics', *Security Studies Quarterly*, 2010: 3–12; Stephen J. Cimbala, 'Minimum Deterrence and Missile Defences: US and Russia Going Forward', *Comparative Strategy* 30(4), 2011: 347–62; Keith B. Payne, 'How Much is Enough? A Goal Driven Approach to Defining Key Principles for Measuring the Adequacy of US Strategic Forces', *Contemporary Strategy* 31(1), 2012: 3–17.
9 Durrani, 'Pakistan's Strategic Thinking', 23–24.
10 This was confirmed by the author's interview with the former Foreign Minister Abdul Sattar, September 2012. Abdul Sattar stated that, 'I was then a foreign minister and second to the president of Pakistan to be responsible for issuing an order of any use of nuclear weapons. I ordered the Pakistani nuclear leadership to be rational in their leadership and avert nonsensical statements of using these weapons for war-fighting purposes so was this message to our adversary. These weapons are not for war-fighting purposes'.
11 Abdul Sattar, Zulfiqar Ali Khan and Agha Shahi, 'Securing the Nuclear Peace', *The News*, 5 October 1999, emphasis added.
12 Ambiguity has both stabilizing and destabilizing deterrent effects when it comes to the command and control of nuclear weapons of both the established and minor nuclear weapon states. Feroz Hassan Khan stated that, 'although ambiguity may serve the purpose of deterrence, this could be dangerous as a crisis unfolds, particularly when an opaque deployment occurs that could be misread by other side. If the region moves closer to deployment, the chance of system failure increases. As questions on safety and security become complicated, the burden on command and control increases': Feroz Hassan Khan, 'Nuclear Command and Control in South Asia During Peace, Crisis and War', *Contemporary South Asia* 14(2), 2005: 171.
13 Author's interview with senior officials of Pakistan's SPD, Khalid Banuri, Adil Sultan and Zafar Ali, 17 September 2012.
14 Interview with Ambassador Tariq Osman Hyder, Foreign Ministry, Islamabad, September 2012.
15 Ibid.
16 Interview with Zafar Iqbal Cheema, September 2012. Cheema pointed out that 'The stated purpose of not formally announcing a nuclear doctrine is to maintain a level of deliberate ambiguity, but Pakistan's nuclear decision making echelon seems to be unaware that ambiguities can be maintained even in copiously written documents: Zafar Iqbal Cheema, 'Pakistan's Posture of Minimum Credible Deterrence: Current Challenges and Future Efficacy', in Zulfqar Khan (ed.) *Nuclear Pakistan: Strategic Dimensions*, London: Oxford University Press, 2011, 44.
17 Rodney W. Jones, 'Pakistan's Nuclear Posture: Quest for Assured Nuclear Deterrence – A Conjecture', *Spotlight* (Regional Studies Islamabad) XIX(1), 2000: 36.
18 Author's interview with Zulfqar Khan, who specializes in nuclear studies and currently works in Pakistan's Ministry of Defence as a security analyst, September 2012.
19 Sattar *et al.*, 'Securing the Nuclear Peace', emphasis added.
20 Interview with a retired Pakistani military official who wished to remain anonymous, September 2012.
21 Rizwana Abbasi, *Pakistan and the New Nuclear Taboo: Regional Deterrence and International Arms Control Regime*, New York: Peter Lang, 2012.
22 Zafar Nawaz Jaspal, 'Evolution of Pakistan's Nuclear Programme: Debates in Decision Making', *Regional Studies* XXX(2), 2012: 18–19. The former Pakistani

Foreign Secretary Abdul Sattar said in this context: 'Most knowledgeable observers of the Pakistani seem to agree that A.Q. Khan had an important degree of autonomy. If nuclear exports had been a consistent state's policy, then it would have been logical that the PAEC had a role in it too, which does not seem to have been the case': Abdul Sattar, *Pakistan's Foreign Policy – 2005: A Concise History*, Karachi: Oxford University Press, 2007, 218. Also, author's interview with Sattar, September 2012.
23 See 'National Command Authority Formed', *Dawn*, 3 February 2000.
24 Durrani, 'Pakistan's Strategic Thinking'; Kenneth N. Luongo and Naeem Salik, 'Building Confidence in Pakistan's Nuclear Security', *Arms Control Today*, 2007, www.armscontrol.org/act/2007_12/Luongo (accessed 14 June 2012); Bhumitra Chakma, *Pakistan's Nuclear Weapons*, London: Routledge, 2009; Naeem Salik, *The Genesis of South Asian Nuclear Deterrence: Pakistan's Perspective*, London: Oxford University Press, 2009; Jaspal, 'Evolution of Pakistan's Nuclear Programme'.
25 Durrani, 'Pakistan's Strategic Thinking', 49.
26 Scott D. Sagan, 'The Perils of Proliferation: Organisation Theory, Deterrence Theory, and the Spread of Nuclear Weapons', *Security Studies* 18(4), 1994: 66–107; Scott D. Sagan, *The Limits of Safety: Organisations, Accidents, and Nuclear Weapons*, New Jersey: Princeton University Press, 1995; Scott D. Sagan, 'The Origins of Military Doctrine and Command and Control System', in S.D. Sagan, J. J. Wirtz and P.R. Lavoy (eds) *Planning the Unthinkable: How New Powers Will Use Nuclear, Biological, and Chemical Weapons*, London: Cornell University, 2000, 16–46; Scott D. Sagan, 'The Perils of Proliferation in South Asia', *Asian Survey* 41(6), 2001: 1064–86; Scott D. Sagan, *Inside Nuclear South Asia*, California: Stanford University Press, 2009; Paul S. Kapur, 'Nuclear Proliferation, the Kargil Conflict, and South Asian Security', *Security Studies* 13(1), 2003: 79–105; Paul S. Kapur, 'India and Pakistan's Unstable Peace: Why Nuclear South Asia is Not like Cold War Europe', *International Security* 30(2), 2005: 127–52; Paul S. Kapur, *Dangerous Deterrent: Nuclear Weapons Proliferation and Conflict in South Asia*, California: Stanford University Press, 2007; Paul S. Kapur, 'Ten Years of Instability in Nuclear South Asia', *International Security* 33(2), 2008: 71–79.
27 Kenneth Waltz, *The Spread of Nuclear Weapons: More May Be Better*, Adelphi Paper No. 171, London: International Institute for Strategic Studies, 1981; K. Sundarji, *Blind Men of Hindustan: India-Pak Nuclear War*, New Delhi: UBS Publishers, 1993; Kenneth Waltz, 'Proliferation of Weapons of Mass Destruction and the Security Dimensions in South Asia: An Indian View', in W.H. Lewis and S.E. Johnson (eds) *Weapons of Mass Destruction: New Perspectives on Counter Proliferation, National Defence*, Washington, DC: University Press, 1995; M.K. Arif, 'Retaining the Nuclear Option', in T. Jan (ed.) *Pakistan's Security and the Nuclear Option*, Islamabad: Institute of Policy Studies, 1995, 121–29; Muhammad Aslam Beg, *Development and Security: Thoughts and Reflections*, Rawalpindi: Foundation for Research on National Development and Security Press, 1994; K. Subrahmanyam, 'The Emerging Environment: Regional Views on WMD Proliferation', in W.H. Lewis and S.E. Johnson (eds) *Weapons of Mass Destruction: New Perspectives on Counter Proliferation, National Defense*, Washington, DC: University Press, 1995; Devin Hagerty, 'Nuclear Deterrence in South Asia: The 1990 Indo-Pakistani Crisis', *International Security* 20(3), 1995: 79–114; Peter R. Lavoy, 'The Strategic Consequences of Nuclear Proliferation: A Review Essay', *Security Studies* 4(4), 1995: 695–753; Sumitt Ganguly and Devin T. Hagerty, *Fearful of Symmetry: India-Pakistan Crises in the Shadow of Nuclear Weapons*, New Delhi: Oxford University Press, 2005.
28 Luongo and Salik, 'Building Confidence in Pakistan's Nuclear Security'.
29 Jordon Seng, 'Less is More: Command and Control Advantages of Minor Nuclear States', *Strategic Studies* 6(4), 1997: 89–90.

30 Naeem Salik, 'Minimum Deterrence and India-Pakistan Nuclear Dialogue: Case Study on Pakistan', www.centrovolta.it/landau/content/binary/01.%20Naeem%20Salik-Minimum%20deterrence%20and%20India%20Pakistan%20dialogie,%20PAKISTAN.%20Case%20Study%202006.pdf (accessed 18 June 2012), 5.
31 Sattar *et al.*, 'Securing the Nuclear Peace', emphasis added.
32 Zafar Iqbal Cheema states: 'Pakistani nuclear planners are likely to build an arsenal of forty-five to sixty nuclear warheads … Pakistan probably has the capability to produce seventy-five to one hundred weapons of various yields … this force would include an *adequate second-strike capability* against even the most extreme contingencies Pakistan is likely to face': Z.I. Cheema, 'Pakistan's Nuclear Use Doctrine and Command and Control', in S.D. Sagan, J.J. Wirtz, J. James and L.R. Peter (eds) *Planning the Unthinkable: How New Powers will Use Nuclear, Biological, and Chemical Weapons*, London: Cornell University, 2000, 179.
33 For details, see IISS Strategic Dossier, 'Pakistan's Nuclear Oversight Reforms', in *Nuclear Black Market Dossier: A Net Assessment*, www.iiss.org/publications/strategic-dossiers/nbm/nuclear-black-market-dossier-a-net-assesment/ (accessed 11 July 2012).
34 Zafar Ali, 'Pakistan's Nuclear Assets and Threats of Terrorism: How Grave is the Danger?' 2007, www.stimson.org/books-reports/pakistans-nuclear-assets-and-threats-of-terrorism-how-grave-is-the-danger/ (accessed 28 June 2011), 10.
35 Ibid., 13: This was confirmed to the author by Zafar Ali of Pakistan's SPD, September 2012. For detailed and effective analysis, see Feroz Hassan Khan, 'Nuclear Security in Pakistan: Separating Myth from Reality', *Arms Control Today*, 2009: 12–20.
36 Munir Ahmed Khan, 'Nuclearisation of South Asia and its Regional and Global Implications', *Regional Studies* 26(4), 1998: 3.
37 Ibid., 3.
38 Federation of American Scientists, *Status of World Nuclear Forces*, 2 March 2012, www.fas.org/programs/ssp/nukes/nuclearweapons/nukestatus.html (accessed 2 March 2012); for these estimates, see M. Hans Kristensen and S. Robert Norris, 'Nuclear Notebook: Pakistan's Nuclear Forces, 2011', *Bulletin of the Atomic Scientists* 67(4), 2011: 91–99.
39 Interview with former Pakistani Ambassador Tariq Osman Hyder, Foreign Ministry, September 2012.
40 Interview with Khalid Banuri, Adil Sultan and Zafar Ali, SPD, September 2012.
41 Kristensen and Norris, 'Nuclear Notebook; Zia Mian, 'Pakistan', 2012, www.princeton.edu/sgs/faculty-staff/zia-mian/Pakistan-nuclear-modernization-2012.pdf (accessed 27 June 2012); David Albright and Robert Avagyan, 'Construction Progressing Rapidly on the Fourth Heavy Water Reactor at the Khushab Nuclear Site', Institute for Science and International Security, 2012, isis-online.org/isis-reports/detail/construction-progressing-rapidly-on-the-fourth-heavy-water-reactor-at-the-k/ (accessed 22 June 2012).
42 Mian, 'Pakistan', 55.
43 Haroon Rashid, 'Pakistan Reveals Defence Spending', BBC News, 11 June 2008, news.bbc.co.uk/1/hi/world/south_asia/7449179.stm (accessed 15 June 2012).
44 Saleem Shahid, 'Musharraf Rules out Rollback of N-Plan', *Gwadar News*, 13 September 2004, www.gwadarnews.com/newsdetail.asp?newsID=341 (accessed 15 June 2012).
45 For details, see Khalid Iqbal, 'India Triggers an Arms Race', *The Nation*, 2012, www.nation.com.pk/pakistan-news-newspaper-daily-english-online/columns/26-Mar-2012/india-triggers-an-arms-race (accessed 15 June 2012); Asif Ezdi, 'India's Military Spending', *The News*, 2012, www.thenews.com.pk/Todays-News-9-99572-Indias-military-spending (accessed 15 June 2012); Laxman K. Behera, 'India's Defence Budget 2012–13', *IDSA Comment*, 2012, www.idsa.in/idsacomments/

IndiasDefenceBudget2012-13_LaxmanBehera_200312 (accessed 15 June 2012); and 'Pakistan Defence Budget Goes up by 10 Percent', *The Times of India*, 1 June 2012, timesofindia.indiatimes.com/world/pakistan/Pakistan-defence-budget-goes-up-by-10-per-cent/opinions/13707742.cms (accessed 15 June 2012).
46 Author's interview with Rahul Roy Chaudhury, Senior Fellow on South Asian Studies, International Institute for Strategic Studies (IISS), London, 16 July 2012.
47 Author's discussion on this aspect with SPD, Foreign Ministry, MoD and leading nuclear experts, September 2012.
48 Author's detailed discussion with Zafar Iqbal Cheema, Mansoor Ahmed and Rizwana Abbasi, who specialized in nuclear studies, September 2012.

4 Pakistan's policy of minimum credible deterrence
Why minimum is not the minimum?

Introduction

With the nuclear weapon tests in May 1998, Pakistan unveiled the nuclear opacity that it had been pursuing for decades. Islamabad considers the 'basic tenets' of its self-proclaimed nuclear policy: 1 nuclear threats warrant nuclear responses; 2 nuclear forces will act as multipliers to balance the conventional forces of the adversary; and 3 finding regional solutions to non-proliferation issues.[1] These variables seem consistent with the essentials of minimum deterrence. This chapter traces out Pakistan's initial policy of minimum deterrence. In the aftermath of Pakistan's nuclear weapon tests, it was considered that minimum deterrence would suffice. Later, Pakistan could not sustain minimum deterrence because of perceived security threats and changed security dynamics in South Asia. Moreover, Pakistan seems preoccupied with the issues of credibility, survivability and invulnerability. Therefore, Pakistan brought about a subtle shift in its nuclear policy orientation, adding the modifier 'credible' to minimum. Minimum deterrence (MD) changed into minimum credible deterrence (MCD).

Pakistan currently follows the nuclear policy of 'minimum credible deterrence'. It keeps its policy options in a 'calculated ambiguity', which is deliberate, intending to keep the adversary guessing about the deployment and employment of nuclear forces. Pakistan deliberately does not want officially to declare and make its nuclear policy public when it comes to the number, design, miniaturization, expansion and fitting of its nuclear weapons into either missiles or aircraft. The MCD stays vague and ambiguous. In the meantime, Pakistani officials' statements from the NCA, the SPD, and the conceptual analysis of experts on the issue are considered a reasonable explanatory and comparative approach to the understanding of *why minimum is not the minimum*. More than a decade and a half after the nuclear tests, minimum deterrence remains indeterminate. Credibility as a modifier adds complexity within Pakistan's nuclear policy which needs to be determined clearly. This chapter explores various tangible and intangible factors responsible for why Pakistan adds 'credibility' to the minimum and why the minimum is not minimal. Why could Pakistan not sustain the minimum deterrence it conceptualized earlier?

Before examining Pakistan's policy of MCD and the factors responsible for its nuclear policy shift from MD to MCD, it is important to understand broadly minimum deterrence, to set a context for Pakistan's policy of MCD.

Understanding minimum deterrence

When it comes to nuclear weapon use, no one is sure how much infliction the adversary accepts and how much is unacceptable. Leaving aside contemporary sophisticated nuclear weapon systems, it is considered that the use of even one nuclear weapon could cause a greater infliction which may not be acceptable to any adversary. Therefore, measuring deterrence as an inflicting force by maximizing the number is not a viable strategy because of the fact that even the *minimum* can cause unacceptable damage.[2] During the Cold War period, both the USA and the Soviet Union planned a greater number of nuclear operations. Their proposed nuclear missions were based upon *assured destruction*, which encouraged the adversaries on both sides of the Atlantic to expand, modernize and hold their nuclear forces on hair-trigger alert for 'warfighting' purposes. For the survival and absorption of the first strike, the adversaries were in a consistent search for a secure 'second strike' capability to retaliate with unacceptable damage, which in turn required large, survivable, reliable nuclear forces.

Deterrence, albeit difficult and expensive for the Cold War adversaries, could be achieved by keeping the *maximum or offensive deterrence forces* with a fuller spectrum.[3] However, the rationale of offensive deterrence did not convince the international community. Critics opposed this approach and echoed the language of the *minimum*, which provided an innovative conceptual rationale that a small number of nuclear forces can deter, while the maximum can cause an unending arms race, more crises, unacceptable inflictions, and the danger of nuclear escalation.[4] The genesis of *minimum* deterrence can be traced in the outcry of a few amidst many who favoured the *maximum* to achieve deterrence capabilities. There is no fixity when it comes to minimum deterrence and this might vary from one nuclear weapon state to another. For many nuclear strategists the term minimum deterrence can best be placed somewhere between 'assured destruction and nuclear abolition'.[5] Cimbala keeps the concept of minimum deterrence limited to the USA and present-day Russia when it comes to their command, control, communications, computers, intelligence, surveillance and reconnaissance (C4ISR) of nuclear weapons for strategic stability. Cimbala states that, 'for present purposes, minimum deterrence in today's world implies that US and Russia arsenals would be limited to a maximum number of 1,000 operationally deployed strategic nuclear weapons, or fewer if possible'.[6] This minimum calculation may not be applicable to the deterrent forces of South Asian nuclear rivals. The proposed 1,000 minimum calculation for the USA and Russia may look offensive for the South Asian nuclear weapon states. Minimum nuclear deterrence is an unwieldy and sketchy concept between the

South Asian nuclear adversaries. Up to now both India and Pakistan have not been clear on their self-proclaimed minimum credible or credible minimum nuclear deterrence. On the one hand the adversaries claim to eschew larger numbers of nuclear forces, while on the other hand there is evidence of a shift of their minimalist postures. For example, India intends to develop a triad[7] of nuclear force capability and use these forces in response to potential biological and chemical weapons attacks. This is a clear departure from its Draft of Nuclear Doctrine in 1999. It is considered that Pakistan seems to be upgrading and expanding its nuclear forces by dint of not taking part in the FMCT.[8]

Many in Pakistan do not even consider the FMCT a formal international treaty.[9] The concept of nuclear deterrence becomes blurred and confusing. The language of 'minimum credible nuclear deterrence' amidst the few authoritative definitional statements does not fully cover the meaning of such a vaguely defined strategy. For instance, Baylis and Booth define the emerging term in simple nuclear strategy language: 'Minimum Deterrence is an attempt to prevent enemy attack through reliance on a small nuclear retaliatory force capable of destroying a limited number of key targets.'[10] This definition demonstrates that even a small risk can deter the adversary whilst keeping a small number of nuclear forces to target key adversarial positions. However, it does not say anything on the survivability of minimum deterrence forces. According to this conceptual nuclear strategy, the 'central assumption generates a wide array of strategic rules: a few nuclear weapons are adequate for deterrence to be effective; deployment is not necessary except under conditions of grave threat; numerical balances or imbalances are meaningless; one "leg" of a potential Triad is enough to deter; and the risk of escalation makes a counterforce-counter-value distinction irrelevant'.[11]

The smaller number of nuclear forces with the unique feature of their destructive power can cause unacceptable damage to the adversary, so it makes sense not to go for a bomb-for-bomb and missile-for-missile development against the adversary. 'If a small number of weapons can produce such sobriety on our part, why do we need thousands? A small number of nuclear weapons is all that is needed for states to achieve a relative security.'[12] The true spirit of minimum deterrence embodies a smaller number of nuclear forces against the key targets of the adversary without further expansion and development.[13] For instance, China's smaller nuclear forces in the Cold War deterred both the USA and the Soviet Union because these forces, with greater strategic impact, could hit both the USA and the USSR, creating a sense of fear that China's small nuclear forces could even cause greater damage if China were militarily attacked.[14] In a similar vein, if Pakistani minimum nuclear forces could successfully deter its adversary in the 1980s and 1990s, then the minimum could deter after the overt nuclear tests. The phenomenon of keeping the 'minimum' embraces a true spirit of minimum deterrence without necessarily embodying a large number of nuclear forces. Any expansion, modernization and maximization of nuclear forces would go against the language of an *actual* minimum deterrence.

Yet the phenomenon of minimum deterrence in the South Asian nuclear context is unclear for the security planners of both the South Asian nuclear adversaries. The term minimum is blurred by adding certain qualifiers, such as 'credible'[15] and 'defensive'.[16] Recently, the Pakistani military General Pervaiz Musharraf created ambiguity by adding a new conceptual term, 'minimum defensive deterrence'.[17] Even though both adversaries have proclaimed minimum deterrence, it is not clear what this concept means. For instance, Indian Minister of External Affairs Jaswant Singh stated in an interview that, '*Minimum deterrence is not quantification, it is not fixity. It is the enunciation of fixity.* The principle is codified in the Cold War phraseology. It is to be determined in accordance with the reality and an assessment of the security situation. And as the security situation alters with time determination of minimum deterrence also deters'.[18] Minimum deterrence becomes more of an umbrella concept where the fixity and quantity are undetermined. A number of factors can affect the sustainability of the minimum. These are discussed later in this chapter. First, it is important to analyse critically how Pakistan treats the minimum and whether or not the term minimum is transparent in its declaratory nuclear policy.

Pakistan's stance on minimum credible deterrence

Although it is difficult to understand clearly the complexity of Pakistan's stance on minimum deterrence, since the term minimum is not fully determined, it is important to understand how the term minimum is played out in the nuclear politics of South Asia. On the one hand Pakistan claims to pursue minimum deterrence against its adversary without necessarily expanding nuclear and conventional forces, while on the other hand it equally emphasizes that the minimum is not 'static' and 'dormant'. Until the term minimum is fully justified, ambiguity and complexity will remain the focal points of Pakistan's MCD. Abdul Sattar stated:

> The concept of minimum deterrence is not static and fixed. It changes in accordance with the changed strategic reality. The estimated number of nuclear forces Pakistan possessed in 2000 would not be sufficient in 2012 in accordance with the logic of minimum deterrence. To meet the requirements of minimum, the minimum should meet the traditional parameters of the deterrence. The minimum has to be credible. As long as minimum is credible, the number can be any. Minimum, if it is credible, has worked in the past. It should work now and in the future.[19]

This seems consistent with Sattar's earlier statements.[20]

In January 2010 Pakistan's NCA reiterated maintaining MCD against its adversarial approach of increasing and modernizing conventional capabilities. India vowed to speed up its arms purchases, which in turn became a cause of concern for Pakistan. The NCA stated: 'Pakistan would not compromise on its security interests and the imperative of maintaining a credible minimum nuclear deterrence ... massive retaliations of advanced weapons systems including installation of ABMs [anti-ballistic missiles], build-up of nuclear arsenal and delivery system ... tend to destabilise the regional balance.'[21] Islamabad's immediate reaction to its adversary's arms deals with major powers indicates, first, that minimum credible deterrence does not remain minimum and/or static. If India increases and modernizes its conventional capabilities, it pressurizes Pakistan to increase its nuclear weapon capability. Second, this scenario indicates the conformity of Pakistan's specificity regarding the adversary. Third, this further adds to the danger of an unending arms race in South Asia, which engenders more violence and increases the risks of military escalation. The Indian nuclear posture of *massive retaliation* with unacceptable damage and Pakistan's stance on maintaining the MCD lead the adversaries into unending nuclear tension, which could have far-reaching economic, political and strategic implications for the South Asian region. Pakistan realizes that it will suffer more than its adversary in this arms race because of its economic weakness and political fragility.[22]

Almeida, a Pakistani newspaper columnist, impresses on the Pakistani nuclear leadership that the MCD in relation to India needs to be defined because the military-bureaucratic establishment could stretch the numbers game from hundreds to thousands. In other words, say, if India produces 400 bombs, Pakistan would need 'X' bombs, but in ten years' time India might double the figure by producing 800, and then Pakistan would need '2X'.[23] From this analysis, there seems to be no nuclear end game, which in turn increases the reliance on nuclear weapons. As both the South Asian nuclear adversaries increase their nuclear weapons force, they would certainly rely more on the tactical and strategic development of nuclear weapons amid a crisis.[24] Thus, hypothetically, the more the nuclear weapon states increase and rely on nuclear weapons, the more they become responsible for managing these weapons, and the greater the chances of intensifying military conflicts because each adversary would then put their nuclear management team on high alert to use nuclear weapons for deterrence purposes. Khan stated:

> Nuclear weapons, instead of deterrent capability, have become a liability for Pakistani security planners. How much we need and for what purpose? Pakistan cannot go beyond what it should have. There would certainly be problems of maintenance of the increased nuclear forces. Nuclear forces require regular maintenance. One needs to be rational in one's perception when it comes to sustainability of nuclear weapons.[25]

If the concept of a minimum remains ambiguous and both the South Asian nuclear adversaries keep upgrading and expanding their nuclear weapons capability, say, in search of developing second-strike capability, then consequently this results in an unending arms race in the region. It appears as if 'ambiguity will remain [an] important element of Pakistani nuclear doctrine ... this has been an important factor in the Pakistani government not announcing a nuclear use doctrine'.[26] The concept of the *minimum* remains viable, credible and flexible in terms of the refinement and upgrade of Pakistan's nuclear programme. It does not remain static. The minimum deterrence needs to be contextualized. That is, it is not inert, but remains dynamic in accordance with the changed strategic reality.[27] A Pakistani security analyst stated: 'The size and quality of the deterrent forces cannot be fixed. It has to be flexible so as to change with time ... but the requirement of credibility can raise minimality ... it is just that need that a nuclear race is made of.'[28] The present Pakistani view on minimum deterrence appears to be a departure from the earlier version of the minimum conceptualized in the immediate aftermath of the 1998 nuclear tests. The question that arises is, why? At present, its minimum strategic calculus is largely set up by various factors affecting *why the minimum is not the minimum*. The remainder of this chapter focuses on tangible and intangible factors that broadly determine the discourse of minimum deterrence for Pakistan in general and South Asia in particular.

Is the minimum sustainable? Obstacles and obsessions

From the observation analysed above, it appears that the term minimum is deliberately exploited and played out in South Asian nuclear politics. Minimum deterrence, in actuality, has never been substantially justified in its true spirit in Pakistan's nuclear policy. Feroz Hassan Khan states that 'the term minimum is *tricky* when it comes to the MCD'.[29] The continuous and consistent arms race between the South Asian nuclear adversaries has never been reduced, nor has it been the agenda of the contemporary confidence-building measures (CBMs) between India and Pakistan. Although the Cold War ended and both the USA and Russia plan for unilateral, bilateral and multilateral reductions of conventional and nuclear forces, an arms race and the expansion of deterrent forces are active at an alarming level in South Asia. According to a recent report in *The Military Balance* from the IISS, Asia has the largest arms growth rate, exceeding Europe for the first time in modern history.[30] Although the central theme of this chapter is Pakistan's policy of minimum credible deterrence as it traces out why the minimum is not minimal, 'the India factor' in the South Asian context is contextualized particularly in the remainder of this chapter to build a better understanding of Pakistan's nuclear policy shift to the MCD. What are the obstacles that prevent the adversary from keeping the minimum truly 'minimum'? Why is the term minimum not fully and clearly defined? Does the minimum really deter?

The addition of credibility

In the aftermath of the May 1998 nuclear tests, Islamabad gradually became aware that the minimum cannot be quantified. Therefore, it added the qualifier 'credible' to articulate the future security situation of the South Asian region. Credibility requires flexibility and dynamism depending on the adversarial intention of arms build-up. Pakistan's foreign minister at the time stated in November 1999 that 'Pakistan will have to maintain, preserve, and upgrade its capability in order to ensure survivability and *credibility* of the deterrent'.[31] Years later, General Musharraf stated: 'The rationale behind our nuclear policy is purely security and we only want to maintain a minimum *credible* deterrence to deter any aggression against our homeland. Pakistan unlike India does not harbour any ambitions of regional and global status'.[32] This would provide Pakistan with a psychological comfort, add ambiguity to its nuclear policy, and provide leverage for the arms race.[33] It appears that the addition of credibility would keep the minimum flexible, that is, the minimum fluctuates in accordance with the evolving strategic environment of South Asia. Pakistani deterrent forces accentuate credibility with the minimum, which largely reflects the security condition of Pakistan. To thwart the evolving threat scenario, Pakistani officials consider preserving and upgrading its deterrent forces. A former Pakistani ambassador, Ali Sarwar Naqvi, stated: 'Pakistan is passing through a critical period ... Pakistan upgrades and preserves its nuclear weapons program to its comfort level.'[34] Thus, the addition of 'credibility' to deterrence meant to 'induce flexibility in Pakistan's nuclear posture and in its force-building plans'.[35]

The statements by Pakistani officials reflect that Pakistan's nuclear forces will not remain static, but largely depend on the adversary's evolving nuclear posture. This will be directly proportionate to India's military advancement. While analysing the concept of the minimum in the context of Pakistani nuclear deterrence, Zeb noted that 'Minimum is not lower or less in this case, but a logical as well as dynamic concept that will improve and diversify with time and need'.[36] It means that Pakistan tends to modify its nuclear doctrine in the context of the 'minimum' depending on the adversary's increase of nuclear forces.

Pakistan will restrain its military advancement as long as India does so. Therefore, credibility with the concept of the 'minimum' means for Pakistan that it would not only absorb India's first strike, but also be capable of striking back, hitting all the major targets.[37] Pakistani security planners deliberated that the minimum remains dynamic to meet Pakistan's security interests. Pakistan intends to acquire *credible deterrence* capability, which is a shift from its earlier conceptualized minimum deterrence. This is exercised against the potential increase of the adversary's nuclear and conventional forces, which in turn pressurizes Pakistan to meet its security and parity objectives.[38] On the strategic stability and parity of South Asia, Naqvi stated that, 'if there is no equilibrium and stability in the region, we cannot keep on saying that Pakistan requires to maintain minimum deterrence. Pakistan seems interested in dropping the word minimum from deterrence'.[39] Changes in the region's strategic environment force both the adversaries to modify their nuclear force postures which indicate that the 'minimum is not quite the minimum'.[40]

Given the arrival of credibility, the minimum may not be sustainable in the near future until the South Asian nuclear rivals mutually agree on some sort of arms control and disarmament mechanism and help establish an arms control regime (ACR). This could slow down the arms build-up of the two adversaries. However, it may not guarantee the actual practice of a minimum.

The absence of an ACR

One of the major obstacles for Pakistan and its adversary when tracing the concrete meaning of minimum deterrence, thus, keeping the limited number of nuclear and conventional forces, is the sheer absence of an ACR in South Asia. The absence of a regime encourages the countries on both sides of the border to develop various types of weaponry whenever they desire and deem fit. The absence of an ACR also enables the adversaries to expand more conventional and nuclear weapons through indigenous and exogenous means. Although various multilateral efforts have been undertaken for nuclear restraint, there is no serious effort to build a bilateral or regional ACR in South Asia.

Several bilateral confidence-building agreements are in place between India and Pakistan. For example, on 31 December 1988 there was an agreement which stipulated that they would not attack each other's nuclear installations and facilities. Both India and Pakistan would also facilitate the exchange of lists of their nuclear installations and facilities every year. A few important strategic agreements between the South Asian adversaries have included an agreement on advance notification of military exercises, manoeuvres and troops movements on 6 April 1991; an agreement on the prevention of airspace violations and permitting over-flights and landings by military aircraft on 6 April 1991; a joint declaration on the complete prohibition of chemical weapons on 19 August 1992; an agreement on the advance notification of ballistic missile tests on 3 October 2005; and an agreement on reducing the risk of accidents in connection with nuclear weapons on 21 February 2007.[41]

In addition to these agreements, there are several other confidence-building measures such as the 1999 Lahore Declaration and the 2004 composite dialogue to reduce military tensions and normalize the relationship between the adversaries.[42] However, these talks failed to deliver because of mistrust, limited war and other minor skirmishes between the South Asian nuclear rivals.[43] The level of mistrust and uncertainty continues, despite the current CBMs. These talks do not include substantially and more specifically the creation of an ACR. The key question arises: is it possible to establish an ACR against the backdrop of several nuclear and other atmospheric CBMs between India and Pakistan? Zafar Iqbal Cheema stated that, 'the establishment of arms control regime between India and Pakistan is possible, but at present its existence is unlikely because of the absence of strategic culture and prudent civilian strategists upon which the regime could be built. The cultural horizon in relation to an ACR is not of the level of the Cold War adversaries'.[44] The political leadership talk about the CBMs, but there are no talks on arms reduction. There is an absence of this type of issue in discussions between the two nuclear adversaries, which certainly has become a cause of concern for their future stable nuclear relationship. Even if there are talks, they are considered of 'diplomatic and political utility' to attract the attention of the major power states,[45] and most of the military and non-military agreements between the two sides of the border are never implemented, which has *'created a credibility crisis for the CBM process'*.[46] Conceptually speaking, one of the hurdles in this could be that the South Asian adversaries are in a formative phase of deterrent force build-up. To be sure, the Cold War nuclear rivals built thousands of nuclear forces in their formative phases. Although both India and Pakistan are in the development stage of their nuclear forces, they may not plan what their predecessors did.

The formative phases of deterrent force building

Both India's and Pakistan's deterrent force building are in the *formative phase*,[47] which requires them to maintain, upgrade and expand their deterrent forces. Though a decade and a half has already passed since their nuclear tests, they are actively pulled into arms building, particularly missile systems.[48] The South Asian adversaries tend to be highly competitive in terms of developing nuclear weaponry systems. In this context, Khan elaborated:

> The nuclearized environment and the logic of the South Asian nuclear weapon states are similar to that of the Cold War period albeit there are differences in between the two streams. Even though the South Asian environment is different, the Cold War-type logic is applicable when it comes to arms expansion of both the South Asian adversaries. So we cannot be dismissive about the early Cold War period.[49]

In a formative phase of arms build-up, any substantive talks on either arms reduction or keeping the nuclear forces minimum remain a pipe dream, at least for the near future. For any formidable change in connection to the limitations of nuclear forces, both the adversaries would need to come out of a formative phase. Ensuring a second-strike capability either by building a triad or keeping one's minimum deterrent forces safe and secure in exchange for a triad could help the two sides to surpass a formative phase of their nuclear force building.

From first- to a second-strike capability

Like their nuclear predecessors, both India and Pakistan look for a secure second-strike capability. In order to achieve this capability, both would obviously tend to increase and develop sophisticated deterrent forces, including both conventional and nuclear warheads, going beyond the minimum deterrence of this study. Pakistan has not defined the actual number and type of nuclear weapons required for its minimum deterrent forces. According to the Federation of American Scientists (FAS), Pakistan could have between 90 and 110 nuclear warheads, which is slightly ahead of its adversary (80–100).[50] It is interesting to see that Pakistan could reach 150–200 warheads in a decade, despite its political instability and economic crisis.[51]

Reports and estimates by the US Defence Intelligence Agency, FAS and IISS indicate that Pakistan is on the road to a second-strike capability. Khan, while elaborating on the Pakistani perspective on the issue of a low or high number of deterrent forces, stated: 'Should the perceived conventional imbalance between the two countries continue to favour India, Pakistan may find itself with two options: 1) secure an assured second strike capability … , or 2) prepare for the operational deployment or readiness of its existing nuclear arsenals.'[52] Both seem critical. First, in the struggle for a second-strike capability Pakistan requires a robust economy, which it does not have currently. Second, the readiness of its nuclear forces increases the possibility of pre-emption, miscalculation and inadvertence. What could possibly be affordable? Maria Sultan contends that 'a second strike is not always a triad. The small number of deterrent forces and secure command and control system can also provide a second strike capability'.[53] One reasonable solution to these emerging issues could be the adoption of *a true non-deployed minimum deterrence* (cost-effective option). The contemporary upgrade and expansion of deterrent forces on both sides of the border indicate the inconsistencies of minimum deterrence. This could be linked to a possible policy shift on both sides of the adversaries' border.

Policy shifts on both sides of the border

The competitive arms building and the nuclear policy shifts both in India and Pakistan create more inconsistencies with their understanding of nuclear weapon issues. For example, Pakistan is preoccupied with worries about the US-Indian nuclear deal, the development of India's military cold start doctrine (CSD), its pursuit of a triad, building a ballistic missile defence system, and India's subtle policy shift from 1999 to 2003 of a doctrinal draft in which India indicated that it might use nuclear weapons if it were attacked by chemical and biological weapons. The Pakistani strategic community views this as India's policy shift from a no first use (NFU) to first use (FU) option, although India pursues an NFU option as part of its nuclear use doctrine.[54] Nevertheless, Pakistan feels that these policy changes would have security implications for the region's strategic environment. Similarly, Pakistan's policy shift from MD to MCD, the construction of more nuclear reactors, and the upgrade of missile systems in particular to the development of tactical nuclear weapons as a response to India's CSD may also worry India. India may also worry about Pakistan's propensity towards fighting a limited war at the sub-nuclear level using proxies. Analysts consider that this could lead to a military escalation to the nuclear level. These changes in the strategic environment of South Asia contradict the basics of minimum deterrence. Also, this indicates the reality of minimum deterrence – that is, that a true minimum deterrence does not exist in South Asia. The policy shifts on both sides of the border posit a different treatment of minimum deterrence.

In the context of Pakistan's deterrent force building, the reality of the minimum remains a complex phenomenon. For example, Pakistan's President Musharraf stated: 'In the past we used to keep it quantified in the conventional weapons and now, ever since we have faced the nuclear and missile threat, in response we also quantified that – we quantified the minimum level. And today, I have been very pleased to announce that – we have *crossed that minimum deterrence level*.'[55] Islamabad blurred the term minimum. It is not clear what is meant by 'crossing the minimum deterrence'. One meaning could be of keeping no minimum deterrence rather than going beyond the minimum level of deterrence. This also could posit a march towards a 'sufficient' or an 'offensive-deterrence posture'. On a nuclear policy shift, an analyst serving at Pakistan's Ministry of Defence stated: 'Pakistan needs to review its nuclear posture in accordance with the changed circumstances. The doctrinal reviews would largely depend on the existing Indian factor as Pakistan's entire nuclear program is Indian-centric. If India expands and develops its deterrent forces, then Pakistan needs to go at the proportionate level rather than weapon to weapon given its poor economic condition.'[56]

The continuous arms competition, albeit not at the level of the Cold War adversaries, and the war-like doctrinal postures make the minimum deterrence slippery and unwieldy. Two things may help define the minimum deterrence when it comes to nuclear weapons development in South Asia. First, both the adversaries might acquire a survivable second-strike capability.[57] Unless they do this, the adversaries will not be satisfied with the existing nuclear force postures. This may also discredit the essence of minimum deterrence because the adversaries may upgrade and expand deterrent forces in the quest for a second-strike capability. Second, both the adversaries could limit the pace of increasing the number of warheads they have attained in just a short period of time. This is somewhat unlikely at present, since both states appear more competitive in terms of developing their deterrent forces and they are in a formative phase of arms building. The trust necessary to hold and sustain mature talks is missing.

Trust deficit

The absence of trust, the pragmatic resolution of outstanding issues including the core issue of Kashmir, and politically consistent talks on the reduction of deterrent forces make the region more volatile. This causes the adversaries to go beyond the minimum. The political rivalry between the two nuclear adversaries of South Asia has become so intensified that there seems to be little political will for the resolution of all issues. This further causes both states to develop sophisticated forces undermining the minimum. In the presence of a trust deficit, a Pakistani official stated, 'both India and Pakistan talk, but these talks remain less productive which result in the failure of confidence building agreements'.[58] The Kargil Crisis in 1999, the military stand-off in 2001–02 between India and Pakistan, and the Mumbai terrorist attack in 2008 have further created a gap in terms of building trust between India and Pakistan.

Terrorism is still a major issue between India and Pakistan and the core issue of Kashmir is yet to be resolved. New Delhi insists that without resolving the issue of terrorism emanating from Pakistan, there cannot be any fruitful talks between the two countries. It is feared that terrorism could cause crisis instability and provoke an Indo–Pakistani nuclear confrontation.[59] India does not consider any talks as being productive without discussing and resolving this issue. The political disagreement and mistrust on the resolution of security-related issues have intensified the conflict between India and Pakistan. Terrorism has become the outstanding issue while discussion on the resolution of the Kashmir problem has slowed. In the meantime, 'the prospect for normalisation of Indo-Pakistani relations is dim. The core issue in Indo-Pakistani relations – the Kashmir dispute – still remains unresolved and no helpful sign is visible of its resolution in the foreseeable future'.[60] One wonders how a true minimum deterrence could be maintained in South Asia without considering the external factor between India and Pakistan.

External factors limiting an actual minimum

The issue of external influence is a key obstacle to the minimum being truly minimal in South Asia. Chakma calls this an 'extra-regional link factor' which encourages the two states to develop deterrent forces: 'What happens outside the region, therefore, has a profound bearing on the South Asian strategic developments ... Pakistan's security concerns are India-specific; India's strategic worries are tied to China and China's to the United States.'[61] In terms of nuclear proliferation, these states are linked together. The tense and strained relationship between the USA and China puts pressure on the minor nuclear weapon states (India and Pakistan), which in turn causes the arms build-up between them. Thus, in this extra-regional link scenario one can assume that 'the key driver of India's nuclear weapons program is China. Beijing launched its nuclear weapons program because of the fear of US nuclear arsenal',[62] whilst the Pakistani nuclear weapons programme, since its inception, has been India-specific. Tariq Osman Hyder verifies the external factor affecting the actuality of the minimum in the South Asian region. 'Whether or not there would be an actual nuclear minimum deterrence in South Asia, it would largely depend on a *global factor*.'[63] In a related way, one of the Pakistani nuclear analysts stated that Pakistan's policy of minimum deterrence and other sub-policies related to the MCD are subject to the external factor.[64]

In addition, as India is *allergic* to the Pakistan-China nexus for the development of nuclear and conventional forces, Pakistan, likewise, has concerns over the US-Indian nuclear deal.⁶⁵ External factors such as the Indian-US nuclear deal, its military CSD and the plan for a ballistic missile defence system, make the minimum deterrence disproportionate in South Asia. The validity of Pakistani policy statements exists in a wider strategic circle of Pakistan. For example, a Pakistani leading nuclear strategist recently stated:

> the most fundamental international developments which have deeply affected Pakistan's MD, are the Indo-US nuclear agreement; the NSG unconditional exemption to India to purchase nuclear materials from NSG members; and the IAEA's India specific safeguards ... will far outstrip Pakistan's quantities of fissile material and pose a serious challenge to Pakistan in maintaining its nuclear force level adequate for an equilibrium that can assure the efficacy of minimum credible deterrence.⁶⁶

Given this external factor, Cheema points to *a reappraisal* to Pakistan's MCD to meet the emerging challenges posed to its nuclear deterrence capability and the safety and security of the related materials competitively.⁶⁷ That said, the extra-regional factor disturbs not only the strategic balance between the South Asian nuclear rivals, but also impinges upon maintaining the minimum as a 'minimum'. This factor, as Cheema asserts, could eventuate Pakistan's position from the institution of minimum deterrence to a regime of 'sufficient deterrence'.⁶⁸ The extra-regional factor prevents the South Asian nuclear weapon states, including the established nuclear weapon states like China, from crafting a better framework for maintaining a true minimum deterrence in the South Asian region.

Conclusion

Pakistan keeps the term minimum deterrence ambiguous and open to discussion. This means that if the adversary increases and upgrades its weapons, Pakistan will follow suit. The number is not defined in actual terms. It may increase depending on the security milieu in the South Asian region. This chapter traced out several problems for Pakistan maintaining MD, among which are: Pakistan's search for the acquisition of secure second-strike capability; the addition of credibility to the minimum; the gradual policy shifts in South Asia; the absence of an ACR; political disagreement and mistrust; the formative phases of arms building in South Asia; and above all, the extra-regional linkage factor. All these factors force Pakistan to preserve, upgrade and sustain its deterrent forces, which in turn undermines minimum deterrence. In these changed strategic circumstances in South Asia, Pakistan appears to have difficulty in sustaining minimum deterrence, and its policy of MD has shifted to MCD.

Since exact numbers have not been defined, the true spirit of 'minimum' is exploited and undermined. As long as the danger of arms building and nuclear weapons use exist in the conflicting South Asian region, more opportunities will attract Pakistan to develop and upgrade deterrent forces. The march for a second-strike capability – a triad means the acquisition of more deterrent forces. Pakistan is currently preserving and upgrading its force building to meet the principles of MCD, but what force building does Pakistan have in mind, and why is it developing the propensity to build these forces?

Notes

1 It is interesting to note that Pakistan's doctrinal posture still remains officially undeclared after one and a half decade of nuclear tests. The basic tenets of Pakistani nuclear weapons policy have been stated in various forms, by officials of the Pakistani government. Minimum credible deterrence, albeit not fully defined and transparent, remains the key principle of Pakistan's nuclear policy. Many officials who are connected within Pakistan's nuclear weapons programme agree with four Pakistani nuclear policy objectives: 1 deter all forms of external aggression; 2 deter through a combination of conventional and strategic forces; 3 deter counter-force strategies by securing strategic assets and threatening nuclear retaliation; and 4 stabilize strategic deterrence in South Asia. See Farah Zahra, 'Pakistan's Road to a Minimum Nuclear Deterrent', *Arms Control Today*, July/August 1999: 1–8; Paul K. Kerr and Mary Beth Nikitin, 'Pakistan's Nuclear Weapons: Proliferation and Security Issues', Congressional Research Service, 2011, www.fas.org/sgp/crs/nuke/RL34248.pdf (accessed 28 February 2012). For interesting analysis, see Rodney W. Jones, 'Pakistan's Nuclear Posture: Arms Race Instabilities in South Asia', *Asian Affairs, an American Review* 25(2), 1998: 67–87; Zafar Iqbal Cheema, 'Pakistan's Nuclear Use Doctrine and Command and Control', in S.D. Sagan, J.J. Wirtz and P.R. Lavoy (eds) *Planning the Unthinkable: How New Powers Will Use Nuclear, Biological, and Chemical Weapons*, London: Cornell University, 2000, 158–81; Mahmud Ali Durrani, 'Pakistan's Strategic Thinking and the Role of Nuclear Weapons', 2004, www.cmc.sandia.gov/cmc-papers/sand2004-3375p.pdf (accessed 18 June 2012); Bhumitra Chakma, 'Pakistan's Nuclear Doctrine and Command and Control System: Dilemmas of Small Nuclear Forces in the Second Atomic Age', *Security Challenges* 2(2), July 2006: 115–33.
2 Robert Jervis, 'Why Nuclear Superiority Doesn't Matter', *Political Science Quarterly* 94(4), 1979: 617–33.
3 For useful studies on this aspect, see for example, Albert Wohlstetter, 'The Delicate Balance of Terror', *Foreign Affairs* 37(1), 1958: 211–23. Wohlstetter stated on increasing the number of US forces: 'Since sputnik, the United States has made several moves to assure the world (that is, the enemy, but more especially our allies and ourselves) that we will match or overmatch … ' (212); 'On our side we must consider an enormous variety of strategic weapons … ' (215); and 'The most important conclusion is that we must expect a vast increase in the weight of attack which the Soviets can deliver … ' (217): J.F. Dulles, 'Policy for Security and Peace', *Foreign Affairs* 32(3), 1954: 353–64; J.F. Dulles, 'The Evolution of Foreign Policy', *Department of State Bulletin*, July 1954: 107–10; Samuel F. Wells, 'The Origin of Massive Retaliation', *Political Science Quarterly* 96(1), 1981: 31–52.
4 For interesting accounts critiquing 'war-fighting' strategies, see Thomas Schelling, 'Nuclear Strategy in Europe', *World Politics* 14(3), 1962: 421–32; Bernard Brodie, 'Nuclear Weapons: Strategic or Tactical', *Foreign Affairs* 32(1/4), 1954: 217–22; Anthony Buzzard, John Slessor and Richard Lowenthal, 'The H-Bomb: Massive Retaliation or Graduated Deterrence', *International Affairs* 32(2), 1956: 148–65; P.M.S. Blackett, 'A Critique of Defence Thinking', *Survival* 3(3), April 1961: 126–34;

P.M.S. Blackett, *Studies of War: Nuclear and Conventional*, London: Oliver & Boyd, 1962. For more recent accounts proposing that the major nuclear weapon states, particularly the USA, maintain the minimum deterrence by reducing their nuclear forces, see James Wood Forsyth Jr, Chance B. Saltzman and Gary B. Schaub Jr, 'Minimum Deterrence and its Critics', *Security Studies Quarterly*, 2010: 3–12; Forsyth *et al.*, 'Remembrance of Things Past: The Enduring Value of Nuclear Weapons', *Security Studies Quarterly*, 2010: 74–89.
5 Stephen J. Cimbala, 'Minimum Deterrence and Missile Defences: US and Russia Going Forward', *Comparative Strategy* 30(4), 2011: 352.
6 Ibid., 352.
7 The term 'triad', in nuclear deterrence forces, is the combination of submarine-launched ballistic missiles (SLBMs), intercontinental ballistic missiles (ICBMs), and nuclear-armed long-range bombers. This conceptual strategy was first carried out by the USA during the Cold War in order to provide its deterrence forces with the military options of placement of various delivery vehicles to discourage the opponent from undertaking the first strike.
8 For example, Michael Krepon has observed that the term 'minimum', which the Pakistani security planners used to incorporate with their nuclear weapons strategy, is not being used consistently. In other words, the modifier 'minimal' is recently less likely used. Krepon stated: 'In the past, Pakistani authorities talked about a minimal, credible deterrent, but a government press statement after the December 2010 National Command Authority meeting notably dropped the modifier "minimal". When explaining his country's continued opposition to the initiation of fissile material cut off negotiations on January 25th, Pakistan's Ambassador to the Conference on Disarmament, Zamir Akram, used the following formulation: "We believe that we need to build a capacity that is a credible deterrence at the lowest levels." Are these mere semantics?' For details, see Mark Jansson, 'The New "Minimum" in Pakistan', 2011, csis.org/blog/new-minimum-pakistan (accessed 20 February 2012).
9 Interview with Zafar Nawaz Jaspal, September 2012.
10 John Baylis and Ken Booth (eds), *Contemporary Strategy: Theories and Policies*, New York: Holmes & Meier, 1987, 312.
11 Rajesh M. Basrur, 'Nuclear India at the Crossroads', *Arms Control Today*, 2003, www.armscontrol.org/act/2003_09/Basrur (accessed 25 February 2012); Rajesh M. Basrur, *Minimum Deterrence and India's Nuclear Security*, California: Stanford University Press, 2006.
12 Forsyth *et al.*, 'Minimum Deterrence and its Critics', 3.
13 For an interesting account of the conceptual development of minimum deterrence, see Abdul Sattar, Zulfiqar Ali Khan and Agha Shahi, 'Securing the Nuclear Peace', *The News*, 5 October 1999; P.R. Chari, Pervez Iqbal Cheema and Stephen P. Cohen, *Perception, Politics, and Security in South Asia: The Compound Crisis of 1990*, London: Routledge Curzon, 2003.
14 Gurmeet Kanwal, 'Nuclear Defence – Shaping the Arsenal', New Delhi: IDSA, 2001, 110–11; Naeem Salik, 'Minimum Deterrence and India-Pakistan Nuclear Dialogue: Case Study on Pakistan', 2006, www.centrovolta.it/landau/content/binary/01.%20Naeem%20Salik-Minimum%20deterrence%20and%20India%20Pakistan%20dialogie,%20PAKISTAN.%20Case%20Study%202006.pdf (accessed 18 June 2012); Forsyth *et al.*, 'Minimum Deterrence and its Critics'.
15 For Rajesh Basrur minimum deterrence may not require credibility as a small number of nuclear forces in the event of its positive uses can cause a greater amount of damage, thus, has both the capability and credibility to deter the opponent. Basrur stated: 'India's stress on the "credibility" of deterrence reflects a lack of clarity as to what exactly constitutes deterrence. Because of the enormity of their effects, nuclear weapons need not be certain to inflict massive damage. Even a

small risk of large-scale devastation suffices to deter': Basrur, 'Nuclear India at the Crossroads'.
16 For interesting accounts on how both of the South Asian nuclear adversaries add the term credible to minimum deterrence, see Swaran Singh, 'India Nuclear Doctrine: Ten Years since the Kargil Conflict', in Bhumitra Chakma (ed.) *The Politics of Nuclear Weapons in South Asia*, London: Ashgate, 2011, 62; Bhumitra Chakma, 'Pakistan's Post-Test Nuclear Use Doctrine', in Chakma (ed.) *The Politics of Nuclear Weapons in South Asia*, 76.
17 See Pervaiz Musharraf's address to the 6th National Security Workshop at the National Defence College, 2 March 2006, presidentmusharraf.wordpress.com/2005/01/09/6th-national-security-2006/ (accessed 25 February 2012). See also other addresses, speeches and interviews of former President of Pakistan General Pervaiz Musharraf at presidentmusharraf.wordpress.com/chronicle/ (accessed 25 February 2012).
18 'An Interview with Shri Jaswant Singh, Minister for External Affairs', *India Today*, 11 January 1999, www.indianembassy.org/inews/February99/feature.html (accessed 25 February 2012), emphasis added.
19 Author's interview with Abdul Sattar, former foreign minister, 18 September 2012.
20 Sattar *et al.*, 'Securing the Nuclear Peace'.
21 *Dawn International*, 'India to Speed-up Arms Purchase after Plane Deal', 2010, www.dawn.com/wps/wcm/connect/dawn-content-library/dawn/news/world/18-india-to-speed-up-arms-purchase-after-scrapping-plane-deal-am-02 (accessed 8 September 2010).
22 Munir Ahmed Khan, 'Nuclearisation of South Asia and its Regional and Global Implications', *Regional Studies* 26(4), 1998: 3.
23 Cyril Almeida, 'Uncontested Dominance', 2010, www.dawn.com/wps/wcm/connect/dawn-content-library/dawn/the-newspaper/columnist (accessed 2 September 2010).
24 According to the current estimates released by the Federation of American Scientists, both India and Pakistan are expanding their nuclear weapons programme including their strategic deterrence forces. For example, it was estimated that 'Pakistan has produced 90–110 warheads. None of these are thought to be deployed but kept in central storage, most in Southern parts of the country. More warheads are in production'. See 'Status of World Nuclear Forces', 5 March 2012, www.fas.org/programs/ssp/nukes/nuclearweapons/nukestatus.html (accessed 5 March 2012).
25 Author's interview with Feroz Hassan Khan, former director of arms control and disarmament affairs within Pakistan's SPD, September 2012.
26 Chakma, 'Pakistan's Post-Test Nuclear Use Doctrine', 89.
27 Author interviews with senior officials and experts on the subject of this project within the SPD, Khalid Banuri, Adil Sultan and Zafar Ali, 17 September 2012.
28 A. Siddiqui, quoted in Chakma 'Pakistan's Nuclear Doctrine and Command and Control System', 124.
29 Author's interview with Feroz Hassan Khan, September 2012.
30 For details, see IISS, *The Military Balance*, www.iiss.org/publications/military-balance/ (accessed 19 March 2012); see also the Stockholm International Peace Research Institute (SIPRI) *Military Expenditure Database*, www.sipri.org/databases/milex (accessed 19 March 2012).
31 Sattar *et al.*, 'Securing the Nuclear Peace', emphasis added.
32 Quoted in Salik, 'Minimum Deterrence'.
33 Sadia Tasleem, 'Towards an Indo-Pak Nuclear Lexicon-II: Credible Minimum Deterrence', *Nuclear South Asia*, The IPCS Nuclear Security Program Quarterly, 2011, www.ipcs.org/Nuke_Quarterly-Jan-Mar_2011.pdf (accessed 18 June 2012), 12.
34 Interview with Ali Sarwar Naqvi, former Pakistani ambassador and executive director, Centre for International Strategic Studies Islamabad, September 2012.

35 Chakma, 'Pakistan's Post-Test Nuclear Use Doctrine', 76.
36 Rizwan Zeb, 'David versus Goliath? Pakistan's Nuclear Doctrine: Motivations, Principles and Future', *Defence & Security Analysis* 22(4), 2006: 391.
37 Cheema, 'Pakistan's Nuclear Use Doctrine', 179.
38 Saqib Mehmood, 'Our Nuclear Strategy', *Pakistan Observer*, 2012, pakobserver.net/detailnews.asp?id=119075 (accessed 18 June 2012).
39 Interview with Ali Sarwar Naqvi, September 2012.
40 Interview with Feroz Hassan Khan, former director of arms control and disarmament within the SPD, September 2012.
41 Bhumitra Chakma, 'Nuclear Arms Control Challenges in South Asia', *Indian Review* 9(3), 2010: 371–72.
42 For details of these provisions and other proposals, see Peter R. Lavoy, 'Civil-Military Relations, Strategic Conduct, and the Stability of Nuclear Deterrence in South Asia', in Scott D. Sagan (ed.) *Civil-Military Relations and Nuclear Weapons*, Stanford: Center for International Security and Arms Control, 1994, 80; Salik 'Minimum Deterrence'.
43 For example, Pakistan's Foreign Ministry blames the adversary on the other side of the border for the failure of strategic regime-related talks. Interview with Pakistani Ambassador Tariq Usman Hyder, September 2012. One of the failures and weaknesses of the talks in connection to these composite dialogues is the 'level of effectiveness'. Each side blamed the other for violations of the provisions, for simply not being honest and committed to the agreed provisions, thus making these levels of talks ineffective.
44 Author's interview with Zafar Iqbal Cheema, September 2012.
45 Rodney W. Jones, 'Prospects for Arms Control and Strategic Stability in South Asia', *Contemporary South Asia* 14(2), 2005: 206.
46 Zafar Nawaz Jaspal, *Nuclear Risk Reduction Measures and Restraint Regime in South Asia*, New Delhi: Manohar, 2005, 102–3, emphasis added.
47 I have borrowed the term 'formative phase' from an analytical piece by Bhumitra Chakma on arms control challenges. See Chakma, 'Nuclear Arms Control Challenges in South Asia'. I have, however, contextualized this term for the purpose of elaborating the argument that since both the South Asian nuclear adversaries are young nuclear weapon states and youth ultimately needs maturity, it is likely expected that they will increase and develop more sophisticated deterrence forces. Therefore, it becomes one of the obstacles for keeping the true minimum in South Asia.
48 On the one hand, for instance, Pakistan is active in producing short-range missile technology (e.g. Nasr or Hatf-9), which can be tipped with TNWs and most likely be used on the battlefield when they achieve the forward-edged capability; on the other hand, its counterpart is going beyond this. That is, India is looking ahead to building an ICBM with greater range (e.g. Agni V ranging 5,000 km plus). See 'India Tests Nuke-capable Missile Able to Hit China', *Yahoo News*, 19 April 2012, news.yahoo.com/india-tests-nuke-capable-missile-able-hit-china-034308390.html (accessed 19 April 2012); and 'India Tests Long-Range Nuclear-Capable Missile', *Dawn*, 19 April 2012, dawn.com/2012/04/19/india-tests-long-range-nuclear-capable-missile-source/ (accessed 19 April 2012).
49 Interview with Feroz Hassan Khan, September 2012.
50 Federation of American Scientists, 'Status of World Nuclear Forces', 2 March 2012, www.fas.org/programs/ssp/nukes/nuclearweapons/nukestatus.html (accessed 2 March 2012).
51 Hans M. Kristensen and Robert S. Norris, 'Nuclear Notebook: Pakistan's Nuclear Forces, 2011', *Bulletin of the Atomic Scientists* 67(4), 2011: 91–99.
52 Feroz Hassan Khan, 'Minimum Deterrence: Pakistan's Dilemma', *RUSI Journal* 156(5), 2011: 48.

53 Interview with Maria Sultan, September 2012.
54 Basrur, *Minimum Deterrence*.
55 General Pervaiz Musharraf's public speech 2005, quoted in B. Chakma, *Pakistan's Nuclear Weapons*, London: Routledge, 2009, 59, emphasis added.
56 Interview with Zulfqar Khan, nuclear analyst working in the Ministry of Defence, September 2012.
57 Since the act of accomplishment of second-strike capability becomes one of the important requirements of nuclear deterrence, Pakistan would look for this ingredient to achieve its deterrent capability. However, Pakistan and its adversary alike blur the true spirit of minimum deterrence. For the essential requirements of nuclear deterrence, see Scott D. Sagan, 'The Perils of Proliferation in South Asia', *Asian Survey* 41(6), 2001. Sagan stated: 'There are three requirements for stable nuclear deterrence: prevention of preventive war during periods of transition when one side has temporary advantage; the development of survivable second-strike forces; and avoidance of accidental nuclear war' (p.1065).
58 Interview with Dr Aman Rashid, director-general disarmament, Foreign Ministry, September 2012.
59 Andrew Phillips, 'Horsemen of the Apocalypse? Jihadist Strategy and Nuclear Instability in South Asia', *International Politics* 49(3), 2012: 297–317.
60 Chakma, 'Nuclear Arms Control Challenges in South Asia', 377.
61 Ibid., 378.
62 Ibid., 378–79.
63 Interview with Tariq Osman Hynder, September 2012.
64 Interview with a Pakistani nuclear analyst who served in the armed forces, Ghulam Mujaddid, September 2012.
65 Jones, 'Prospects for Arms Control'; Chakma, 'Nuclear Arms Control Challenges in South Asia'.
66 Z.I. Cheema, 'Pakistan's Posture of Minimum Credible Deterrence: Current Challenges and Future Efficacy', in Zulfqar Khan (ed.) *Nuclear Pakistan: Strategic Dimensions*, London: Oxford University Press, 2011, 77.
67 Ibid., 76.
68 Ibid., 74.

5 Pakistan's nuclear force building

Introduction

Pakistani policy makers and the strategic community initially viewed that a low number of nuclear forces would be sufficient to meet security requirements. In the aftermath of Pakistan's nuclear tests, a nuclear force-building plan was chalked out, based on the principles of minimum deterrence. That is, the deterrent force build-up would not be based on the logic of parity. Presumably, a larger number and size of deterrent forces, a nuclear triad and sophisticated delivery systems were not the focus of Pakistan's force-building strategy in the aftermath of its nuclear weapon tests. Islamabad reportedly adopted a long-term 15–20-year plan for force building. A short-term plan for 2000–05 was also adopted in order to build its deterrent forces. At the end of a five-year force-building strategy, Islamabad claimed in 2005 that it had reached a planned force-building threshold which meant that Islamabad quantified its deterrent forces.[1]

In the meantime, it was also viewed that Islamabad would not be able to sustain the low force build-up it initially planned because of various tangible and intangible factors, as elaborated in the preceding chapter. Minimum became an undefined concept both at the theoretical and practical levels in the making of Pakistan's nuclear policy. The immediate shift from MD to MCD was based on three reasons: 1 India is huge geographically and Islamabad is not yet satisfied with its ability to inflict unacceptable damage; 2 given the first use option, Islamabad is probably tempted by a flexible response and escalation dominance; and 3 large deterrent forces will protect Pakistan against the risk of an Indian first strike.[2] Therefore, Islamabad adopted a 10–20-year plan to improve the survivability, penetrability and command and control capabilities of its deterrent forces. This indicates that Pakistan's force building would much depend on changed strategic calculations in the South Asian region. It is considered that Pakistan is rapidly upgrading its deterrent forces in relation to its adversary, which contradicts the notion of minimum deterrence earlier conceptualized by the Pakistani elite.[3] Why is Pakistan building up its nuclear forces, and what has it done for its nuclear force building since the 1998 nuclear tests under the policy of minimum deterrence? These points will be elaborated later. First, it is important to understand the force-building process.

There are various theoretical explanations that detail why a state builds weapons. Conceptually, Barry Buzan has developed three models of force building by a state: 1 the action-reaction model; 2 the domestic structure model; and 3 the technological imperative. According to the action-reaction model, 'states strengthen their armaments because of the threats they perceive from other states'. In this process, states will either increase security to be more defensive or increase power to be offensive against the threats posed. This model assumes the international system as anarchic, where each state feels threatened by other states. Therefore, each state acts defensively or offensively for survival, independence and welfare against the encroachment of others. The volume of forces, timing, awareness and motives are the rudimentary ingredients of the action-reaction model. Second, the domestic structure model also plays an important part in a state's force building. The internalization and institutionalization of nuclear forces cause a state's security planners to build certain kinds of forces and delivery systems. The domestic bureaucratic personnel and people associated with these bureaucratic and organizational set-ups within the state increase pressure either to build or forego deterrent forces. Third, the technological imperative no doubt helps speed up arms procurement. It is viewed that technology has played an important role in the arms race, especially in the development process of nuclear weapons and their delivery systems. There is a significant role of technology in weapons development, deployment and employment. With modern technology, states upgrade, modernize and also dispose of ageing strategic forces.[4]

Amongst these models, the action-reaction model best explains Pakistan's armed procurement and its nuclear weapons development programme. The action-reaction syndrome has dominated South Asian politics of force building since the onset of independence in India and Pakistan. Pakistan considers that it was its adversary that created a security dilemma and caused Pakistan to build its deterrent forces, especially to acquire nuclear weapons. Pakistani analysts in general believe that Pakistan reacted against India's missile development programme and its nuclear weapons tests in May 1974 and 1998. Jaspal stated: 'Pakistan upgrades and expands its nuclear forces because of the changed strategic environment of South Asia where Pakistan is being pulled into arms build-ups.'[5] Zulfqar Khan stated: 'Pakistan's strategic review of its nuclear forces is largely based on its adversary's sophisticated arms build-up which pushes Pakistan to increase its deterrent forces at the proportionate level.'[6] The action-reaction phenomenon which is security oriented increases the arms competition in South Asia. This is elaborated in the following sections to understand how Buzan's conceptual action-reaction model is best exercised in South Asia, and how this model enhances the nuclear force building in Pakistan under the policy of minimum deterrence.

This chapter discusses Pakistan's nuclear force-building process. In particular, it explains what Pakistan has done to upgrade its nuclear forces; why Pakistan upgrades and preserves its nuclear forces (e.g. missile systems, air force, submarines, and uranium and plutonium enrichment); the significance of these nuclear forces; whether this means a shift in Pakistan's doctrinal policy; and if these arms build-ups meet the essentials of minimum deterrence.

Pakistan's MCD and its force building

Taking the action-reaction syndrome into consideration, Pakistan has not only acquired and tested nuclear weapons, but has also developed the delivery systems such as various types of missile systems and has procured aircraft for deterrence purposes. Pakistan also plans to develop nuclear submarines in order to build a second-strike capability against its adversary and to achieve a nuclear triad.[7] The minimum deterrence capability requires certain deterrence components such as the miniaturization of nuclear warheads, employment and deployment of nuclear forces, and delivery systems. Maria Sultan stated: 'Pakistan attempts to meet the parameters of its deterrent forces. These are effective force posture, survivability of these forces, better command and control, and the ability to penetrate in the adversarial territory at time of military strikes.'[8] The rudimentary components of Pakistan's minimum credible nuclear deterrence forces include the 'bomb design, miniaturisation, and fitting of nuclear devices onto ballistic missiles'.[9]

Nuclear forces can be delivered by a triad of air-, land- and sea-based delivery systems. The aerial mission requires modern, sophisticated bombers, the land one requires technologically advanced and sophisticated missiles, and the sea-based delivery system requires submarines such as the submarine ballistic nuclear-powered system. Even though Pakistan does not have the technological and financial resources to embark upon the triad delivery of nuclear forces, it is widely believed that it can carry out the nuclear mission by two possible delivery vehicles: bombers and missiles. It is important to understand how Pakistan plans to exercise its nuclear forces through two important existing delivery systems. First, Pakistan can use the US-supplied F-16 fighter aircraft, which are under the control of the Pakistan Air Force (PAF). Second, Pakistan can also use missile capability for a nuclear mission. The surface-to-surface missile systems, which come under the direct command and control of the Pakistan Army, are considered one of the two legs of Pakistan's nuclear mission. Pakistan is interested in expanding and modifying both of these systems, including the would-be nuclear submarine, to sustain the credibility of minimum deterrence. Before this chapter discusses the delivery systems, it is important to know about the fissile materials for which Pakistan is striving, which would help build the deterrent forces and make them ready for delivery systems.

Uranium and plutonium enrichment

There are two routes for the production of nuclear forces. First, uranium, a naturally occurring element, requires various types of technological means. It is a difficult and exhaustive process. Second, plutonium, which is not a naturally occurring element, is produced in a nuclear reactor. The USA was the first country to embark upon this development in the 1940s; subsequently, other nuclear weapon states followed suit.[10] When India tested its first nuclear weapon in 1974, Pakistan reacted in both the uranium enrichment and plutonium routes to acquire nuclear capability. Initially, the PAEC, headed by Munir Ahmed Khan, opted for the plutonium route in terms of building nuclear weapons. Khan, who served the IAEA for many years, was a plutonium expert. Although Pakistan adopted the plutonium route, progress remained slow largely due to the initiation of safeguards on fissile materials after the Indian nuclear tests.[11] Pakistan's KANUPP was under IAEA safeguards. The ineffectiveness of KANUPP for the fast production of plutonium made the PAEC postpone the plutonium route, leaving the uranium option for Pakistan to develop its nuclear weapons programme. According to the IISS dossier on A.Q. Khan, 'A CANDU-type heavy-water-moderated 50MWt reactor at Khushab, built with Chinese assistance and unsafeguarded, began operating in April 1998. Able to produce enough irradiated fuel for about 10–15 kg of plutonium per year, it significantly increased Pakistan's fissile material production capabilities'.[12] In subsequent years, Pakistan was successful in constructing the Khushab II and Khushab III nuclear plants, which increased the capacity of producing enough fissile material.[13] According to reliable sources, Pakistan has been constructing its fourth Khushab nuclear reactor, which will have the capability to produce a large amount of plutonium.

This nuclear infrastructure includes uranium mining; uranium enrichment; nuclear reactor fuel fabrication; nuclear reactor construction; and spent fuel reprocessing for plutonium recovery.[14] The significance of the fourth Khushab nuclear reactor is that Pakistan would be able to produce lighter, smaller nuclear weapons with a higher yield. Although there are no substantial details on Pakistan's production of fissile material, it is believed that Pakistan has achieved the capability to produce plutonium from the existing nuclear infrastructure. Whilst elaborating the significance of plutonium production, Mansoor Ahmed asserted that, 'Every country with nuclear weapons has preferred plutonium because it has a significant smaller critical mass with higher yield ... as it takes five times less amount of this material by weight per warhead compared to highly-enriched uranium. This helps in making advanced, compact, and miniaturised warheads for ballistic and cruise missiles'.[15] Pakistan has always expressed its concerns about the US-Indian nuclear deal which, Pakistan believes, increases its adversary's capacity to produce more plutonium fissile material for the production of more weapons. Since then, Pakistan has focused on increasing its deterrent forces and upgrading its nuclear infrastructure at the proportionate level to achieve a strategic balance in the South Asian region. However, this rapid production of fissile material has triggered an arms build-up in South Asia, with neither India nor Pakistan signing the NPT, and consistently disagreeing on the FMCT.

Pakistan's series of Khushab nuclear reactors, including the fast build-up of Khushab IV, is believed to have a similar capacity of producing 6–12 kg per

76 *Pakistan's nuclear force building*

year of weapons-grade plutonium depending on the level of efficiency. At the start of 2012, Pakistan was estimated to have produced 140 kg of plutonium. Assuming 5 kg per warhead, this is enough to produce 30 nuclear warheads. The International Panel on Fissile Materials (IPFM) estimated in 2010 that Pakistan had the inventory for producing 2,600 kg of highly enriched uranium (HEU) and roughly 100 kg of weapons-grade plutonium, which is enough to produce 200 warheads.[16] It is difficult to figure out how much HEU and plutonium a country produces for warheads per year. This is estimated by certain variables such as the amount of weapons-grade fissile material produced, warhead design proficiency, production rates, governmental official statements, etc.[17] With the increased production of plutonium fissile material, it becomes challenging for Pakistan to build delivery systems for this number of warheads because it is secretive about its nuclear weapons programme and its nuclear warheads. It often uses the terms 'warheads' and 'weapons' interchangeably. Nevertheless, the amount of plutonium Pakistan requires would largely depend on the scientific skills, the warhead design and the desired yield.[18] Pakistan seems interested in improving its nuclear infrastructure by replacing the uranium-based warheads with plutonium fissile materials, which it thinks would increase deterrence capability.

The increase of Pakistan's fissile material stockpiles and its reluctance to withdraw its veto from the FMCT negotiations represents a gradual policy shift in Pakistan's nuclear doctrinal posture regarding its adversary. The Indian-US nuclear deal, the CSD, and its adversary's armed boost make the economically and conventionally weak Pakistan vulnerable to strategic pressure to rely on nuclear weapons and strike a similar deal with China. With the US refusal to strike a similar deal with Pakistan, China seems willing to support Pakistan to gain a strategic balance in the region. Pakistan pledges to increase its fissile material stockpile not only to increase the yield of its warheads from uranium to plutonium, but also to boost the lethality and accuracy of its deterrent forces. Pakistan is currently increasing both the number and quality of its warheads. Although China has called for a similar deal by seeking approval from the NSG, the Group has failed to support Pakistan.[19]

It was recently reported that both China and Pakistan struck a secret deal in February 2013 in which China agreed to sell Pakistan a 1,000-MW nuclear reactor. This will be located at Chashma (Punjab province) in addition to two other Chashma nuclear reactors which were also supported by Beijing. This nuclear deal was chalked out while China was the rotating head of the NSG in 2013.[20] China joined the NSG in 2004. The international community, particularly the USA, has expressed concerns that China, being a member of the NSG, cannot sell nuclear reactors as they are not safeguarded. However, China calls these allegations 'groundless'. The deal, until it was recently revealed, had been kept secret to avoid international pressure. Apparently, there is less US diplomatic and political pressure on both China and Pakistan.[21] This could be for a number of reasons. The USA has recently developed better diplomatic relations with China in terms of having China play a constructive role in halting Iran from developing a nuclear weapons capability. Also, the USA needs China to play a positive role in terms of the denuclearization of the Korean peninsula. Second, the USA requires Pakistan not only to play a constructive role in the political and economic reconstruction of Afghanistan after the US withdrawal, but also Pakistan is needed in the global war on terrorism. However, it remains uncertain how the US non-proliferation role in the South Asian region will unfold after it withdraws from Afghanistan. Currently, the USA seemingly remains reluctant to pressurize China and Pakistan on building a nuclear reactor. In the meantime, it is observed that the Beijing-Islamabad nuclear deal will allow Pakistan to produce more fissile material, which in turn enhances Pakistan's capability to increase its deterrent forces. Beijing wants Pakistan to keep its deterrent forces both qualitatively and quantitatively strong. To be sure, the energy-monger China is largely interested in Pakistan's Gwader deep-sea port which Beijing views would meet its energy and economic interests. Presumably, this nuclear deal is a reaction to the Indian-US nuclear deal that Pakistan feels threatens its deterrent capability and, therefore, Islamabad would keep its deterrence credible. With the increasing production of fissile material, Islamabad could enhance its deterrent capability, but it could also face challenges in how Islamabad could manage the delivery systems for these increasing deterrent capabilities. Currently, Pakistan has two delivery systems for its nuclear forces: aircraft and missile systems. It also plans a triad, in reaction to India's recent test of a nuclear submarine system.

Air Force

Aircraft, particularly the modern, sophisticated US-supplied aircraft, have become one of the important legs of Pakistan's nuclear delivery system. Pakistan most likely is interested in using US-supplied F-16 aircraft for nuclear delivery missions.[22] When the USA worked closely with Pakistan to expel the Soviet forces from Afghanistan in the 1980s, it promised to sell Pakistan F-16 aircraft. Pakistan got the first batch of F-16s in the 1980s, and paid for more, but delivery was delayed. The US government cancelled the immediate sale of these aircraft under the Pressler Amendment because of the suspicion that Pakistan was preparing to acquire nuclear weapons, and that it could use the F-16s for nuclear delivery missions. The US Administration then denied these aircraft were capable of carrying out nuclear missions.[23]

Pakistan continued its efforts to get F-16 aircraft with important modifications from the USA. Its plan for the expansion of its aircraft fleet was meant to reduce its reliance on the USA. In the late 1980s, it was believed that Pakistan had designed a bomb that could be carried by the aircraft and many test missions were conducted in this regard to improvise the delivery of the bomb via aircraft.[24] Pakistan is currently in possession of more than 50 US-supplied F-16s, having increased the number,[25] according to the latest figure, to 86.[26] In the wake of the terrorist attacks on the USA on 11

September 2001 (9/11), when Pakistan once again became an important US ally in the 'war on terror', the USA promised to support Pakistan both militarily and economically. The US Congress agreed to provide Pakistan with 28 F-16s in 2006. Half of these have already been delivered, with the second half underway. The USA supplied three more F-16s to Pakistan in 2012.[27] With these sophisticated aircraft, Pakistan could hit most of its adversary's military installations and nuclear facilities.[28] However, it is not clear what proportion of these aircraft could be used for nuclear delivery missions. Pakistan may also use Mirage V aircraft for nuclear delivery purposes (see Table 5.1).[29]

Recently, Pakistan's Army chief of staff stated that India's CSD increases the possibility of 'sudden spiral escalation'.[30] In addition to the Azm-e-Nau III military exercise, the Air Force conducted a war-fighting exercise named 'High Mark 2010'. For the first time, Pakistan successfully conducted landing and take-off operations from the motorway to meet the emergency security needs against the adversary's offensive military posture envisioned in its CSD. Pakistan is now one of a few countries able to use its motorways in the event of war-like emergencies.[31] Both of the Pakistani motorways (M-1 and M-2) have four emergency runway sections which can be operationalized in time of emergency, and the Air Force used the M-2 in 2000 and 2010 during its air-war exercises. For example, the PAF has used its two fighter aircrafts Miraj III and F-7P, as well as the Super Mushak Trainer and C-130 aircraft, to land, refuel and take off to accomplish the war-like operation exercises.[32] Besides the economic purposes, motorways seem to play a critical role in future contingency plans and could provide a rapid air-fighting capability if these motorway sections are properly repaired and maintained on a regular basis. In Pakistan, the motorway build-up stretches from north to south (Peshawar to Gwadar) and would not only provide fast economic growth, but some of its sections could also be used for 'flexible operations'.[33]

Missile systems

At the start of the 21st century, the Carnegie Endowment for International Peace conducted studies on the rise and decline of missile systems on a global scale. The study revealed that the level of production of highly sophisticated missile systems was alarmingly high in the 1980s, but this number dropped in the 1990s.[34] Against this backdrop of assessment, it is interesting to observe that the South Asian adversaries consistently strived to improve their medium- and long-range ballistic missile systems throughout the 1990s, and

Table 5.1 Pakistan's nuclear-capable aircraft

Type	Range (in km)	Suppliers	Deployment	Quantity
F-16 A/B/C/D	1,600	USA	1998	86
Mirage V	2,100	France	1998	82

continue to do so. Missiles are a key component of Pakistan's arsenal. It emphasizes the development of a missile system as an important part of its deterrence capability.[35] Pakistani missile systems are capable of carrying out the nuclear missions with heavy payloads, and Pakistan is believed to be still developing and upgrading its missile capability (see Table 5.2). Recently, the US director of national intelligence stated that Pakistan is developing new missile capability which will boost its missile development programme, and this will enable Pakistan 'to strike a variety of targets at ranges of 200–2000 kilometres with both conventional and nuclear payloads'.[36] Next, we will look at various Pakistani missile systems in detail.

Hatf-I

Hatf-I is Pakistan's first battlefield-range ballistic missile with a range of 50–90 km. It is a single-stage solid propellant missile and has a capability of carrying up to a 500-kg payload. This was first tested in 1989. This missile confronted several unsuccessful tests which were then halted by security planners to plan for more tests until the beginning of the 21st century. There is no clear explanation why it was kept dormant for such an extended period of time, or why it reappeared. Chakma stated: 'A plausible explanation for reviving Hatf I missile is, perhaps, that after the experience in the 1999 Kargil War a tactical delivery vehicle was felt to be necessary.'[37] It is believed that Pakistan has about 80 Hatf-I missiles. The commencement of the Hatf series at the start of the 21st century, with the involvement of both North Korea and China, made it possible for it to be more sophisticated, precise, and possibly able to carry both conventional and nuclear payloads.

Table 5.2 Pakistan's missile forces

Delivery system	Range (in km)	Deployment
Ballistic missiles		
Hatf-1	50–90	1989
Abdali (Hatf-2)	180	2012
Ghaznavi (Hatf-3)	400	2004
Shaheen-1 (Hatf-4)	> 450	2003
Ghauri (Hatf-5)	1,200	2003
Shaheen-2 (Hatf-6)	2,000	2011
Nasr (Hatf-9)	60	2012
Cruise missiles		
Babur (Hatf-7)	600	2011
Raad (Hatf-8)	350	2012

Source: (Compiled from various sources, including Mian 2012; Chakma 2009; Salik 2009; and Kristensen and Norris 2011: 93)

Hatf-II/Abdali

This missile system is a two-stage solid propellant missile which has a range of 70–200 km and can carry a 450-kg payload.[38] Hatf-II was tested in early 1989 simultaneously with Hatf-I. There were no activities relating to this missile system for a decade. No reasons were given by Pakistani officials. Chakma notes that there were several reasons for this: first, the nascent missile programme faced technical constraints, due to which Pakistan suspended its development programme. Second, this project merged into another missile project involving M-11 missiles which China supplied to Pakistan in the early 1990s. A decade later, Pakistan developed a series of Hatf missile systems.[39] Currently, Pakistan seems to be getting rid of old missiles and upgrading the Hatf missile series. It has recently developed a Hatf-II (Abdali) short-range ballistic missile with a range of 180 km, which is capable of carrying both conventional and non-conventional weapons.[40]

Hatf-III/Ghaznavi

This is also a solid-fuel single-stage ballistic missile with a maximum range of 290 km, with the capability of carrying 800-kg payloads. This was first tested on 26 May 2002, although press reports suggest that Pakistan started working on this type of missile capability in 1997.[41] This is an improvised version of the first two Hatf missile systems which Pakistan tested in the early 1989, but then halted further development for unknown reasons. This missile is capable of carrying both conventional and nuclear weapons. This missile system was formally inducted into Pakistan's strategic forces in 2004.

Hatf-IV/Shaheen-1 and Hatf-VI/Shaheen-2

Hatf-IV, named Shaheen-1, was first tested in April 1999 and was inducted into Pakistan's Strategic Forces Command in March 2003. This is an improved version of the M-11 missile supplied by China. This is a solid-fuel road-mobile missile system which can carry up to 850 kg of warheads with a maximum range of 650 km. Hatf-VI/Shaheen-2 is the improved version of the Shaheen-1 missile system. This missile system has a maximum range of 2,200 km and is capable of carrying a 1,100-kg payload warhead. This was first tested in March 2004. China has assisted Pakistan in the development of this missile system.

Hatf-IV/Shaheen-1A

In addition to these missiles, Pakistan recently tested the Hatf-IV/Shaheen-1A which is the upgraded version of Shaheen-1. It is a nuclear-capable intermediate-range missile with a payload up to 1,000 kg and has a range of 750 km. The exact range was not revealed when the missile was tested on 25 April

2012. However, a Pakistani retired General stated that this intermediate-range missile could reach targets up to 2,500–3,000 km away. Head of SPD Khalid Ahmed Kidwai has stated that Shaheen-1A is the improved version of the Shaheen-1 missile and that it has enhanced Pakistan deterrence capabilities.[42] It is interesting to note that Pakistan tested this missile system after India had tested its long-range missile system Agni-V, which has a range of 5,000 km and can hit any part of its adversary, China or parts of Europe.[43]

Hatf-V/Ghauri-I and Hatf-VI/Ghauri-II

Pakistan increased not only the sophistication of the Hatf missile system, but also its range, accuracy and payload capabilities.[44] Hatf-V/Ghauri has a range of 1,300 km with a 680-kg maximum payload. Before Pakistan tested its nuclear weapons, it had already tested the Hatf-V/Ghauri missile in April 1998. This missile was in response to India's development of the Prithvi missile system. Since this missile looks similar to the North Korean Nodong missile, it is thought that Pakistan might have taken the design and technology from North Korea in the early 1990s in exchange for Pakistan's assistance to North Korea's clandestine uranium enrichment programme. This type of missile was inducted into Pakistan's Strategic Forces Command (SFC) in January 2003. Pakistan tested Ghauri-II in April 1999 after one year of Ghauri-I tests, of which it is the improved version. It has a maximum range of 1,800 km and is capable of carrying 1,500 kg of payload.

Hatf-VII/Baber

Baber is also an important part of the Hatf series of missiles. It is a low-level, subsonic, terrain-hugging cruise missile system. It was tested on 12 August 2005 with a range of 500 km. It closely resembles the American BGM-109 Tomahawk missile system.[45] After modifications, it could be launched from submarines and aircraft. Islamabad probably has started to upgrade this missile system in recent years (see Table 5.2).

Hatf-VIII/RAAD

This is an air-launched cruise missile (ALCM) with a range of 350 km. Hatf-VIII is capable of carrying both conventional and nuclear warheads.[46] The continuing tests of these missile systems indicates that Pakistan is improving and upgrading its deterrent force capability and credibility.[47]

Hatf-9/Nasr[48]

Pakistan recently tested a short-range tactical missile system called Hatf-9/Nasr in April 2011. This has a range of about 60 km and reportedly can deliver 'nuclear warheads with high accuracy'.[49] This missile system has 'shoot and scoot attributes' – that is, it can be quickly moved after shooting a missile. From a short range with tactical capability, this missile system is assumed to counter India's 'cold start' military doctrine,[50] and is called a tactical nuclear weapon (TNW). In response to Nasr, India's Defence Research and Development Organisation tested its Prahar missile system in July 2011, which has a range of 150 km.[51] Pakistan's SPD does not agree to the notion that the Prahar missile test was a reaction to Pakistan's Nasr missile test. Zafar Ali at SPD stated: 'India tested the short-range missile within two weeks of Pakistan's test of Nasr. How is it possible for India to test its short-range missile within two weeks of Pakistan's Nasr test? This indicates that India had already acquired the capability of TNWs. It was just short of testing.'[52] According to a report released by the US Naval Postgraduate School, 'The introduction of Nasr (Hatf-9), in April and Prahar in July indicates that both Pakistan and India have possibly succeeded in miniaturizing their nuclear weapon designs. If so, in the foreseeable future these missiles could be launched on a variety of land-based system, artillery shells, cruise missiles, or naval systems like torpedoes and ship-to-ship missiles'.[53] One interesting element in the development of this missile system is to counter India's nascent CSD. The CSD has been developed by India to wage a limited war.[54] In addition to aircraft and missile delivery systems, Pakistan plans to develop a nuclear submarine system to keep its deterrent forces credible vis-à-vis its adversary.

Nuclear submarine

The Pakistan Navy is considered a 'coastal or brown water' navy, which means it is small and can only manoeuvre relatively close to base at all times. However, with the diffusion of technology, 'navies are categorised as global, blue water, regional or coastal'.[55] The significance of the development of submarine-based nuclear weapons is that it is regarded the *safest*, particularly if the submarines are powered by nuclear generators that allow them months of undetected submerged operations.[56] Another significance of the nuclear-based submarine is that it adds to a second-strike capability, which in turn acts as a stabilizer of mutual deterrence.[57] The plan for a nuclear submarine system is in response to India's development of nuclear submarines. With the commissioning of a Russian-origin INS *Chakra*, India is also planning to induct the INS *Arihant* into the Indian naval forces. These two nuclear-capable submarines would patrol the blue seas by the end of 2012.[58]

These developments and the induction of nuclear-powered submarines have subjected Pakistan to strategic pressure and concerns. Pakistan's Naval Chief Muhammad Asif Sandila stated in reaction to the induction of India's nuclear-capable submarines that 'the strategic dimension of India's naval build-up is a cause for concern. We are mindful of this development and taking necessary measures to restore the strategic balance'.[59] Pakistan's defence analyst Dr Farrukh Saleem stated on local TV, while debating India's nuclear submarine, that India's launch of a Russian nuclear-powered submarine is a *non-event* as far as Pakistani security is concerned. His assertion is based on the following: 1 it is a non-attack submarine and can merely be used for deterrence purposes; 2 it is not Pakistan-specific, but is rather made to contain China; 3 it was launched 3,000 km away from Pakistan; 4 it is merely a symbolic deterrence gesture by India's naval force, and India had already deployed a Russian-origin nuclear-powered submarine in 1988; and 5 these submarines are based on Russian technology and many Russian submarines of similar technology sank before reaching their deterrence periods. Pakistan, therefore, needs to maintain its MCD without plunging into a vicious cycle of force building with its adversary.[60] In a similar fashion, Maria Sultan stated: 'For a triad, much depends on how secure a state's nuclear forces are.'[61] In connection with these growing security concerns, the *Margalla Paper* stated: 'Any future threat scenario against Pakistan shall most probably have complex multidimensional facts i.e. sub-conventional and un-conventional actors too. Therefore, to cover such a large spectrum of threat dimensions, a reappraisal of Pakistan's nuclear capabilities as well as policy is urgently required.'[62]

Of eight submarines, the Pakistan Navy (PN) has been working on at least five to tip them with missiles (Hatf-VII). These missiles are likely to be deployed in the PN's French-built Agosta-class submarines. The PN is operating five Agosta-class submarines: PNS *Hashmat*, PNS *Hurmat*, PNS *Khalid*, PNS *Saad* and PNS *Hamza*. Currently, all five submarines are armed with the French anti-ship SM39 Exocet missile.[63] Although there is no specific elaboration on why Pakistan should not arm these submarines with nuclear-capable missiles such as Baber, Brain Cloughley, a military defence expert, critiqued Pakistan's naval move and urged the country's security planners to upgrade the existing submarines and increase their number to 14.[64] The PN plans to build a nuclear-powered submarine within five to eight years.[65] Khan recommends that Pakistani security planners seek the China-based PLAN Xia-class nuclear-powered submarine with Pakistan naval officers trained to operate the submarines. Khan stated: 'The national maritime objectives or the task assigned to [the] PN may not merit a nuclear submarine. Nonetheless, preservation and credibility of deterrence value obligates such a consideration particularly in the evolving geo-politics of the IOR [Indian Ocean Region]'.[66]

Conclusion

Pakistani security planners initially thought that a low number of deterrent forces would suffice to meet its security needs. Islamabad even planned for both short- and long-term arms building. Pakistan claimed within a few years that it possessed minimum deterrent forces. In the meantime, there was a realization within the Pakistani strategic community that the minimum deterrence could not be quantified. Islamabad could not sustain the MD.

This chapter traced out various factors due to which Islamabad could not sustain the small number of nuclear forces it conceptualized in the initial years of force building. Islamabad believes that nuclear weapons and missile systems have enabled Pakistan to attain MCD vis-à-vis India. In addition, Pakistan is fast upgrading its delivery systems for these warheads to make its deterrent forces credible. Although missiles and aircraft are the main delivery systems for Pakistan's deterrent forces, it also plans to build a nuclear submarine. Islamabad's force building posits that minimum deterrence cannot be sustained. In other words, the fast upgrade and expansion of Pakistani nuclear reactors is a departure from MD to MCD.

Given the changes in the region's strategic environment and evolving security dynamics, Pakistan feels threatened. In seeking strategic parity, Pakistan not only increases its fissile material stockpile, but also relies on nuclear weapons use for stability and deterrence purposes. To counter both its adversary's conventional and nuclear attacks, Pakistan opts for nuclear first use. The conventionally weak Pakistan believes that with this policy option, it has deterred its adversary from crossing the LOC. However, there is an ambiguity within this declaratory policy which is contentious.

Notes

1 For details see, 'Nuclear Black Market Dossier: A Net Assessment', 2007, www.iiss.org/publications/strategic-dossiers/nbm/nuclear-black-market-dossier-a-net-assesment/ (accessed 20 March 2013), 31–33.
2 Ibid., 34.
3 Naeem Salik, 'Minimum Deterrence and India-Pakistan Nuclear Dialogue: Case Study on Pakistan', www.centrovolta.it/landau/content/binary/01.%20Naeem%20Salik-Minimum%20deterrence%20and%20India%20Pakistan%20dialogie,%20PAKISTAN.%20Case%20Study%202006.pdf (accessed 18 June 2012); Zafar Iqbal Cheema, 'Pakistan's Nuclear Use Doctrine and Command and Control', in S.D. Sagan, J.J. Wirtz and L.R. Peter (eds) *Planning the Unthinkable: How New Powers Will Use Nuclear, Biological, and Chemical Weapons*, London: Cornell University, 2000, 158–81.
4 Barry Buzan, *An Introduction to Strategic Studies*, London: Macmillan, 1987, 74–113.
5 Interview with Zafar Nawaz Jaspal, who specialized in nuclear studies, September 2012.
6 Interview with Zulfqar Khan, who specializes in nuclear studies and currently serves in Pakistan's Defence Ministry, September 2012.
7 See 'Pakistan's 21st Century Naval Modernisation Program', 15 May 2012, pakdefenceunit.wordpress.com/2012/05/15/pakistans-21st-century-naval-modernisation-programme-indian-nuclear-submarine-programme/ (accessed 21 June 2012).
8 Interview with Maria Sultan, director-general of South Asian Strategic Studies Institute (SASSI), Pakistan, September 2012.
9 Farah Zahra, 'Pakistan's Road to a Minimum Nuclear Deterrent', *Arms Control Today*, July/August 1999: 1–8.
10 Joel Ullom, 'Enriched Uranium Versus Plutonium: Proliferant Preferences in the Choice of Fissile Material', *Non-Proliferation Review*, Fall 1994: 1.
11 See 'Pakistan', www.nti.org/country-profiles/pakistan/nuclear/ (accessed 16 February 2013).
12 Ibid.
13 For details on Pakistan's Khushab nuclear plants, see isis-online.org/isis-reports/imagery/category/pakistan/ (accessed 16 February 2013).

14 Zia Mian, 'Pakistan', 2012, www.princeton.edu/sgs/faculty-staff/zia-mian/Pakistan-nuclear-modernization-2012.pdf (accessed 27 June 2012), 53.
15 Mansoor Ahmed, 'Understanding Pakistan's Plutonium Option', 2011, weeklypulse.org/details.aspx?contentID=706&storylist=2 (accessed 29 November 2012); Khurshid Ahmed, 'Summation: Capping the Nation', in Tariq Jan (ed.) *Pakistan's Security and the Nuclear Option*, Islamabad: Institute of Policy Studies, 1995, 145–58.
16 For details, see International Panel on Fissile Materials, 2010, fissilematerials.org/countries/pakistan.html (accessed 27 June 2012).
17 Hans M. Kristensen and Robert S. Norris, 'Nuclear Notebook: Pakistan's Nuclear Forces, 2011', *Bulletin of the Atomic Scientists* 67(4), 2011: 92.
18 Ibid., 92.
19 Mark Hibbs, 'Moving Forward on the US-India Nuclear Deal', 2010, www.carnegieendowment.org/2010/04/05/moving-forward-on-u.s.-india-nuclear-deal/5ww (accessed 9 February 2012); Mark Hibbs and Shahid Rehman, 'NSG, US Will Not Accommodate New Pakistan-China Commerce', *Nucleonics Week*, 2 March 2006, www.pakstop.com/pmforums/f83/nsg-us-wont-accommodate-new-pakistan-china-commerce-21814/ (accessed 28 June 2012).
20 Bill Gertz, 'China, Pakistan Reach Secret Nuclear Deal Reactor Deal for Pakistan', *The Washington Times*, 2013, www.washingtontimes.com/news/2013/mar/21/china-pakistan-reach-secret-reactor-deal-pakistan/?page=all (accessed 14 April 2013).
21 Ananth Krishnan, 'Pak, not China, Likely Source of N-Korea n-Plan, Says Kerry', *The Hindu*, 2013, www.thehindu.com/news/international/world/pak-not-china-likely-source-of-n-korea-nplan-says-kerry/article4613550.ece (accessed 14 April 2013).
22 However, Cheema observed that: 'The United States took special care not to provide Pakistan with any equipment that would facilitate nuclear delivery missions, especially electronic mechanism necessary for safe maintenance, transportation and delivery of nuclear weapons by F-16s'. Cheema, 'Pakistan's Nuclear Use Doctrine and Command and Control', 166. For more details on this premise, see 'Weapons Proliferation in the New World Order', hearing before the US Senate, Committee on Government Affairs, 102nd Congress, 2nd session, 15 January 1992, 20–25.
23 For detailed discussion on the fiasco of Pakistan's F-16 aircrafts, see Christine Fair, 'The Militants Challenge in Pakistan', *Asia Policy*, 11, Washington, 2011. Also, see some useful links in connection to Pakistan's failed quest for F-16 aircrafts: 'The Pressler Amendment and Pakistan's Nuclear Weapons Program', Senate, 31 July 1992, www.fas.org/news/pakistan/1992/920731.htm (accessed 28 February 2012).
24 'Pakistan's Atomic Bomb', *Foreign Report*, 12 January 1989: 1.
25 For exact number, see IISS, *The Military Balance*, March 2012, www.iiss.org/publications/military-balance/the-military-balance-2012/ (accessed 28 February 2012).
26 See 'List of Aircrafts of the Pakistan Air Force', en.wikipedia.org/wiki/List_of_aircraft_of_the_Pakistan_Air_Force (accessed 17 February 2013).
27 For details, see 'Pakistan Negotiating for More F-16s with US', www.indianexpress.com/news/pakistan-negotiating-for-more-f16s-with-us/759952/ (accessed 28 February 2012); 'Pakistan Plans to Buy More F-16s', www.dawn.com/2011/03/10/pakistan-plans-to-buy-more-f-16s.html (accessed 28 February 2012); and 'Pakistan Received 3 More US F-16 Aircrafts', www.nation.com.pk/pakistan-news-newspaper-daily-english-online/national/06-Feb-2012/pakistan-receives-3-more-us-f-16-aircraft (accessed 28 February 2012).
28 Cheema, 'Pakistan's Nuclear Use Doctrine and Command and Control', 167.
29 Paul K. Kerr and Mary Beth Nikitin, 'Pakistan's Nuclear Weapons: Proliferation and Security Issues', Congressional Research Service, 2011, www.fas.org/sgp/crs/nuke/RL34248.pdf (accessed 28 February 2012); Naeem Salik, *The Genesis of South Asian Nuclear Deterrence: Pakistan's Perspective*, London: Oxford University Press, 2009, 215.

30 For details on General Ashfaq Kiyani analyses, see Cyril Almeida, 'Uncontested Dominance', 2010, www.dawn.com/wps/wcm/connect/dawn-content-library/dawn/the-newspaper/columnist (accessed 2 September 2010).
31 Lubna Umar, 'Azm-e-Nau and Renewed Security Trends', *Pakistan Observer*, 2010, pakobserver.net/detailnews.asp?id=24748 (accessed 6 April 2012).
32 Sannia Abdullah, 'Cold Start in Strategic Calculus', *IPRI Journal* XII(1), Winter Issue, 2012: 1–27.
33 See 'PAF Jets Undertake Landings on Motorway', September 2005, www.defencetalk.com/paf-jets-undertake-landings-on-motorway-3359/ (accessed 6 April 2012); also see the video link 'PAF Fighter Jets Successfully Undertake Landings on Motorway During Exercises High Mark 2010', www.youtube.com/watch?v=bkkRLyrsZkI (accessed 6 April 2012); and 'Pakistan Conducts Fighter Operations from Motorway', April 2012, www.paf.gov.pk/press_release/uploaded/MOTORWAY-RELEASE02-04-10.pdf (accessed 6 April 2012).
34 Josef Cirincione, 'The Declining Ballistic Missiles Threat', 2005, www.carnegieendowment.org/pdf/The_Declining_Ballistic_Missile_Threat_2005.pdf (accessed 29 February 2012).
35 Mahmud Ali Durrani, 'Pakistan's Strategic Thinking and the Role of Nuclear Weapons', 2004, www.cmc.sandia.gov/cmc-papers/sand2004-3375p.pdf (accessed 18 June 2012), 20.
36 For details on the hearing, see Ronald L. Burgess, 'World-wide Threat Assessment', 2011, armed-services.senate.gov/hearings2011.cfm?h_month=3#month (accessed 28 February 2012).
37 Bhumitra Chakma, *Pakistan's Nuclear Weapons*, London: Routledge, 2009, 63.
38 See 'Hatf-II-Pakistan Missile Special Weapons Delivery Systems', *Federation of American Scientists*, www.fas.org/nuke/guide/pakistan/missile/hatf-2.htm (accessed 29 February 2012).
39 Chakma, *Pakistan's Nuclear Weapons*, 64.
40 'Pakistan Test Fires Short-range Ballistic Missile', 5 March 2012, www.dawn.com/2012/03/05/pakistan-test-fires-short-range-ballistic-missile.html (accessed 5 March 2012).
41 For detail description on this aspect, see 'Hatf 3', www.missilethreat.com/missilesoftheworld/id.50/missile_detail.asp (accessed 29 February 2012).
42 See Inter-Services Public Relations, 'Press Release', 25 April 2012, www.ispr.gov.pk/front/main.asp?o=t-press_release&id=2043#pr_link2043 (accessed 25 April 2012).
43 For details, see 'Pakistan Successfully Test Fires Hatf-IV Ballistic Missile', 25 April 2012, dawn.com/2012/04/25/pakistan-successfully-test-fires-hatf-iv-ballistic-missile/ (accessed 25 April 2012).
44 Pakistan has recently tested the Hatf V (Ghauri) to keep its missile system modified and accuracy and range assured, see www.ispr.gov.pk/front/main.asp?o=t-press_release& id = 2208#pr_link2208 (accessed 28 November 2012).
45 Robert Hewson, 'Cruise Missile Technology Proliferation Takes Off', *Jane's Intelligence Review* 17(10), 2005: 41–45.
46 For details of these missile tests, see Inter-Services Public Relations, www.ispr.gov.pk/front/main.asp?o=t-press_release&id=2088#pr_link2088 (accessed 5 June 2012).
47 'Pakistan Tests Hatf-VIII (RAAD)', 31 May 2012; for details see, www.ispr.gov.pk/front/main.asp?o=t-press_release&id=2080#pr_link2080 (accessed 31 May 2012).
48 Although this missile system is considered a dangerous development, one of the speakers at the conference held by the US Naval Postgraduate School viewed the Nasr missile development as a response to India's 'cold start' strategy. See Feroz Hassan Khan and Nick M. Masellis, 'US-Pakistan Strategic Partnership: a Track II Dialogue', 2012, www.dtic.mil/cgi-bin/GetTRDoc?AD=ADA555421 (accessed 9 April 2012). The report stated in the view of this speaker that, 'As long as India

continues to challenge Pakistani deterrence, such tactical innovations will continue in the future as well' (p.30).
49 See 'Pakistan Launches Nuke-Ready Missile in Trail', 19 April 2011, www.nti.org/gsn/article/pakistan-launches-nuke-ready-missile-in-trial/ (accessed 8 March 2012).
50 See 'Test of Pakistan's Hatf-9 Nasr Missile Seen as Response to India's 'Cold Start' Strategy', 22 April 2011, www.terminalx.org/2011/04/test-of-pakistans-hatf-9-nasr-missile.html (accessed 8 March 2012).
51 For details, see 'India Successfully Test Fires Surface to Surface Prahar Missile', *The Indian Express*, 21 July 2011, www.indianexpress.com/news/india-successfully-test-fires-surfacetosur/820344/ (accessed 8 March 2012).
52 Interview with Zafar Ali, SPD, September 2012.
53 However, the report stated that Pakistan, in comparison to India's 'colossal investment in its military arsenals' because of its growing economy, cannot involve itself in an arms race with its adversary and defeat radicalism. Therefore, Pakistan has little choice but to implement counter-measures in the form of nuclear weapons, TNWs in order to balance such efforts: Khan and Masellis 'US-Pakistan Strategic Partnership: A Track II Dialogue', 27–28.
54 Charles E. Costanz, 'South Asia: Danger Ahead?' *Strategic Studies Quarterly*, 2011: 92–106; Zafar Khan, 'Cold Start Doctrine: The Conventional Challenge to South Asian Stability', *Contemporary Security Policy* 33(3), 2012: 577–94.
55 Muhammad Azam Khan, 'The Indian Undersea Nuclear Deterrence and Pakistan Navy', *IPRI Journal* X(2), 2010: 101.
56 Ibid., 94.
57 Shireen M. Mizari, 'India's Arihant: Upping the Psychological Ante', 2009, pakistankakhudahafiz.wordpress.com/2009/07/30/india%E2%80%99s-arihant-%E2%80%94-upping-the-psychological-ante/ (accessed 21 June 2012).
58 See 'India Inducts Russia Made Nuclear Submarine into Navy', *The Times of India*, 4 April 2012, articles.timesofindia.indiatimes.com/2012-04-04/india/31286733_1_akula-ii-nuclear-submarine-ins-chakra (accessed 21 June 2012); and 'India Inducts New Russian-Made Nuclear Submarine', *The Tribune*, 4 April 2012, tribune.com.pk/story/359577/india-inducts-new-russian-made-nuclear-submarine/ (accessed 21 June 2012).
59 See 'Pakistan's 21st Century Naval Modernisation Program', 15 May 2012, pakdefenceunit.wordpress.com/2012/05/15/pakistans-21st-century-naval-modernisation-programme-indian-nuclear-submarine-programme/ (accessed 21 June 2012).
60 See 'India's Nuclear Submarine to Trigger Arms Race: Pakistan to Maintain its Minimum Deterrence', www.youtube.com/watch?v=YjSm6IKknbc&feature=BFa&list=PLB5EBDDD31ACB3152 (accessed 22 June 2012).
61 Interview with Maria Sultan, September 2012.
62 For details, see 'Nuclear Pakistan: Ten Years On', *Margalla Paper*, Special Edition, 2008, www.ndu.edu.pk/publications/pub_margalla2008_se.php (accessed 22 June 2012).
63 'Pakistan Hints at the Existence of Submarine Launched Variant of the Babur (Hatf-VII)', 24 May 2012, www.defence.pk/pakistan-hints-existence-submarine-launched-variant-babur-hatf-vii-780/ (accessed 22 June 2012).
64 Ibid.
65 'Pakistan: Navy Plans to Design Own Nuclear-Powered Submarine', 16 February 2012, navaltoday.com/2012/02/16/pakistan-navy-plans-to-design-own-nuclear-powered-submarine/ (accessed 21 June 2012); and 'Pakistani Navy to Develop Nuclear Powered Submarines', 13 February 2013, www.defensenews.com/article/20120211/DEFREG03/302110003/Pakistani-Navy-Develop-Nuclear-Powered-Submarines-Reports (accessed 22 June 2012).
66 Khan, 'The Indian Undersea Nuclear Deterrence and Pakistan Navy', 110.

6 Pakistan's doctrine of nuclear first use

Introduction

Each nuclear weapon state adopts its nuclear weapon use. It can either be first use (FU) or no first use (NFU). Nuclear weapon use doctrine is adopted to thwart the security threat in order to achieve political and military objectives. It is viewed that the security threat, organizational interests and military bias, national and global strategic culture are the rudimentary conceptual factors that determine a state's doctrine of nuclear weapon use. Although Pakistan has not yet officially declared its nuclear weapon use doctrine, it declares that Pakistan would follow the FU option to deter both conventional and nuclear attacks. The FU option has been deeply inherent in Pakistani deterrence assumption since the onset of its nuclear weapons programme in the 1970s. This can be assumed from Prime Minister Zulfiqar Ali Bhutto's argument that his country needed nuclear weapons to deter both India's conventional and nuclear attacks.[1] In the 1990s, it was revealed that Pakistan had attained a nuclear delivery system (F-16 aircraft), which was kept ready if India carried out air strikes on Kashmir.[2]

In the aftermath of Pakistan's nuclear weapons tests, the Pakistani Prime Minister Nawaz Sharif declared: 'These weapons are to deter aggressions, whether nuclear or conventional.'[3] This implies that Islamabad would use its nuclear weapons *first* to deter all forms of aggression. Islamabad's FU option was also affirmed when Foreign Secretary Shamshad Ahmed rejected India's offer of an NFU agreement, which he categorically stated as 'unacceptable'.[4] The Pakistani security planners view FU as an important factor for the country's minimum credible deterrence. Islamabad viewed the FU option as cost effective and consistent with minimum deterrence. At the same time, it was thought that FU would enhance the credibility of Pakistan's deterrent forces. Nevertheless, a much closer look at the existing literature on Pakistan's nuclear weapon use traces out ambiguity in Pakistan's nuclear weapon use option. While Islamabad views that it would use its nuclear weapon first, but it is not clear when, where and how exactly it would use nuclear weapons. Meanwhile, many believe that Islamabad would use its nuclear weapon as a last resort, which creates ambiguity.

This chapter provides a critical analysis of Pakistan's doctrine of FU. It examines why Pakistan opts for the FU option and why it claims simultaneously to use its nuclear weapons as a last resort. Keeping the usability of its deterrent forces, it examines how Islamabad postures for the targeting option, that is, whether Islamabad would opt for counter-value or counter-force targeting, followed by a critique of these two targeting options. Also, this chapter explores the obstacles for Pakistan to rescind the FU option, followed by various benefits ideally tilting towards an NFU option. Before analysing Pakistan's doctrinal FU option, it is important to examine the debate on FU and NFU in the Cold War era between the USA and the Soviet Union. I briefly commence the chapter by analysing this important debate as a backdrop to set the stage for this chapter.

Debating no first use and first use of nuclear weapons

It is important to understand the debate on FU and NFU. The debate started in the USA, which pursued the policy of FU from the start of the Cold War. The proponents of an NFU contend that the USA and the North Atlantic Treaty Organization (NATO) no longer require the FU option because of the sophisticated conventional capabilities and modernization of their conventional forces which could deter any challenger without necessarily using nuclear weapons. However, the opponents of an NFU option argue: 1 foreswearing FU means a departure from the US security assurances and guarantee to its allies that are vulnerable to Russia in Europe and North Korea and China in Asia; and 2 the renunciation of FU could increase the possibility of adversarial chemical and biological attacks, including nuclear weapons, on US soil. The critics of NFU believe that it is the FU option which has deterred adversaries from using both conventional and non-conventional (including nuclear) weapons.

This argument was advanced by the USA in the early 1950s, when it heavily relied on nuclear weapons use in relation to the former Soviet Union. The US National Security Council Document (NSC-68) stated that, 'in our present situation of relative unpreparedness in conventional weapons, such a declaration would be interpreted by the USSR as an admission of *great weakness* and by our allies as a clear indication that *we intended to abandon them*'[5] The document further read: 'it is doubtful whether such a declaration would be taken sufficiently seriously by the Kremlin to constitute an important factor in determining whether or not to attack the United States. It is to be anticipated that the Kremlin would weigh the facts of our capability far more heavily than a declaration of what we proposed to do with the capability.'[6] Decades later Joffe stated in a similar vein: 'Nations plan for war not by listening to their rivals' commitments but by looking at their capabilities.'[7] Hence, Washington opposes the proposal of an NFU by stating that if the USA needed to achieve its political and military goals, it would need to maintain its FU option or attain high conventional superiority regarding the adversary.

The debate continues on whether the USA should pursue the FU or NFU option. Before an influential article on a nuclear-free world by Henry Kissinger, Sam Nunn, William Perry and George Shultz, famously known as the 'four horsemen',[8] the debate was already heating up when four former influential US Administration members, McGeorge Bundy, George Kennan, Robert McNamara and Gerard Smith, famously known as the 'gang of four', advocated that the US-led NATO adopt the policy of NFU. They proposed that Washington and its NATO allies modify the FU option after studying closely the previous strategic plans in Europe which were based upon the notion of massive retaliation, flexible response and assured destruction. These warlike nuclear strategies could lead to 'devastating exchanges ... and ... carry with it a high and inescapable risk of escalation into the general nuclear war which would bring ruin to all and victory to none'.[9]

Given this, Bundy *et al.* argued that, 'The one clearly definable firebreak against the worldwide disaster of general nuclear war is the one that stands between all other kinds of conflict and any use whatsoever of nuclear weapons. To keep that firebreak wide and strong is in the deepest interest of all mankind'.[10] The gang of four justified their basic argument in support of an NFU on the following grounds. Fist, an NFU would avert the danger of an all-out nuclear war between the two adversaries. Second, this would prompt both the USA and NATO to improve conventional forces in relation to their adversary. Third, the adoption of this policy would not mean US departure from its security assurances to its allies. The NFU 'policy is the best one available for keeping the Alliance united and effective'.[11] That is, the USA could still keep an alternative option of 'no early first use'. It continues: 'A policy of NFU would not and should not imply an abandonment of this extraordinary guarantee – only its redefinition.'[12] Last but not least, the gang of four justifies this policy proposal on the basis that all previous US Administrations made fascinating departures from early strategic policies: that is, James Byrnes's learning of international arms control; John Foster Dulles's retreat from his proposed massive retaliation; Dwight D. Eisenhower's rethinking on bans of nuclear tests; John F. Kennedy's modified views on targeting doctrine; Lyndon B. Johnson's shelving the proposed multilateral forces; and Richard Nixon's agreement on a limited role for anti-ballistic missiles.[13]

A decade earlier, Richard Ullman came out in support of an NFU policy before the gang of four heated the debate. Whilst citing various examples in connection with the first use of nuclear weapons, Ullman proposed that non-nuclear attacks should be responded to likewise and the FU of nuclear weapons should only be considered when the adversary used its nuclear weapons.[14] Ullman stated: 'The granting of congressional authorization, should it take place, would be equivalent to a formal announcement rescinding a prior "no-first use" commitment, unilateral or multilateral. Such authorization (or the rescinding of a prior "no-first use" commitment) would, in fact, constitute in itself an important diplomatic instrument.'[15] Did the Ullman and Bundy *et al.* NFU proposal convince the USA and its allies?

There were certain concerns both in the USA and Europe whether or not they would be more secure by adopting an NFU doctrinal option. Kaiser *et al.* responded in Europe to the gang of four immediately. They took great pains in reading and analysing cover to cover Bundy *et al.*'s proposal on an NFU. They responded in the manner that the US policies of massive retaliation, flexible response and assured destruction suited the US allies and the coupling of conventional and nuclear weapons inflicted a *fear* which deterred Soviet conventional and nuclear forces. Kaiser *et al.* were not fully convinced and presented the following justifications. First, any renunciation of the FU policy would avert the policy of war prevention based upon the existence of these weapons. Second, the abandonment of FU would provide opportunity to the Soviet armed forces to accept a risk of waging war in Europe. The adversary would no longer be in fear of US nuclear forces. Third, it would cause more damage than cure to the US allies contributing to the 'internal health of the Western alliance itself'. Finally, the renunciation of FU would mean the abandonment of the US security guarantee to its non-nuclear allies in the event of a Soviet attacks, making 'conventional war in Europe possible'. Therefore, the renunciation of FU would mean renouncing the US nuclear guarantee and its credibility of sustaining security assurances for its allies.[16]

Did this debate have an influence on minor nuclear weapon states? Did this convince the leadership of the established nuclear weapon states to renounce the FU option as part of a nuclear policy option? Since the USA influences the policies of other states in connection with both military and nuclear postures, any modifications to the nuclear policy of the established nuclear weapon states, particularly the USA, would interestingly have an impact on the strategic perceptions of minor nuclear weapon states.[17] Having analysed the FU debate as a backdrop, the following section discusses Pakistan's option of FU and the ambiguity within it. On the one hand, Pakistan declares that it would use nuclear weapons first, but on the other hand, insight of the higher echelons in Pakistan informs us that nuclear weapons would be a last resort, blurring the two arguments. Pakistan's 'calculated ambiguity' of nuclear weapons use is analysed against the backdrop of this important and influential debate.

Pakistan's nuclear use doctrine: ambiguity between the FU and last resort

In light of the nuclear use debate, it is interesting to see what Pakistani security planners, analysts and scholars think of nuclear weapons use as part of policy options, and what the strategic implications of these policy options are. The Cold War debate on the FU and NFU nuclear options indicated that the proponents of an NFU failed to convince either the established nuclear weapon states or the minor ones to rescind the FU to offset conventional vulnerabilities. So long as the established nuclear weapon states, particularly the USA, retain the FU option as a sole military and political instrument, minor nuclear weapon states might not adopt a policy of NFU.

In order to sustain the minimum credible deterrence, Pakistan adhered to the FU option. A Pakistani nuclear analyst stated: 'a quest to ensure a credible deterrent is also a major factor in Pakistan's refusal to sign a "no-first strike" pact with India.'[18] According to Rodney Jones, 'A first-strike doctrine would be chosen not because it could disarm India (this would not be technically plausible), but because it would signify that Pakistani escalation, as a last resort, would be sudden and all out, with catastrophic consequences'.[19] Looking closely at the US nuclear posture reviews (NPRs) since 9/11, one can assess the elements of the US consistent interest in retaining the doctrine of nuclear FU against its adversaries for deterrence purposes.[20] Other nuclear weapon states do not seem to be convinced by the US arms control and disarmament endeavours and expect the USA to do more before nuclear weapon states are convinced to follow suit.[21] What makes Pakistan retain the FU option and how do Pakistani security planners consider this effective and credible when it comes to deterring the effects of nuclear weapons? First, it is important to analyse why first use, then examine the important segment of Pakistan's declaratory nuclear use policy – that is, the option of last resort. This dichotomy creates ambiguity.

The FU option

Like the USA and unlike India (albeit India has recently started thinking of using its nuclear weapons first under some conditions), Pakistan lays out the FU option in order to offset its adversary's superior conventional forces. Feroz Hassan Khan stated: 'Pakistan follows the example of the US and NATO which follow the FU option. Pakistan cannot rescind the FU option because of its weakness in the conventional forces.'[22] Islamabad views that Pakistan cannot foreswear the FU option because of conventional weaknesses vis-à-vis India. Even India has differing views about whether or not it would retain an NFU option. Pakistan rejects it, however. In this context, Abdul Sattar, Agha Shahi and Zulfiqar Ali Khan stated: 'India's declaration that it would not be the first to launch a nuclear strike is a cost free exercise in sanctimonious propaganda.'[23] Sattar recently said that 'leadership on both sides of the border need to be rational in their decisions how to use nuclear weapons. These weapons are not for war-fighting rather than for deterring purposes'.[24] Ideally, the root of this argument takes us beyond any use of nuclear weapons. That is, the rationality of nuclear leadership on both sides of the border depicts that nuclear weapons should never be used in war. The FU option entails uncertainty and ambiguity. It is not certain when, where and how nuclear weapons would be used.

Pakistan considers that ambiguity, uncertainty and a doctrinal flexibility of the Cold War era may deter the adversary. Given massive conventional force differences, geographical proximity and a lack of strategic depth, Pakistan retains the FU option as the USA did to protect its European allies against the Soviet's conventional forces during the Cold War.[25] Even at the start of the 21st century, the USA maintains its traditional policy of FU. In a similar vein, Pakistan deliberately retains ambiguity in its FU option. Pakistani security planners consider that uncertainty and ambiguity could also have a deterrent effect. In the words of an Indian nuclear strategist, 'in the strategic literature of the fifties, sixties, and seventies of deterrence has been derived mostly from factors of *certainty* in punishing retaliation. It has been overlooked that factors of *uncertainty can also function as a deterrent*'.[26] However, deterrent uncertainty and ambiguity could also harm the credibility of nuclear forces at some stage.

To overcome this issue, states could be certain where, how and when to consider using nuclear weapons. This would enhance credibility and ensure the will to deter. Vijai Nair stated that deterrence requires 'both the *ability* and the *will* to respond promptly'.[27] Nair speaks of both capability and credibility of nuclear deterrence that should be free from ambiguity and uncertainty of deterrence in terms of using nuclear weapons in the event of a crisis. On credibility of nuclear deterrence, Nair stated that 'credibility is a function of an unambiguous communication of: a demonstrated capability backed up by a visible production capacity; a competent strategic infrastructure system; and a demonstrated political will to achieve any and all measures to defend the nation'. This stance was confirmed by a Pakistani strategic analyst: 'Pakistan needs to unveil its nuclear ambiguity as its nuclear weapons program gets matured. It needs to review its nuclear posture and announce clearly its red-lines when to use nuclear weapons to increase its nuclear deterrence capability.'[28] In a similar vein, Maria Sultan stated: 'Pakistan is to make it clear when, how, where, and why it should use its nuclear weapons.'[29] Can a weaker conventional side be more unambiguous in its nuclear force use? It is not exactly certain when, where and how Pakistan would use nuclear forces. Some Pakistanis consider that Pakistan should retain the FU option. Others view that nuclear weapons are for deterrence purposes and should not be used for war fighting. Still others consider that nuclear weapons could be used in 'extreme conditions'. That is, there should be an option of last resort.

The option of last resort

Since ambiguity is a central part of Pakistan's nuclear weapons programme, there seems to be a conceptual dichotomy when it comes to its nuclear weapons use. The posture of the first use of nuclear weapons, but as a last resort is confusing and contentious. This raises many questions. What factors will drive Pakistan to use nuclear weapons? Will Pakistan use nuclear weapons first in the event of war, or will it use nuclear weapons as a last resort when deterrence fails? Perhaps, 'this perception of the value of ambiguity is debatable given that one needs to communicate the threat as unambiguous as possible in a deterrence situation. Also, fudgy red lines can keep moving further back when it comes to the crunch and in Pakistan's situation, perhaps a clearly enunciated one-rung escalation ladder – given the prevailing asymmetries – may be more useful'.[30]

This perception becomes challenging as the red lines are not clear cut as a matter of nuclear policy. Most Pakistani security analysts believe that there are certain circumstances that could cause Pakistan ultimately to use nuclear weapons as a last resort. In this context, retired Air Commodore Tariq Ashraf relayed certain security threat scenarios that could cause Pakistan to use nuclear weapons: 1 penetration of Indian forces beyond a certain defined line or crossing of a river; 2 imminent capture of an important Pakistani city like Lahore or Sialkot; 3 destruction of Pakistan's conventional armed forces or other assets to an unacceptable level; 4 attack on any of Pakistan's strategic targets, such as dams or nuclear installations like Tarbela, Mangla, Kahuta, Chashma, etc.; 5 imposing a blockade on Pakistan to an extent that it strangles the continued transportation of vital supplies and adversely affects the war-waging stamina of the country; and 6 India crossing of the LOC to a level that threatens Pakistan's control over Azad Kashmir.[31]

Ashraf's formulation seems vague and carries loopholes that cannot be the *actual* and optimal nuclear policy option of Pakistan in relation to its nuclear weapons use. It is not robustly clear when and at what stage exactly Pakistan would use nuclear weapons against the adversary. He does not explicitly explain the parameters of 'certain lines' and does not mention which 'river' in Pakistan. For instance, when it comes to India's military forces crossing the LOC, the whole posture becomes blurred because Pakistan lacks the strategic depth. The LOC between the two adversaries is not exactly defined. In other words, it would be difficult to draw a definite line in a disputed area of Kashmir. Similarly, Pakistani nuclear leadership may not opt for nuclear weapons use by merely facing a sea blockade. In the event of war, Pakistan could seek economic assistance from the Islamic world, such as Iran, Saudi Arabia or other Middle Eastern countries connected via both land and sea. This would not severely strangle Pakistan's economy and its capability for war fighting. The assertion in relations to nuclear weapons use needs robustness and revision.

In a similar vein, Lt General (retired) Khalid Kidwai, director-general of the SDP, stated in an interview to an Italian research group, Landau Network (Ramusino and Martellini) that Pakistan would use nuclear weapons if: 1 India attacks Pakistan and conquers a large part of its territory; 2 India destroys a large section of its land and air forces; 3 India proceeds to strangle Pakistan's economy; and 4 India pushes Pakistan into political destabilization or creates large-scale internal subversion.[32] Given that Pakistan is a conventional weak nuclear weapon state, some of the scenarios described by Ashraf and Kidwai make sense for Pakistan's usability of nuclear forces which indicate 'extreme conditions'. It is interesting to note that Kidwai denies what the Landau Network asserted.[33] The Landau Network's assertion does not exactly depict the complete nuclear use scenario that Pakistan has kept ambiguous. Therefore, the assertion remains controversial and does not indicate whether or not Pakistan would actually use its nuclear forces as a last resort. Chakma questions one of the segments of the Network's assertions: 'what are the operational parameters of such notions such as political destabilisation, large-scale internal subversion, and economic strangulation ... these are subjective notions in Pakistan-India context and may mean different things in different time and situations.'[34] Given the Landau Network's vague interpretation of Kidwai's interview, it raises more questions than answers. That is, would a crisis in parts of Pakistan such as political instability, economic meltdown, terrorist acts, etc., with the involvement of foreign hands, say India, let Pakistan use nuclear weapons against its adversary? These crises have become daily routine in Pakistan. Terrorist acts and various forms of violence have strangled Pakistan's economic and political conditions severely which, unfortunately, has shown doubt in world opinion on the survival of Pakistan as a state in general and the safety and security of its nuclear weapons in particular. The contemporary layer of social, political and economic crises in Pakistan contradicts what the Landau Group asserts in its interview with Kidwai. This injects more ambiguity within Pakistan's use of deterrent forces.

Such ambiguity in Pakistan's nuclear uses either first or last can be assumed still further in a statement from Pakistan's Foreign Ministry. Tariq Osman Hyder said:

> Pakistan has not officially announced that it would first use its nuclear weapons. No nuclear weapon state uses aggressive words when it comes to nuclear weapons use. Every nuclear weapon state says that these are the weapons for strategic peace. However, Pakistan could use nuclear weapons in extremis conditions, that is, against any aggression.[35]

Given the ambiguity, Pakistan's FU option becomes widely challenged, which needs to be reformulated, revisited and formally modified – that is, Pakistan may have to come out of its nuclear ambiguity and officially declare nuclear policy. This could have some positive outcomes: first, this would not only help streamline the nuclear policy of Pakistan under the banner of minimum deterrence, but also avoid an inadvertent nuclear war between the two adversaries. Second, Pakistan could successfully refute the ambiguous Landau Network-type controversial assertions. Third, it would open a debate amongst the policy analysts both within and outside Pakistan for a more transparent picture on Pakistan's policy options. Last but not least, it could allow Pakistan to uncover the counter-argument about the suspicion on Pakistan's minimum credible deterrence.[36]

The Pakistani security planners consider and believe that Pakistan could use nuclear weapons, as a last resort, if the territorial integrity and sovereignty of Pakistan were threatened. This can be assumed from Musharraf's statement in an interview to German magazine *Der Speigel* in 2002:

> Nuclear weapons are the last resort. I am optimistic and confident that we can defend ourselves with conventional means, even though the Indians are buying up the most modern weapons in a megalomaniac frenzy ... if Pakistan is threatened with extinction, then the pressure of our countrymen would be so big that this option, too, would be considered.[37]

Prior to this interview, the military ruler made it clear to the world on 28 May 2000 that, 'Pakistan's nuclear tests, after Indian [nuclear] blasts, were to protect its security and sovereignty'.[38] This clearly asserts that Pakistan would try to use all other options in the event of war before considering the nuclear use option. Thus, the assertion between the two different options of nuclear weapons use makes the usability of nuclear forces contentious.

Critiquing the debate: first use and last resort

In Pakistan, the debate in terms of nuclear weapon use seems deliberately blurred to keep the adversary guessing at what point Pakistan would use its nuclear forces. That is, Pakistani security planners would closely observe its strategic environment which would shape Pakistan's nuclear use options. The consistency of Pakistan's option of FU and its renunciation of an NFU make it clear that Pakistan relies on nuclear weapons for deterrence purposes. Pakistan's current preservation and upgrade of nuclear forces become fundamental to the assertion that Pakistan retains its nuclear use options open. On the other hand, the option of last resort in the given statements by Pakistani leadership and security analysts tend to provide a conceptual analysis that Pakistan may not use nuclear weapons early during a military crisis against its adversary. Presumably, this provides the clues on Pakistan's possible departure from an *absolute first use* to 'no early first use', which could incline to an NFU. To use nuclear weapons as a last resort means that Pakistan would first try all its conventional capabilities, including the exploitation of the immediate role of the international community, particularly the USA, in de-escalating the crisis. If all these options fail and Pakistan's security condition reaches extreme conditions and its *existence as a state is threatened*, then it could consider using nuclear forces. One of Pakistan's anonymous freelance security analysts stated:

> Since going nuclear would be an option of last resort, only an imminent scenario of abject defeat could force Pakistan to that stage. In this sort of critical situation, Pakistan's leadership would have exhausted all other options of averting defeat and would have their backs to [the] wall. Also, Pakistan's nuclear threshold would have been over-stepped by India.[39]

Conceptually, the international community may not afford the failure of deterrence in South Asia, which could unleash the accidental and unwanted use of nuclear weapons; nor would it be in the interest of either of the South

Asian adversaries to threaten each other's existence, given the fear of nuclear weapon use. In addition, the international community is well aware of the conflicting past of India and Pakistan. It also knows that the two nuclear rivals are in possession of nuclear weapons albeit with de facto nuclear status. The international community would not desire that either of the adversaries reach the stage of nuclear use. It would probably act quickly to end the military crisis before any use of nuclear weapons. However, the danger of inadvertent and unwanted nuclear weapon use exists as long as the nuclear weapons remain in the states' military discourse.[40] In this scenario, last resort likely embraces the option of an NFU or 'no early first use', which discourages the states' leadership to use nuclear weapons in the event of a crisis.

Although Pakistan has nuclear weapons and will continue to do so for deterrence purposes with the possible option of FU, it is still ambiguous and debateable whether Pakistan would pursue an FU or an NFU utility of nuclear weapons to avert a military crisis. In fact, neither Pakistan nor its adversary has used nuclear weapons in any military crisis against each other. To be sure, Pakistan developed the capability of nuclear weapons in the late 1980s and its adversary achieved nuclear weapons capability in 1974. Given the past military crises and military exercises on both sides of the border, Pakistan used conventional forces against its adversary and kept its nuclear weapons non-deployed. In both the Kargil episode in 1999 and the military standoff in 2001–02 between the two nuclear adversaries, both sides readied their conventional forces before any application of nuclear weapons. We have no substantial clues of the adversarial states' readiness of nuclear weapons first. However, the threat of the use of nuclear weapons, either first or in retaliation, existed. The threat continues to exist. We have experienced through empirical evidence that Pakistan used conventional means, waited for the immediate role of the international community, especially the USA, and attempted a hotline mechanism between the two states to avert military escalation to a nuclear level.[41] Although the political and military uses of nuclear weapons may have a deterrent capability, it is not clear whether or not nuclear weapons averted these crises.

In this scenario the role of nuclear weapons in either FU or NFU does not amount to a greater significance. Other forces are more unambiguous and are tried first. This is considered humane, just and pragmatic in both waging and terminating wars. Nuclear weapons are not used to terminate wars. The FU of nuclear weapons has neither historically terminated an already-waged war, nor has it been used as a policy option to begin a war – at least in the South Asian region.[42] Many may claim the deterrent effects of FU of nuclear weapons to avert the war in the first place, however. Nuclear weapon states with the FU option may not attack an adversary first because of the fear of a retaliatory attack with an unacceptable level of damage, especially when the adversary has already achieved a greater strategic depth and second-strike capability. In either case, it really does not matter which policy option is used: both deter reciprocally at the end of the day. A state in possession of second-strike capability and strategic depth deters the other, and a conventional weak state with the policy option of FU, although ambiguous, convinces the adversary not to strike or wage a war because nuclear weapons become the sole option for its survival. Since achieving second-strike capability is difficult, if not impossible, a nuclear weapon state in possession of second-strike forces and strategic depth can either renounce the FU or limit the use of nuclear weapons in a future military crisis. Thomas Schelling's substantial work on deterrence theory explanations suggests the limitation of one's options which can be beneficial for both deterrence and strategic stability.[43] In addition, Pakistan needs to posture the use of nuclear weapons, that is, whether or not it would use nuclear forces for military purposes in the event of a crisis – the setting for counter-force or counter-value targeting.

The FU option: counter-value or counter-force targeting

The utility of Pakistani nuclear weapons is not clearly defined due to ambiguity in its minimum credible deterrence. It is not clear whether it would use nuclear forces on population centres or military infrastructure. Nuclear strategists have commonly described two kinds of nuclear targeting: 1 counter-value targeting includes the use of nuclear weapons against people and property; 2 counter-force targeting includes the use of nuclear weapons against the adversary's military facilities and industrial components.[44]

It is uncertain whether Pakistan would opt for counter-value or counter-force targeting in the event of war. However, there are certain factors that might drive Pakistan towards counter-value attacks against its adversary: 1 India has an advantage of greater geographical depth than Pakistan, and most of its weapons are dispersed, which, therefore, makes it difficult for Pakistan to opt for counter-force targets; and 2 as the geographical proximity enables Pakistan's nuclear warheads to access major cities and industrial centres, counter-value becomes a natural option for Pakistan.[45] It is interesting to note that the current Pakistani development of TNWs is considered a reaction to the adversarial CSD. This indicates that TNWs can be used against the CSD's military forces once CSD is developed and launched for a limited war. That said, it is uncertain whether the arrival of and dependence on TNWs and a war-fighting doctrine CSD could mark strategic stability in the South Asian region. This reminds us of the US nuclear policy of *massive retaliation* and *assured destruction* in the 1950s and the 1960s, which included both the cities and major installations of its adversary.[46] Pakistan, just like the USA at the onset of its nuclear policy, relies much on nuclear weapons when it comes to its survival. Even though the USA planned for counter-force targeting, its declaratory nuclear doctrine exclusively focused on counter-value targeting to deter the Soviet Union's conventional attacks, both on the USA and its allies in Western Europe.

Although Pakistan pursues the FU option, like the USA against the superior Soviet conventional forces during the Cold War, it has not declared

US Cold War-type nuclear options, such as assured destruction, massive retaliation, etc. This would require a larger number of nuclear forces and a stronger economy, both of which Pakistan lacks. It is unclear whether Pakistan would shift from counter-value targeting as its adversary's nuclear and conventional forces grow. Even with a policy option of counter-force targeting, India and Pakistan could cause non-military damage because most air and military bases in both countries are close to cities. The academic distinction between the two targeting options becomes uncertain in a real war-fighting scenario. Any use of nuclear weapons either for counter-value or counter-force purposes would most likely target cities. Pakistan's nuclear policy remains largely unwritten, closed and ambiguous. It could be considered that given the countries' close proximity, India's development of a limited war-fighting CSD, nuclear ambiguity on both sides of the border, and Pakistan's TNWs make both counter-value and counter-force targeting challenging to South Asian strategic stability.

Critiquing counter-value versus counter-force targeting

Both India and Pakistan could be deterred when considering seriously the scenario of using their nuclear weapons for counter-value targeting and their environmental repercussions on each side of the border. Their cities are just a few minutes' flight apart. The cost of using these weapons for counter-value is more than the benefits each side plans against each other, however deterrent these nuclear options may be. Also, the counter-value targeting option becomes questionable for Pakistan considering the Muslim population in India. It is estimated that 220 million Muslims live in India, more than the entire population of Pakistan, which is estimated at 180 million.[47] Chakma questions 'how Pakistan would carry out counter-value attacks on India given that they [Indian cities] are inhabited by a large Muslim population'.[48] In a similar vein, India, the largest democracy and self-declared secular state, may also not use strategic nuclear weapons on Pakistani cities because the larger Muslim population in India, although considered a large minority yet bigger than the Pakistani Muslim population, could go against the option of counter-value targeting. That is, the Muslim population including the majority public opinion of both the nuclear adversaries could reject counter-value targeting.[49]

Having said this, both India and Pakistan are self-deterred. Pakistan needs to address the counter-value/counter-force targets dilemma in its nuclear policy. This seems to drive the theoretical concept of neo-culturalism into the limelight of Pakistan's nuclear leadership when one puts concerns on Pakistan's nuclear policy of counter-value targeting. It is not clear whether the values of neo-culturalism – which influence states' decisions not to use nuclear, biological and chemical weapons on the basis of moral norms – exist in the highest echelon of Pakistan's nuclear leadership. While the moral norms of neo-culturalism may be accepted through realism, this is only when national security and a state's sovereignty is not gravely threatened. Realism may undermine the neo-cultural theoretical explanation at times when a state's existence is threatened by the adversary. The concept of strategic neo-culturalism, which was developed in the 1990s, entails two-prong conceptualizations: 1 neo-culturalists develop domestic constraints on the military organization at the time of formulating or modifying the military doctrine; 2 they try to promote the moral norm issues into the limelight of military echelons and thereby influence the military decision in the event of nuclear weapons use.[50]

To sum up, it is not clear whether Pakistan would use its nuclear weapons for its survival against counter-value or counter-force targeting since Pakistan's official nuclear policy has not been made public. However, the current upgradation and preservation of Pakistan's deterrent forces indicate the country's consideration of TNW build-up like that of the USA-led NATO during the Cold War period to chalk out counter-force targeting.[51] Even a counter-force targeting approach could engulf cities and millions of people could be killed. Counter-force targeting would then differ little from counter-value targeting. If Pakistan increases its nuclear weapons capability in terms of TNWs, then it becomes logical that these weapons could be used for counter-force targets – a departure from counter-value targeting. Until Pakistan is open on this stance by making its nuclear policy public, the obstacles to renouncing its FU option remain part of its ambiguous MCD.

Obstacles to Pakistan's renunciation of first use

Pakistani officials have indicated that the country follows an FU doctrine. At the same time, they have stated that Islamabad would use nuclear weapons as a last resort, which means that Pakistan would use all other options before seriously considering nuclear weapons use, and that would be in extreme conditions. This is ambiguous and requires elaboration. However, given Pakistan's conventional weakness and changes in the South Asian strategic environment, many nuclear analysts think Pakistan might not rescind the FU option. This section assesses the obstacles to the renunciation of nuclear FU.

The fear of pre-emption

Many security analysts point out that Pakistan lacks strategic depth to protect its forces fully from any possible pre-emptive strike.[52] It would obviously retain its FU option as part of its nuclear policy, that is, *use it or lose it*. Pakistan has observed that its adversary could pre-empt its deterrent forces before Pakistan even uses them, or develops a second-strike capability. Pakistan observes that its adversary attempted preventive strikes against Pakistan's nascent nuclear weapon capability in the 1980s and in the late 1990s before Pakistan overtly tested its nuclear weapons. Israeli preventive strikes on nuclear facilities in Iraq at Osirak in 1981 and Syria at Al-Kibar in 2007 are evidence feeding this fear of renouncing FU of nuclear weapons. Neither Iraq nor Syria reacted against Israel's preventive strikes. Pakistani security planners accept the conceptually developed deterrent effects of nuclear weapons vis-à-vis its adversary. They consider that their nuclear adversary was deterred during various military crises and border confrontations from waging a total war because of the existence of nuclear weapons.[53] This means that the adversary does not cross the LOC, nor intrude into Pakistan over the national border in the event of a crisis because of Pakistan's reliance on nuclear weapons and its FU option. Sattar *et al.* stated that 'an NFU posture could invite aggression', which would possibly prompt pre-emption.[54] The reliance on nuclear weapons for deterrence purposes strengthens the notion that the renunciation of the FU option could weaken Pakistani deterrence credibility and a conventionally weak Pakistan would become more vulnerable to pre-emptive strikes.

Conventional weakness

Pakistan is conventionally weaker compared to its adversary. Its conventional forces, although of standard, war-fighting quality, still lag behind its adversary in number and modernity. Considering the weaker conventional position in relation to the adversary, a Pakistani retired Air Commodore Tariq Ashraf stated that:

> Being on a weaker military footing as compared to India, Pakistan's nuclear employment doctrine should assert that since she would be fighting for her survival as an independent nation-state in any future war, it could not renounce the policy of first use as India has done in her draft nuclear doctrine. Pakistan while announcing and emphasising the deterrent basis of its nuclear employment doctrine *must reserve the right of first use of nuclear weapons* and this assertion should be made as a part of her nuclear employment doctrine.[55]

In a similar context, Qadar Baksh Baloch stated: 'Owing to Pakistan's lack of strategic depth, imbalances in conventional forces, and location of its main population centres in proximity to its Eastern borders, NFU nuclear posture could invite aggression and leave Pakistan highly vulnerable to India in any long drawn out conventional war.'[56]

Since it would take a large economy and technological assistance to make conventional improvements, Pakistan could keep upgrading and expanding its nuclear weapons programme. It also consumes a large part of Pakistan's national budget. Zafar Iqbal Cheema stated: 'If Pakistan does not confront conventional disparity vis-à-vis its adversary, it would possibly have an NFU option.'[57] During the Cold War if the USA had renounced the FU option, then it would have had to build greater conventional capability against its adversary. John Mearsheimer argued that this was a flawed option and 'would not guarantee that the balance would shift in NATO's favour'.[58] In the age of tightened budgets and careful spending, Pakistan may exchange improvements to its conventional capabilities for those to its nuclear forces.[59] Lack of a technological shift to Pakistan and huge financial constraints would keep the country's conventional forces weaker than those of its adversary, whose economic boom, political stability and arms deals with major powers have become challenging to Pakistan and are making India a regional power. Even if Pakistan improves its conventional capabilities against its adversary at the cost of renouncing the FU option, it is not clear how much its adversary could advance its nuclear and conventional capabilities. It is also neither clear nor guaranteed, to follow Mearsheimer's argument on NATO, that adversarial conventional forces would be offset by pursuing an NFU option.

Therefore, a *conventional weakness* becomes one of the major obstacles for Pakistan in renouncing its declared nuclear FU option. Renouncing the FU option means a thorough transformation in military doctrinal and nuclear policy options,[60] which will take both time and a bigger budget. This would also mean the transformation of both Pakistan's security posture, which could include the de-emphasis of the role of nuclear weapons; detachment of nuclear weapons from their actual bases; refraining from using nuclear weapons at the forward position; improving its conventional forces with high, modern technology; and making moves towards the de-nuclearization of South Asia, such as signing the NPT and CTBT.

However, this would not mean that Pakistan would be completely deprived of the use of nuclear weapons unless it were attacked by nuclear weapons; it means that unless Pakistan were assuredly attacked by the adversary's nuclear weapons, it could retain an NFU option. The modern applicability of high technology in the contemporary conventional forces, say, of India, makes strikes as destructive and powerful as the possible use of nuclear weapons in the battlefield.[61] If a state's nuclear reactor were hit with piercing, destructive use of conventional forces causing the release of nuclear radiation and possibly a nuclear explosion, would it mean the FU of a nuclear weapon on a state?[62] Given the financial constraints and political instability, Pakistan remains unlikely to improve its conventional capability, replacing the FU option with an NFU, irrespective of any moral argument against the FU of nuclear weapons.

Although a global NFU is based on the law of morality, this scenario undermines the law of survival. According to Yu and Guangqian, 'NFU policy may conform to the rule of morality, but it does not necessarily conform to the law of survival. This is perhaps the most serious paradox facing an NFU policy'.[63] As long as the conventional forces remain asymmetrical between the two South Asian nuclear adversaries, this will remain a stumbling block to the possible renunciation of FU. Nuclear weapons and FU are deemed essential for offsetting India's conventional superiority and generating a conventional balance between the two adversaries.[64] Conceptually, the more the adversary increases and modernizes its conventional forces, the more it provokes Pakistan to strengthen its policy of MCD, which means upgrading and expanding its nuclear weapons technology *proportionally* to its adversary, and the more the reliance on nuclear weapons increases for deterrence purposes. Usman Iqbal Jadoon stated: 'For its existence and survivability, Pakistan would use its nuclear forces for deterrence purposes. Therefore, it is logical for Pakistan to keep the FU option given its weakness in conventional forces vis-à-vis its adversary.'[65] The solution here, perhaps, is not in Pakistan's conventional transformation of development and deployment of deterrent forces, but rather in the creation of an ACR in the South Asian region to restrain the two antagonistic nuclear weapon states from further conventional and nuclear modernity and expansion.

The civil-military dilemma

The long-embedded civil-military dilemma in Pakistan creates yet another obstacle for any possible shift in Pakistani policy option. The Pakistan Army has ruled the country for more than 30 years and has become part of Pakistan's nuclear development discourse since its inception for peaceful purposes. The Pakistan Army has learnt how and when to rule the country, given the weak political environment where civilian regimes are no longer trusted and the army is thought to be stronger and more disciplined. Presumably, it is considered that the army exploits the weakening condition of civilian government and claims to be the 'saviour of Pakistan', which is just about acceptable to the majority of Pakistanis. The army is the strongest institution within Pakistan, and thus the major stakeholder in the foreign policy decision-making processes including military and nuclear affairs.

The Pakistani military is projected to be the most reliable and least corrupt institution in Pakistan, compared to the civilian or bureaucratic organizations. However, Ayesha Siddiqa called this a 'Milbus' – a term which she defines in relation to the military elite's influence in Pakistani politics: 'Milbus refers to all activities that transfer resources and opportunities from the public and private sectors to an individual or a group within the military, without following the norms of public accountability and for the purposes of personal gratification.'[66]

There has been a civilian-military dilemma since the creation of Pakistan. On the one hand, the military justifies its intervention in state affairs because of civilian regime failures to sustain a stable government; on the other hand, the civilian leadership criticizes, if not challenges openly, the military institution for weakening the political structure of the country. Therefore, it becomes difficult for a common observer to find a genuine and long-lasting democratic process in Pakistan. Direct military intervention is considered one of the factors of the failure of democracy in Pakistan. Moreover, Siddiqa criticized the fact that none of the civilian leadership has seriously challenged the military force in Pakistani politics.[67] One of the reasons why these civilian governments could not directly challenge the military rule is because they themselves are the product of a transitional period after a direct military rule and largely fear being ousted from the political system. Rizvi stated: 'The elite [military] is prepared to support a government as long as it ensures stability and effectively performs its duties towards the citizenry and the state, and does not threaten military interest ... the military option increases if the government's political and economic performance falters, if it faces a crisis of legitimacy aggravated by popular unrest in the major urban centres, or if political competition turns nasty.'[68]

The Pakistani civilian government keeps the option of an NFU open. This can be assumed based on at least two occasions where the civilian leadership at the highest level has projected an interest in keeping an NFU. First, Pakistan's Foreign Minister Abdul Sattar, whilst speaking at the Carnegie International Non-Proliferation Conference on 18 June 2001, proclaimed that Pakistan had a 'no first use of force' policy.[69] While the term nuclear is not specifically stated, this can be assumed to be an NFU. Second, Pakistani President Asif Ali Zardari has already mentioned at the *Hindustan Times* World Leaders' Summit in November 2008 that, 'we will most certainly not use first'.[70] In contrast, the Pakistan Army has a proclivity to the policy option of FU. This was evidenced when the civilian leadership's plea for an NFU was rejected as flawed by the army. A civil-military dichotomy exists in Pakistan. Although the civilian leadership is included as part of the NCA, it seems that the armed forces have a greater say and influence in terms of the actual command and control of Pakistani conventional and nuclear forces. The SPD, which was established in 2000, and its directorates such as the Directorate of Arms Control and Disarmament,[71] are run by retired armed forces personnel and even the army chief is sometimes (incorrectly) recognized as the general director of the SPD and its related directorates, which comprise more than 20,000 personnel screened for the safety and security of Pakistan's nuclear weapons. Some have highly critical knowledge of these weapons.[72]

The civilian leadership has a tendency to shift in policy option from an FU to an NFU. Since the armed forces dominate the practical and actual command and control structure of Pakistan's nuclear arsenal and the civilian leadership remains weak in Pakistan, it is unlikely that Pakistan will shift to an NFU option in the foreseeable future. If anything were to happen to retain the FU or shift to an NFU, there could be a need for mutual coordination between the army and civilian leadership, given the strategic reality of the South Asian region. This could be possible once there is political stability for a powerful civilian government, which Pakistan has lacked since its inception.

Two things are important in this context, however. First, Pakistan needs a stronger civilian leadership, free from the direct influence of the armed forces, which is only possible if Pakistanis elect the right leadership; there would need to be a free and fair election; and Pakistan would need to sustain an independent judiciary. Second, the civilian government needs to be reassured of its survival in its political term and be re-elected if it has the confidence of the House and the trust of the masses. Conceptually, if a civilian government with a strong, changed leadership governs the state's affairs for more than two consecutive decades, then there is a high probability of the establishment of a genuine democracy in Pakistan. This will affect the security policies and encourage more assertive control of nuclear weapons. Realistically speaking, 'Pakistan has a political system but with poor governance'.[73] Historically, the civilian government has either been dismissed or has not completed its fixed political tenure before the start of another election.[74] The Pakistan People's Party (PPP) democratic government completed its tenure in 2013 for the first time in the history of democracy in Pakistan, although it remained weak and unpopular. No Pakistani civilian government has been elected twice consecutively to establish stronger roots of democracy, whilst the army has ruled for at least a decade, paradoxically, derailing the civilian leadership further. It can be presumed that if the Pakistani democratic system prevails without the direct intervention of the army, then it will have stronger civilian leadership and a significant impact on the security policies of Pakistan. A civilian leadership that cannot survive for a few years for whatever reason is unlikely to bring change to security policy.[75]

The adversary's changed policy options

Last but not least, Pakistani security planners closely observe the security policies of the adversary: how it evolves, strategizes and affects the strategic environment of the South Asian region. The government feels that Pakistan should maintain the MCD (relying on nuclear weapons) if its adversary expands and modernizes its conventional and nuclear forces. It feels that any arms deals its adversary makes with major powers would have direct implications on the nuclear policy of Pakistan and Pakistan would keep its policy options flexible.[76] For example, the US-Indian nuclear deal, India's arms relations with Israel, Russia and, more recently, Australia put more military and political pressure on Pakistan to expand its nuclear forces. This was confirmed by many respondents to the author of this study.[77] This will have direct implications for Pakistan's policy options – that is, retaining an FU option to offset the increasing development and deployment of the adversary's forces. Although India rejects the concerns of Pakistan, noting that all nuclear deals with the USA or Australia are for peaceful purposes to meet its energy requirements, Pakistan is unconvinced and views that this increases India's nuclear capabilities. As a consequence, this provokes Pakistan to enhance the credibility of its deterrent forces. The USA supports the Indian membership of the NSG following its nuclear weapons deal with India. The USA also supports India's membership of the Missile Technology Control Regime (MTCR), the Australian Group and the Wassenaar Arrangement.[78] All these developments, which disturb the strategic balance in South Asian, concern Pakistan's security planners.[79] Pakistan's permanent representative to the UK, Zamir Akram, stated at the Conference on Disarmament that 'Membership of the NSG will enable our neighbour to further expand its nuclear co-operation agreements and enhance its nuclear weapons and delivery capability. As a consequence, Pakistan will be forced to take measures to ensure the credibility of its deterrence', whilst the Pakistani defence analyst Rizvi stated: 'Pakistan is worried that India will be an integral part of the system regulating nuclear technology. If that happens, getting any equipment even such as civilian reactors for power generation will be completely impossible'.[80]

Such developments in terms of India's growing interest in nuclear deals and arms negotiations with major powers affect Pakistan's strategic thinking. These developments would not only increase the arms build-up in the South Asia region, but also provide excuses for Pakistani security planners to keep the country's nuclear options open.[81] Pakistan considers that if India is supported in terms of both its conventional and nuclear development capabilities, then Pakistan will get support from China in order to maintain its MCD.[82] This both increases the dangers of an arms race and encourages Cold War-style war-fighting policies. Consequently, these developments on both sides of the border increase the chances of more military escalations to a nuclear level. To avert these dangers, we need to conceptualize the political and strategic benefits of a true and verified NFU in South Asia. Can Pakistan rescind its FU option?

Ideally, it would be better for Pakistan to opt for an NFU option which could, in turn, discourage the adversary's war-fighting military strategies, promote crisis stability, create incentive for an ACR, work for advanced conventional forces, and avert external pressure. However, in reality Pakistan cannot rescind the FU option, given the challenges it faces as analysed above. Against this backdrop, a Pakistani security analyst stated: 'To avert the first use option in South Asia, there is need for a political solution. We should, but we cannot because of the *trust deficit* between the nuclear rivals of South Asia. India prepares for a limited war option in the presence of nuclear weapons and they can if they find a concrete link of terrorism acts from Pakistan.'[83] Zulfqar Khan stated: 'the political weakness, lack of resources, diplomatic backwardness have got impact on the strategic and security posture of Pakistan and, therefore, Pakistan relies largely on its FU of nuclear option in order to keep the strategic balance and sustain a credible deterrence in the South Asian region.'[84]

Conclusion

Islamabad follows the FU option to thwart both its adversary's conventional and nuclear strikes. This chapter highlights that the FU option has been deeply inherent in Pakistan's deterrence assumption since the beginning of its nuclear weapons programme. It also indicates that FU is cost effective and consistent with minimum deterrence. At the same time, Pakistani officials view that the FU option enhances the credibility of Pakistan's policy of MCD. The nuclear ambiguity can be traced in Pakistan's doctrine of nuclear weapon use when, on the one hand, Islamabad declares that it would use its nuclear weapons first, but on the other hand, others have noted on various occasions that Pakistan would use its nuclear weapon as a last resort. It appears that nuclear ambiguity is intentional and remains an important part of Pakistan's nuclear policy. Ambiguity has served Pakistan's strategic objective in numerous ways and the salience of nuclear ambiguity even exists today. Since Islamabad views that ambiguity has served the country's military and political objectives, it would be unnecessary to announce its nuclear weapon use doctrine officially.

This chapter explores the various obstacles to Pakistan's renunciation of FU. The conventional weakness and the 'India factor' remain dominant. Ideally, Pakistan could opt for an NFU seeking various other benefits, but this would require dramatic changes in the strategic conditions of the South Asian region. Until then, Pakistan's nuclear policy remains dynamic and evolving. The contentious debate between Pakistan's FU and last resort is one of the indicators to such dynamism. Given all, Pakistan still participates in arms control and disarmament-related conferences, but it remains contingent. Pakistan does this to justify the MCD.

Notes

1 Zulfiqar Ali Bhutto, *The Myth of Independence*, London: Oxford University Press, 1969.
2 Devin Hagerty, 'Nuclear Deterrence in South Asia: The 1990 Indo-Pakistani Crisis', *International Security* 20(3), 1996: 102.
3 'Statement by Nawaz Sharif, May 28 1998', printed in *Disarmament Diplomacy* 26, May 1998.
4 See 'India Asks Pakistan to Accept "No-first Use Pact"', *The Independent* (Dhaka), 9 July 1998.
5 See National Security Council, 'A Report to the National Security Council – NSC 68', 12 April 1950, 40, emphasis added, www.trumanlibrary.org/whistlestop/study_collections/coldwar/documents/pdf/10-11.pdf (accessed 3 February 2012).
6 Ibid., 40.
7 Josef Joffe, 'Nuclear Weapons, No First Use, and European Order', *Ethics* 95(3), 1985: 609.
8 This article seems to have been influential, calling for member states including the USA to make the world free from nuclear weapons. See Henry Kissinger, Sam Nunn, William Perry and George Shultz, 'Towards a Nuclear Free World', *Wall Street Journal*, 2008.
9 McGeorge Bundy, F. George Kennan, S. Robert McNamara and Gerard Smith, 'Nuclear Weapons and Atlantic Alliance', *Foreign Affairs*, 1982: 757.
10 Ibid., 757.
11 Ibid., 761.
12 Ibid., 759.
13 Ibid., 763. After one year of this influential article by the gang of four, Robert S. McNamara wrote another article in which he stated: 'nuclear weapons serve no military purpose whatsoever. They are totally useless – except only to deter one's opponent from using them'. See Robert S. McNamara, 'The Military Role of Nuclear Weapons: Perceptions and Misperceptions', *Foreign Affairs* 62(1), 1983: 59–80.
14 Richard H. Ullman, 'No First Use of Nuclear Weapons', *Foreign Affairs* 50(4), 1972: 677.
15 Ibid., 682.
16 Karl Kaiser, George Leber, Alois Mertes and Frans J. Schulze, 'Nuclear Weapons and the Preservation of Peace: A Response to an American Proposal for

Renouncing the First Use of Nuclear Weapons', *Foreign Affairs* 60(5), 1982: 1157–70. Two years after Kaiser *et al.*'s opposition to the renunciation of first use policy initiated by Bundy *et al.*, an American professor, John Mearsheimer, in his in-depth analysis on nuclear weapons, considered Bundy *et al.*'s proposal *dangerous* and *flawed* to the security of both the USA and its allies on the other side of the Atlantic. See John Mearsheimer, 'Nuclear Weapons and Deterrence in Europe', *International Security* 9(3), 1984: 19–46. Mearsheimer concludes that 'This discussion points to the fact that, as long as the superpowers have nuclear weapons, one should never feel confident that they will not be used in a war' (p.43). Therefore, 'unless nuclear weapons can be eliminated altogether or at least radically reduced in number and certainly eliminated from Europe, an NFU policy is positively dangerous' (p. 43). Also, see the editorial notes on no first use. Stanley Kober, David C. Jones, Easl C. Ravenal, Carl N. Anderson and Donald L. Hafner, 'The Debate Over No First Use', *Foreign Affairs* 60(5), 1982: 1171–80. In contrast to Kaiser *et al.*'s and Mearsheimer's insights on the urge not to renounce the US first use of nuclear weapons against any threat from its adversaries, Michael S. Gerson, in his article, reopens the debate proposing that the USA adopt the policy of NFU, stating that 'The traditional case for NFU rests on the argument that the threat of nuclear first use is unnecessary for the United States. US conventional capabilities, NFU proponents contend, are more than sufficient to deter and respond to anything but a nuclear attack': Michael S. Gerson, 'No First Use: The Next Step for US Nuclear Policy', *International Security* 35(2), 2010: 9.

17 The US Administration claims that its policies do not have any influence on other states. For example, see these claims in Linton Brooks, 'An Assessment of the Impact of Repeal of the Prohibition on Low Yield Warhead Development on the Ability of the United States to Achieve its Non-Proliferation Objectives, March 2004 report to Congress', quoted in Christopher F. Chyba, 'Remarks at Carnegie International Non-Proliferation Conference June 22, 2004', iis-db.stanford.edu/pubs/20737/Chyba_CEIP_remarks.pdf (accessed 6 February 2012). However, the USA still seems largely to influence the policies of minor nuclear weapon states. See, for example, Scott D. Sagan, 'The Case for No First Use', *Survival* 51(3), 2009: 175–76.

18 Qadar Bakhsh Baloch, 'Beyond Nuclear Deterrence: The Transformation of Indo-Pak Equation', *Defence Journal*, 2008: 30; also see 'Assessing Pakistan's Nuclear First Use Option', *Defence Journal* (Pakistan), September 2004: 12–15. The freelance security analyst remained anonymous in this piece, stating that, 'Pakistan suffers from some very serious strategic imbalances relative to India which could lead to Pakistan reaching her nuclear threshold in a time frame much earlier (first use) than India; firstly, her limited territorial and geographical depth and secondly, her tremendous conventional inferiority'.

19 Rodney W. Jones, 'Pakistan's Nuclear Posture: Quest for Assured Nuclear Deterrence – A Conjecture', *Spotlight* (Regional Studies Islamabad) XIX(1), 2000: 18.

20 For more details on various US Nuclear Posture Reviews in which the USA retains the option of first use, renouncing NFU for its homeland security against chemical, biological and nuclear strikes and for its security assurances to its allies both in Europe and Asia, see www.defense.gov/news/jan2002/d20020109npr.pdf; www.cfr.org/proliferation/nuclear-posture-review-2010/p21839; www.defense.gov/npr/docs/2010%20nuclear%20posture%20review%20report.pdf (accessed 4 February 2012).

21 For interesting accounts on this, see the academic *Journal NPR* Special Issue on 'Arms, Disarmament and Influence: International Responses to the 2010 Nuclear Posture Review', *The Non-Proliferation Review* 18(1), February 2011: 1–319.

22 Interview with Feroz Hassan Khan, former director of arms control and disarmament, SPD, September 2012.

23 Abdul Sattar, Zulfiqar A. Khan and Agha Shahi, 'Securing the Nuclear Peace', *The News*, 5 October 1999.

24 Interview with Abdul Sattar, former foreign minister, September 2012.
25 Rasul Bakhsh Rais, 'Conceptualizing Nuclear Deterrence: Pakistan's Posture', *India Review* 4(2), 2005: 156.
26 K. Subrahmanyam, 'Nuclear India in Global Politics', *Strategic Digest* 28(12), 1998: 2016, emphasis added.
27 Vijai Nair, 'The Structure of an Indian Nuclear Deterrent', in Amitabh Mattoo (ed.) *India's Nuclear Deterrent, Pokhran II and Beyond*, New Delhi: Har Anand Publications, 1999, 84.
28 Author's interview with a Pakistani strategic analyst who wanted to remain anonymous, September 2012.
29 Interview with Maria Sultan, director-general of South Asian Strategic Studies Institute (SASSI), Islamabad, September 2012.
30 Shireen M. Mizari, 'Understanding Pakistan's Nuclear Doctrine', *Strategic Studies* XXIV(3), 2004: 3.
31 Tariq M. Ashraf, *Aero-Space Power: The Emerging Strategic Dimension*, Peshawar: PAF Book Club, 2003, 148.
32 Khalid Kidwai, 'An Interview with the Italian Research Group Landau Network', in C.P. Ramusino and M. Martellini, *Nuclear Safety, Nuclear Stability and Nuclear Strategy in Pakistan*, 2002, www.pugwash.org/september11/pakistan-nuclear.htm (accessed 13 September 2010), 7.
33 This was confirmed to the author during his interview at SPD, September 2012.
34 Bhumitra Chakma, 'Pakistan's Nuclear Doctrine and Command and Control System: Dilemmas of Small Nuclear Forces in the Second Atomic Age', *Security Challenges* 2(2), July 2006: 127–28.
35 Interview with Pakistan's former Ambassador Tariq Osman Hyder, Arms Control and Disarmament, Foreign Ministry of Pakistan, September 2012.
36 For a useful discussion on thinking for an actual declaration of Pakistani nuclear doctrinal posture, see the latest video programme (in Urdu), 'Thinking Pakistan', anchored by Dr Moeed Pirzada with a panel of four Pakistani security and nuclear experts who conclude that Pakistan is, in fact, in need of exiting nuclear ambiguity and declaring its actual nuclear posture for various reasons: www.youtube.com/watch?v=trFTH5RI1qA (accessed 19 April 2012).
37 'Pervaiz Musharraf's Interview to a German Magazine in 2002', in Peter R. Lavoy, 'Pakistan's Nuclear Doctrine', in R. Dossani and H.S. Rowen (eds) *Prospects for Peace in South Asia*, California: Stanford University Press, 2005, 283.
38 General Pervaiz Musharraf, 28 May 2000 Address to the Nation, in Rifat Hussein, *Nuclear Doctrines in South Asia*, SASSU Research Report, No. 4, 12
39 See 'Assessing Pakistan's Nuclear First Use Option', *Defence Journal* Pakistan, September 2004: 12–15. The freelance security analyst remained anonymous in this piece.
40 This danger is also viable for the established nuclear weapon states as long as nuclear weapons exist in their military and political discourses. See Mearsheimer, 'Nuclear Weapons and Deterrence in Europe'; Gerson, 'No First Use'; Scott D. Sagan, 'The Case for No First Use', *Survival* 51(3), 2009: 175–76.
41 For detail on this perspective, see Rizwana Abbasi, *Pakistan and the New Nuclear Taboo: Regional Deterrence and International Arms Control Regime*, Oxford and New York: Peter Lang, 2012.
42 Nuclear weapons have not been used either to terminate an already waged war, nor to begin one, at least in the South Asian case or during the many military crises of the Cold War era. However, many might say that the USA used nuclear weapons first to terminate a war already being waged, World War II, when two atomic bombs were dropped in Japan, on Hiroshima and Nagasaki, in August 1945.
43 For excellent works on this fundamental tenet of deterrence theory, which was first articulated and popularized by Thomas Schelling, see: Thomas Schelling, *The*

110 *Pakistan's doctrine of nuclear first use*

    Strategy of Conflict, New York: Oxford University Press, 1963, 21–28; Thomas Schelling, *Arms and Influence*, New Haven, CT: Yale University Press, 1966, 35–55.
44 Herman Kahn, *On Thermonuclear War*, (New York: Princeton University Press, 1960); K. Knorr, 'Limited Strategic War', in K. Knorr & T. Read (eds.), *Limited Strategic War: Essays in Nuclear Strategy*, (New York: Pall Mall Press, 1962), pp. 3–31
45 Shireen M. Mizari, 'India's Nuclear Doctrine in Perspective and Pakistan's Option', 1999, www.defencejournal.com/oct99/india-doctrine.htm (accessed 4 March 2012); Farah Zahra, 'Pakistan's Road to a Minimum Nuclear Deterrent', *Arms Control Today*, July/August 1999: 1–8; Chakma, 'Pakistan's Nuclear Doctrine'.
46 In his posited doctrine, US Secretary of State McNamara defined the level of damage needed as the destruction of 'one-quarter to one-third of the Soviet population and about two-thirds of Soviet industrial capacity'. See Desmond Ball, 'The Development of the SIOP, 1960–83', in Desmond Ball and Jeffrey Richelson (eds) *Strategic Nuclear Targeting*, New York: Cornell University Press, 1989, 69.
47 For details, see '2012 World Population Data Sheet', www.prb.org/pdf12/2012-population-data-sheet_eng.pdf (accessed 1 April 2013).
48 Chakma, 'Pakistan's Nuclear Doctrine', 129.
49 In his article Abhijit Singh stated on this premise that, 'there will be a strong ethical constraint that India would feel while counter-attacking with a high yield strategic weapon, in response to a first Pakistani strike by a low yield TNWs (Tactical Nuclear Weapons) … it would be hard for India's political masters to justify the annihilation of a whole Pakistani city by SNW (Strategic Nuclear Weapons)': Abhijit Singh, 'Pakistan: Testing of Tactical Nuclear Weapons', *India Defence Review* 26(3), 2011: 1–4, www.indiandefencereview.com/geopolitics/Pakistan-Testing-of-Tactical-Nuclear-Weapons.html (accessed 23 March 2012).
50 For contributory details on neo-culturalism, see Peter J. Katzenstein (ed.), *The Culture of National Security: Norms and Identity in World Politics*, New York: Columbia University Press, 1996; Peter J. Katzenstein, *Cultural Norms and National Security: Police and Military in Post-War Japan*, New York: Cornell University Press, 1998; Richard M. Price, *The Chemical Weapons Taboo*, New York: Cornell University Press, 1995.
51 This point was raised in the recent conference held at Carnegie Endowment for International Peace entitled *2011 Carnegie International Nuclear Policy Conference*, in which Pakistan's renowned expert on nuclear and security studies stated that there is a growing debate on the introduction of TNWs for counter-force targeting to offset its adversary's conventional forces followed by its war-fighting doctrinal procedure, e.g. CSD. See carnegieendowment.org/2011/03/29/two-triads-india-pakistan-china-and-china-u.s.-russia/2t0t (accessed 11 February 2012). For an interesting account on the US posture of counter-force targeting to use TNWs, see Desmond Ball, *Déjà Vu: The Return to Counterforce in the Nixon Administration*, California: Seminar on Arms Control and Foreign Policy, 1974; Desmond Ball, Counterforce Targeting: How New? How Viable? *Arms Control Today*, 1981.
52 Pakistan fears that its adversary would pre-empt it either by nuclear or conventional forces because of its lack of strategic depth. To pre-empt such a possibility, according to Rifaat Hussein, Pakistan retains its nuclear options open and upgrades its nuclear weapons programme. See, for example, carnegieendowment.org/2011/03/29/two-triads-india-pakistan-china-and-china-u.s.-russia/2t0t (accessed 11 February 2012).
53 The author had confirmation on this point from several of his key respondents in connection to this project: interviews with Zafar Iqbal Cheema, Khalid Iqbal, Feroz Hassan Khan and Rizwana Abbasi, September 2012.
54 Sattar *et al.*, 'Securing the Nuclear Peace'.
55 M. Tariq Ashraf, 'Doctrinal Reawakening of the Indian Armed Forces', *Military Review*, 2004, tamilnation.co/intframe/indian_ocean/ashraf_on_indian_maritime_doctrine.pdf (accessed 15 September 2010), emphasis added.

56 Baloch, 'Beyond Nuclear Deterrence', 31, note 58.
57 Interview with Zafar Iqbal Cheema, September 2012.
58 Mearsheimer, 'Nuclear Weapons and Deterrence in Europe', 33.
59 Recently, a Pakistani Chinese-made F-7PG training aircraft crashed, killing the pilots, which was the seventh aircraft crash in just six months. This indicates how ageing conventional capabilities need quick transformation if Pakistan's security planners are to improve the conventional balance in relation to its adversary. This also indicates how Pakistan, in this age of financial constraint and a weakening economy, cannot simply afford to spend much on modern conventional forces. See 'Pakistan Air Collision Kills Four Pilots', 15 May 2012, dawn.com/2012/05/17/collision-of-pafs-training-aircraft-kills-four/ (accessed 15 May 2012); and 'Pilot Killed in a PAF Plane Crash', www.dawn.com/2012/02/08/pilot-killed-in-paf-plane-crash.html (accessed 9 February 2012).
60 The factor of Pakistan's conventional weakness has been stated by a majority of Pakistani security planners and think tank institutes during the author's field work. For example, the author's interview with Khalid Rehman, director-general of the Institute of Policy Studies, and Shaheen Akther, senior fellow of the Institute of Regional Studies, Islamabad, September 2012.
61 For instance, in the case of the USA's and NATO's possible shifts in security policy options, that is, emphasizing the role of conventional forces with high, modern technology rather than the use of nuclear weapons, many insisted on the development and deployment of modern technology which could bolster the deterrence nature of conventional forces once the modern, sophisticated technology is applied to this effect. See Benjamin F. Schemmer, 'NATO's New Strategy: Defend Forward, But Strike Deep', *Armed Forces Journal International*, 1982: 50–68; B.F. Schemmer, 'Defend Forward, But Strike Deep – Part II', *Armed Forces Journal International*, 1982: 68–73, 92; B.F. Schemmer, 'Defend Forward, But Strike Deep – Part III', *Armed Forces Journal International*, 1983: 48–54; and 'Defending NATO', Editorial, *The Wall Street Journal*, 19 November 1982: 30.
62 It is because of these scenarios and numerous other factors that a number of articles appeared critiquing the applicability of technology and modernity to the then US and NATO conventional forces as being the technical solution to the former Soviet conventional forces. See, for example, Steven L. Canby, *The Conventional Defence of Europe: The Operational Limits of Emerging Technology*, Wilson Centre Working Paper No. 55, Washington, DC, 1984; Daniel Goure and Jeffery R. Cooper, 'Conventional Deep Strikes: A Critical Look', *Comparative Strategy* 4(3), 1984: 215–48.
63 Rong Yu and Peng Guangqian, 'Nuclear No-First-Use Revisited', *China Security* 5 (1), 2009: 86.
64 Brian Cloughley, *A History of Pakistan Army: Wars and Insurrections*, Karachi: Oxford University Press, 1999, 340.
65 Interview with Usman Iqbal Jadoon, director of arms control and disarmament, Foreign Ministry, September 2012.
66 Ayesha Siddiqa, *Military Insurance Inside Pakistan's Military Economy*, London: Pluto Press, 2007, 5.
67 Ibid., 22.
68 For interesting accounts on Pakistan's civil-military dilemma, see Hasan Askari Rizvi, 'Civil-Military Relations in Contemporary Pakistan', *Survival* 40(2), 1998: 110.
69 Timothy D. Hoyt, 'Strategic Myopia: Pakistan's Nuclear Doctrine and Crisis Stability in South Asia', in Lowell Dittmer (ed.) *South Asia's Nuclear Security Dilemma: India, Pakistan, China*, London: M.E. Sharpe, 2005, 120.
70 Sandeep Dikshit, 'Zardari Says he is Against Nuclear Warfare', *The Hindu* (New Delhi), 2008, www.hindu.com/2008/11/23/stories/2008112350260100.htm (accessed 16 October 2012).

71 For interesting accounts on Pakistan's strategy and classification of handling these security policies from a day-to-day basis, see Mahmud Ali Durrani, 'Pakistan's Strategic Thinking and the Role of Nuclear Weapons', 2004, www.cmc.sandia.gov/cmc-papers/sand2004-3375p.pdf (accessed 18 June 2012).

72 For an interesting piece on the SPD, which was previously named the Combat Development Directorate (CDD), see 'SPD & CDD', www.globalsecurity.org/wmd/world/pakistan/spd.htm (accessed 7 February 2012).

73 Author's interview with Dr Aman Rashid, director-general disarmament, Foreign Ministry, September 2012.

74 For details on Pakistan's civil-military relations, see Bindanda M. Chengappa, 'Pakistan: Military Role in Civil Administration', 1995, www.idsa-india.org/an-may9-9.html (accessed 7 February 2012); Talat Syed Hussein, 'Pakistan Hedged on Obvious Bet', *The Nation*, 29 May 1998; Hassan Askari Rizvi, 'Civil-Military Relations in Contemporary Pakistan', *Survival* 40(2), 1998: 96–113; Stephen P. Cohen, *The Pakistan Army*, New York: Oxford University Press, 1984.

75 Rizvi states: 'The military stands a better chance of wielding influence on key policy decisions and allocation of resources from the sidelines. This saves the military from hazards of direct assumption of power and gives space to elected civilians'. Hassan Askari Rizvi, 'On Civil-Military Relations', *Pakistan Today*, December 2011, www.pakistantoday.com.pk/2011/12/27/comment/columns/on-civil-military-relations/ (accessed 23 April 2013).

76 A Pakistani scholar based in Quaid-i-Azam University, Islamabad, whilst answering one of the questions posed on the policy options of Pakistan's nuclear posture at the 2011 Carnegie International Nuclear Policy Conference, stated: 'They [Pakistanis] would like to maintain a posture of credible minimum deterrence and this credible minimum deterrence is actually not very *static*, which essentially means that if India were to engage in a strategic nuclear modernisation, then the number game can actually change. There are several other elements, but this is the main thrust of the nuclear doctrine': Hussein, 2011, 21, emphasis added, carnegieendowment.org/2011/03/29/two-triads-india-pakistan-china-and-china-u.s.-russia/2t0t (accessed 11 February 2012).

77 The author's interviews with various key respondents such as Khalid Banuri, Adil Sultan and Zafar Ali of SPD, and Ambassador Tariq Osman Hyder, Dr Aman Rashid and Osman Jadoon of Pakistan's Foreign Ministry, who agreed somewhat to the preceding points, September 2012.

78 Dean Nelson and Ben Farmer, 'Pakistan Threatens Nuclear Arms Race over India Deal', 2011, www.telegraph.co.uk/news/worldnews/asia/pakistan/8286301/Pakistan-threatens-nuclear-arms-race-over-India-deal.html (accessed 9 February 2012).

79 Author's interview with Mansoor Ahmed, who specializes in nuclear studies, September 2012.

80 Ibid.

81 In addition to the US-Indian nuclear deal, India consistently looks to modernize its conventional forces. The recent Indian-Russian deal on conventional upgrade and nuclear energy worth billions of dollars depicts its evolution of conventional forces which would have an impact on other states such as China and largely on Pakistan. See www.dawn.com/2010/12/21/india-russia-sign-deals-on-fighter-jets-nuclear-energy.html, (accessed 21 December 2010); www.dawn.com/2010/12/22/india-tests-nuclear-capable-missile.html (accessed 22 December 2010).

82 For more details and an interesting account, see Mirza Aslam Beg, 'Responding to Indo-US Defence Pact', 2005, archives.dawn.com/2005/08/11/op.htm (accessed 9 February 2012).

83 Interview with Noman Sattar, Islamabad, September 2012.

84 Interview with Zulfqar Khan, who currently serves at the Ministry of Defence as a strategic analyst, September 2012.

7 Pakistan's policy of arms control and disarmament

A call for an arms control regime in South Asia

Introduction

Although Pakistan became a nuclear weapon state in the aftermath of its nuclear tests, it is not recognized by the NPT. Pakistan is more recently viewed as a de facto nuclear weapon state. In the 1960s, Pakistan had a favourable attitude towards the development process of the NPT. However, it did not sign the NPT when it found that India was not willing to sign it. Until Pakistan carried out nuclear weapon tests in May 1998, it maintained that Islamabad would not sign the NPT unless New Delhi signed it first. Pakistan also did not sign the 1996 CTBT because of the 'India factor' and Islamabad's interest in maintaining nuclear deterrence capability. This defying approach is consistent with Pakistan's policy towards the FMCT. The 'India factor' remains dominant whilst analysing Pakistan's approach towards the non-proliferation regimes.

This chapter highlights that the India factor cannot be the *only* factor responsible for Pakistan's defiance to the NPT, the CTBT and the FMCT. In the immediate aftermath of nuclear tests, Pakistan altered its approach in relation to the NPT and the CTBT. It demanded the formal status of a nuclear weapons state. In other words, Pakistan would now join the non-proliferation regime if it was recognized formally as a nuclear weapon state. On the FMCT, Pakistan's non-adherence is based on its concerns about the 'existing stockpiles' of fissile materials and other regional and international factors that Islamabad thinks affect the country's credibility in deterrent forces. Apparently, Pakistan's post-1998 defiance to non-proliferation regimes, including its non-adherence to the FMCT, may not conform to the idea of MD. In this scenario, the MD looks unsustainable as the Pakistani defiance to the NPT, the CTBT and the FMCT.

This chapter evaluates Pakistan's position and its role in global arms control and disarmament. It discusses how Pakistan supported the international disarmament process and why it later shifted its perception on acquiring nuclear weapons. It analyses Pakistan's policy approaches towards the post-1998 NPT, CTBT and FMCT. It also elaborates concerns on arms control and the disarmament process both at the international and regional levels, which become the obstacles for the creation of an ACR needed for deterrence stability in South Asia. Finally, it evaluates whether Pakistani policy in relation to the NPT, the CTBT and the FMCT conforms to the idea of MD.

Pakistan's policy of arms control and disarmament

To understand the dynamics of Pakistan's policy towards arms control and disarmament in the post-1998 era, it is important to look back at history. Pakistan's policy towards arms control and disarmament was based on equitable and non-discriminatory mechanisms. It desired arms control and disarmament both at the international and regional levels. This normative policy approach existed in Pakistan because it did not have any intention of acquiring nuclear weapons in the 1950s and the 1960s, although the option to acquire nuclear weapons existed. Later, Pakistan gradually shifted from normative to strategic policy approaches. The following sections analyse why Pakistan's normative principles towards its arms control and disarmament process turned into a strategic approach.

Shifting perceptions: Pakistan's normative approach

Pakistan, in its initial years of independence, remained inexperienced in the world politics of major powers. It took time for the fledgling state to learn from its strategic environment and formulate its policy option of arms control and disarmament. Pakistan thought that the early solutions for fast growing conventional and nuclear weapons would emerge out of deliberate efforts of the major powers.[1] For example, in the fourth session of the UNGA in 1949, a Pakistani representative to the UN, Sarwar Hassan, stated that 'the constantly increasing anxiety of the peoples of the world could be allayed only by a genuine agreement providing for effective guarantee amongst the nations possessing atomic energy and atomic weapons'.[2] At the sixth session of the UNGA, Pakistan remained committed and active in proposing arms control and disarmament resolutions which could not only urge member states to control the spread of arms, but also look forward to eradicating the atomic weapons and weapons of mass destruction.[3] On the basis of these proposals, the UNGA adopted the resolution for constituting the Disarmament Commission, which aimed at dealing with the emerging issues of arms control and disarmament amongst the member states.[4] When the USA tested its thermonuclear weapon, Pakistan, along with other members at the Bandung Afro-Asia Conference, urged the UNGA to abolish nuclear and thermonuclear weapons.[5] Pakistan played an important role in the UN Disarmament Commission towards the conclusion of the NPT.

Pakistan's NPT policy option evolved gradually. It adopted a more realistic and pragmatic approach after Pakistan joined the two US-supported security alliances: SEATO in 1954 and CENTO in 1955. Pakistan supported the Western powers in terms of dealing with the issues of nuclear weapons by adopting and setting up the mechanism for concrete inspection and verification of proliferation and disarmament. Pakistan, along with its Western alliance partner, viewed that without these (i.e. inspection, detection, verification, etc.), dealing with arms control and disarmament issues would be difficult, if not impossible. The dramatic shift in Pakistan's policy option of arms control and disarmament issues came after the US-backed security alliances sidelined Pakistan in its major foreign and strategic policy-making process. Pakistan felt isolated and abandoned despite the membership of SEATO and CENTO. It became suspicious of US assistance to India which would soon test a nuclear weapon. This was a major cause of concern for Pakistan in relation to its initial normative approach to the NPT.

Pakistan remained one of the first states of the UNGA that proposed an immediate adoption of the resolution of the NPT which would not only bring arms controls and initiate the disarmament dialogue between the Cold War rivals, but also pave the way for the total prohibition and testing of the spread of nuclear weapons to non-nuclear weapon states.[6] Zulfiqar Ali Bhutto claimed that it was he who proposed to the UNGA passing and adopting a resolution on the formation of a partial ban treaty in his address to a Political Committee of the UNGA in October 1960.[7] When the Partial Test Ban Treaty (PTBT) was formed in 1963, Pakistan became a party to the treaty. However, it did not ratify it until 1988.[8] In the years after signing the PTBT, Pakistan urged the world community that any form of treaty in relation to arms control and disarmament would remain meaningless if there were no attitudinal changes among the major powers and both vertical and horizontal proliferation continued to take place.[9] Islamabad obviously pointed to New Delhi's intention of a nuclear test.

Pakistan tried to convince the UNGA that its adversary would soon carry out an underground nuclear test without violating the NPT. In the mid-1960s, a Pakistani representative to the UNGA, Agha Shahi, informed the UNGA: 'The Government of Pakistan has reason to believe that the Government of India has decided to embark on a program for the production of nuclear weapons and that in order to do so without violating the Test Ban Treaty, a test explosion of a nuclear device will be carried out underground in the near future, ostensibly for peaceful purposes.'[10] In a similar vein, Agha Shahi urged the UNGA: 'the attitude of the potential nuclear weapons states will be of crucial importance. Even if all the non-nuclear weapon states signed and ratified the treaty and the near-nuclear weapon states did not, the main purpose of the treaty would be defeated.'[11] Thus, US arms support to India and India's testing of a nuclear device in 1974 caused Pakistan to shift its normative approach.

Shifting gears: from a normative to a strategic approach

From these official and semi-official statements, one can observe a change in Pakistan's stance on arms control and disarmament from a normative to strategic approach. When Pakistan observed in the late 1960s that India was not willing to sign the NPT because of its over-ambitious resolutions of a complete elimination of nuclear weapons and preparing to carry out a nuclear weapon test in the early 1970s, Pakistan's policy option in relation to a non-proliferation regime became 'Indian-centric'. Pakistan would follow suit if its adversary was to conduct a nuclear test. In the absence of a 'NATO-like security guarantee' and India's preparation for a nuclear test, it became a matter of national interest for Pakistan whether or not to sign the NPT. After India's nuclear weapon tests, Pakistan critiqued the discriminatory approaches and India's non-participation in the NPT. Islamabad expressed its unwillingness to sign the NPT. The country's normative principle on the NPT was replaced by the strategic approach that would accentuate the national interest and formulate the country's NPT policy in accordance with the changed South Asian strategic environment.

At the time of the NPT review conference in 1995, when the NPT was to be extended indefinitely, Pakistan had already started a national debate on whether or not to sign the NPT. The pro-NPT group suggested that Pakistan sign for economic and military benefits. To them, Pakistan's image before the international community would be enhanced at the expense of its adversary. Moreover, the bottom line for this group was that Pakistan could withdraw from the treaty on national security grounds. It was better for Pakistan to sign given its economic fragility, which would get support through incoming economic and military assistance. The anti-NPT group urged the Pakistani government to consider the national interest and geopolitical realities. The Pakistani government concurred with the latter group and did not sign the NPT.

Pakistan's NPT policy approach post-1998

In the aftermath of Pakistan's nuclear tests, it dramatically shifted its NPT policy. Until May 1998, the 'India factor' remained dominant, that is, Pakistan made it conditional that it would not sign the NPT unless India signed it first. The post-1998 nuclear tests changed that scenario. Pakistan demanded nuclear weapon status before signing the NPT. The defiance towards the non-proliferation regimes put Pakistan under external pressures. The international community imposed crippling economic sanctions on Pakistan. The G8 countries urged Pakistan to sign the NPT without conditions (as a non-nuclear state). The European Parliament also adopted a similar resolution, calling upon Pakistan to roll back its nuclear programme and join the NPT. There was lots of external pressure from other parts of the world to convince Pakistan to sign the NPT unconditionally in exchange for a mix of military and economic incentives. Nevertheless, Pakistan resisted all the external pressures and noted that it had already tested nuclear weapons in reaction to its adversary and it was in the best interests of national security and territorial integrity. Today, Pakistan's policy of defiance towards the non-proliferation regimes remains unchanged, responding to the international community that it would make no sense for Pakistan to roll back and join the NPT as a non-nuclear weapon state after testing nuclear weapons.[12]

The change in the US Administration, the events of 9/11 and Pakistan's much-needed role in the US-led 'war on terror' as a frontline state might have played a critical role in changing Pakistan's NPT policy approach. Pakistan exploited the opportunity and the Musharraf administration refused to sign the NPT as a non-nuclear weapon state. A Pakistani diplomat argued:

> In the aftermath of the May 1998 nuclear tests by India and Pakistan, the NPT has become irrelevant, as it recognises only those states as nuclear powers that have manufactured and exploded a nuclear weapon or other nuclear explosive prior to January 01 1967. In order for Pakistan to join the NPT it will therefore have to roll back its nuclear program which is not a practical proposition ... Pakistan cannot afford to give up its nuclear deterrent. Pakistan's reliance on nuclear capability for its independence and territorial integrity is therefore absolute. Pakistan should not be expected to come on board the NPT as a non-NWS [nuclear weapon state].[13]

Although the 'India factor' cannot completely be ruled out, this NPT policy statement is a clear indication to the international community that Pakistan's policy of arms control and disarmament would remain contingent. It also shows that Pakistan would 'wait and see' whether or not India signs the NPT first and the international community recognizes Pakistan as a nuclear weapon state before it actually signs the NPT.

Pakistan also sensed that the international community would put off economic sanctions and the new Administration in the USA would abandon the Clinton Administration's NPT policy of pressing Pakistan (and India) to roll back and sign the NPT. This can be assumed from a statement of the then US secretary of defense, Donald Rumsfeld, that Pakistan and India should be encouraged to 'learn that it is possible to live with nuclear weapons and not to use them'.[14] Later, the USA lifted the economic sanctions on Pakistan and granted it 'non-NATO ally' status, which allowed it to pursue an NPT policy that suited its interests.[15] Just as Pakistan debated the NPT, it also debated whether to sign the CTBT.

Pakistan's CTBT policy approach post-1998

Pakistan's CTBT policy approach remains identical to that of its NPT policy. Like the NPT policy orientation, Pakistan also supported the complete ban of the production of nuclear weapons since the 1950s. Pakistan was ready in 1996 to sign the CTBT, but the circumstances changed and it could not sign without India because Islamabad viewed that it would jeopardize its national security interests. Owing to domestic, regional and international factors (discussed later in this chapter), Pakistan refused to sign the CTBT, although it came very close to joining the CTBT without its adversary. Chakma outlined a few reasons for this: 1 it would erode Pakistan's strategic nuclear deterrent credibility; 2 by not signing the CTBT, it would keep Pakistan's option for nuclear tests open; 3 before the finalization of the CTBT draft in 1996, Pakistan observed that India was planning for a nuclear test, which in turn demanded a more cautious Pakistani approach towards the draft of CTBT; 4 Pakistan played the diplomatic card not to sign the CTBT, prioritizing the 'India factor' condition which served Pakistani national interests aimed at gaining international credibility at India's expense, which would blur international pressure and shift the external pressure on India; and 5 Pakistani domestic political dynamics also played a role in preventing Pakistan from signing the CTBT.[16]

The post-1998 tests brought about an interesting development as far as Pakistan's CTBT policy approach was concerned. Prime Minister Nawaz Sharif pointed out that his government had declared a moratorium on further nuclear weapon tests and would sign the CTBT before September 1999, whether or not India signed it first.[17] He tabled a resolution in the Pakistani parliament which proposed to 'authorise the government to take a decision on the CTBT in the best national interest'.[18]

There was a crucial CTBT debate in Pakistan before it actually signed. The pro-CTBT group highlighted that Pakistan should sign the CTBT to ease external pressure and accept the international economic and military incentives; it would enhance Pakistan's normative stance on the non-proliferation regimes; Pakistan would garner international support in terms of resolving the Kashmir issue once and for all; and signing the CTBT would not affect the credibility of its nuclear weapons because it had already acquired and tested nuclear devices.[19] Conversely, the anti-CTBT group insisted that Pakistan should carry out more nuclear weapons tests as six nuclear weapons were not enough for its deterrence credibility; it would not benefit Pakistan either economically and militarily; and it would be difficult to withdraw from the CTBT once it had joined.[20]

Pakistan failed to sign the CTBT on the promised date (in September 1999) as its defiance of these non-proliferation regimes and goals for enhancing the credibility of its deterrent forces continued. Chakma observed why Pakistan did not sign: 1 in reality, the 'India factor' remained alive despite Pakistan's promised date to sign the CTBT without its counterpart; 2 Pakistani domestic political dynamics once again remained as opposed to signing the CTBT as the NPT; 3 the Pakistani 'wait and see' policy approach also played a role when it observed the discriminatory treatment of the international community serving its adversary better than Pakistan, which in turn affected the initial decision to sign the CTBT and moreover, the 'wait and see' policy approach helped Pakistan draw maximum benefits from the international community; 4 the Pakistani armed forces also played a key role in dissuading the Sharif government from signing the CTBT (traditionally, the army has a great influence on national defence and security issues); 5 India's nuclear policy draft also moved Pakistan's decision further away from signing the CTBT, as Pakistani officials were closely observing these developments and national security interests were prioritized to a normative approach to the non-proliferation regimes; and 6 Islamabad also observed the US Senate disapproval of the CTBT in December 1999, which in turn waned US efforts of non-proliferation in the South Asian region.[21] Pakistan remained defiant of both the NPT and the CTBT, largely to ensure the credibility of its deterrent forces and attain the status of a recognized nuclear weapon state. The question of the credibility of Pakistan's deterrent forces cannot only be traced out in its NPT and CTBT policy approaches, but also its policy approach towards the FMCT.

Pakistan's policy towards the FMCT

Since the conclusion of the CTBT in 1996, it was hoped that the UN-sponsored 65-member state Conference on Disarmament (CD) would be able to lay out a thorough disarmament programme, halting the production of fissile material. The CD functions through a mutual consensus and the veto of a single member can create deadlock. Until now, no substantive discussion has taken place to make the FMCT an effective and verifiable treaty that requires unanimous acceptance by all the CD states. Although Pakistan is viewed as creating the FMCT deadlock, it is considered that the disagreement between the seven nuclear weapons states has rendered the initiative unviable for a formal negotiation.[22] The general disagreement creating the deadlock is on the 'existing stockpiles of fissile materials'. In addition to this, there are other key challenges to the successful enactment of the FMCT: 1 the negative security assurances; 2 the Prevention of an Arms Race in Outer Space (PAROS); and 3 nuclear disarmament. The CD has yet to reach an amicable resolution on these outstanding issues to make the FMCT more effective and verifiable. Pakistan seems to have its own worries in relation to the FMCT. Why is the country viewed as 'spoiling' or defiant on the successful working of the FMCT? This chapter helps trace the rudimentary factors elaborating Pakistan's policy towards the FMCT.

Although Pakistan was close to signing the CTBT in the immediate aftermath of its nuclear tests, the domestic political dynamics on the basis of Pakistan's security concerns prevented the Sharif government from signing the treaty. After the tests, there were external pressures on Pakistan to declare a moratorium on production of fissile material (highly enriched uranium and plutonium). In this context, the UN Security Council passed resolution 1172 on 6 June 1998, which called on both Pakistan and India to halt further fissile material production. The UN urged both Pakistan and India 'to participate, in a positive spirit and on the basis of the agreed mandate, in negotiations at the Conference on Disarmament in Geneva on a treaty *banning the production of fissile material for nuclear weapons* or other nuclear explosive devices, with a view to reaching early agreement'.[23] Pakistan could not comply with the UN resolution on fissile materials. It also blocked the successful negotiation at the subsequent CD. Islamabad views that various factors are responsible for its defying stance on the FMCT.

First, Pakistan says that there is a need for a non-discriminatory and universally verifiable treaty negotiation. Pakistan's then ambassador to the UN, Munir Akram, stated on 11 August 1998 that 'Pakistan has consistently believed that a ban on the production of fissile materials should be promoted through a universal non-discriminatory treaty in the CD and through universal measures'.[24] Apparently, Akram's statement on the FMCT is consistent with the 'Shannon Mandate'.[25]

Second, Pakistan also has reservations about the loose FMCT term 'cut-off'.[26] It does not function in a nuclear disarmament programme but is yet another recipe for the NPT. On 26 December 1998, Pakistan's foreign minister, Sartaj Aziz, stated in the Pakistani National Assembly that Pakistan would support the FMCT if it promoted both nuclear non-proliferation and nuclear disarmament.[27]

Third, Pakistan highlights the issue of the 'existing stockpiles' of fissile material, worrying about an increasing gap on this particular issue between Islamabad and New Delhi. Islamabad urges the CD nations to work on the elimination of the asymmetries in existing stockpiles of fissile material. Masood Khan, Pakistani ambassador to the UN, stated in 2006 that a 'cut-off in the manufacturing of fissile materials must be accompanied by a mandatory program for the elimination of asymmetries in the possession of fissile material stockpiles by various states ... a fissile material treaty must provide a schedule for a progressive transfer of existing stockpiles to civilian use and placing these stockpiles under the safeguards'.[28]

Fourth, Islamabad also believes that the conclusion of the US-Indian nuclear deal and the NSG's special waiver to its counterpart would have far-reaching security implications for the South Asian region. On various occasions, Pakistan has raised this concern and informed the CD nations that due to changed regional security dynamics, Islamabad would maintain the credibility of its deterrence. Pakistan observes that the US-Indian nuclear deal would help India increase its existing stockpile of fissile material, which in turn would assist New Delhi to produce more deterrent forces. Maleeha Lodhi pointed out: 'Given its ambition to acquire hundreds of nuclear warheads (400 in one estimated figure), India faces the dilemma of how to build this arsenal while meeting its civilian nuclear needs. This problem was resolved by its deal with the US.'[29] Also, Islamabad expresses its concerns over the NSG's special treatment of India, which in turn undermines Pakistan deterrence credibility.[30] The NCA stated that Islamabad's policy towards the FMCT would be based on its national security interests and objectives of strategic stability in South Asia. The NCA noted in December 2010:

> Such policies, detrimental as they are to international peace and security, undermine the credibility of the existing non-proliferation regime and are

inconsistent with the national laws and international obligations. Revisionism based on strategic, political or commercial considerations accentuates asymmetries and would perpetuate instability, especially in South Asia.[31]

Despite Pakistan's recent accelerated production of fissile material, it is believed that the gap between Islamabad's stockpile and that of New Delhi remains wide.[32] The increasing asymmetry in fissile material stockpiles between the two countries keeps Islamabad reluctant to withdraw its veto from the FMCT negotiations.[33]

Last but not least, Pakistan views that the region's increasingly altering security environment affects Pakistan's stance on the FMCT. For example, India's development of CSD, its pursuit of a ballistic missile defence (BMD) system in collaboration with the USA and Israel, and its increasing fissile material build-up put pressure on Pakistan's strategic options. These fast-changing security dynamics in South Asia in turn make Islamabad reluctant to withdraw its veto over the current FMCT deadlock. Pakistani leading analyst Jaspal presumed:

> [These] strategic constraints necessitate Islamabad to increase its fissile materials stockpile and rejuvenate its nuclear weapons capability for the foreseeable future. Indeed, the embryonic South Asian strategic environment obligates Pakistan to build more missiles and more warheads which require more fissile materials.[34]

Thus, the issue of the existing stockpile of fissile materials, the US-Indian nuclear deal, the NSG's special waiver to India including the issues of negative security assurances, discriminatory approaches of the FMCT, and an arms race at the global level further move Pakistan away from concluding an FMCT negotiation. Pakistan's reluctance to withdraw its veto over the FMCT negotiation indicates that minimum deterrence is not sustainable for Pakistan. Pakistan's policy of minimum deterrence remains evolving as it demands equal treatment on the fissile material in relation to its adversary. In this context, Pakistan's representative to the UN, Zamir Akram, stated that Islamabad would consent to the FMCT negotiations only when Islamabad was granted an Indian-style NSG waiver.[35] This further shows that Pakistan's policy of arms control and disarmament remains contingent, subject to the region's changes in security environment.

Pakistan's approach to regional nuclear arms control

Pakistan seemingly played a positive role in terms of building an arms control regime in South Asia. In the aftermath of India's nuclear test in 1974, it offered various proposals to India in an effort to establish a regional ACR. These proposals included: 1 the establishment of a nuclear weapons-free zone in South Asia in 1974; 2 a joint declaration renouncing the acquisition or

122 *Policy of arms control and disarmament*

construction of nuclear weapons in 1979; 3 the mutual acceptance of the IAEA safeguards on all nuclear facilities in 1979; 4 a bilateral/regional nuclear test ban in 1987; 5 a conference on nuclear non-proliferation in South Asia in 1991; 6 a zero-missile zone in South Asia in 1993; and 7 a no-war pact in 1997.[36] Although these talks were discussed and theoretically placed between India and Pakistan, Islamabad considers that these measures towards the establishment of a regional arms control regime were both rejected by India and ignored by the international community.

Pakistan links the global factor with its approach towards the regional nuclear arms control process. It believes that regional and international endeavours towards non-proliferation regimes are complementary. The Pakistani officials' view is that unless the regional non-proliferation prospects and issues related to these approaches are resolved, it would be difficult for Pakistan to adhere to the principles of the NPT, and hard for both Pakistan and India to establish an ACR in South Asia.

Loopholes within the NPT

There are weaknesses within the NPT provisions which are exploited by both the NPT member states and the non-NPT nuclear weapon states. These weaknesses have implications for international efforts on arms control and disarmament policies and the South Asian region is no exception.

First, the formation of the NPT is carried out in such a way, due to the impasse created by the USA and the former Soviet Union, that it does not elaborate the complete mechanism for the elimination of nuclear weapons. There is a lack of discussion on the transfer of US nuclear weapons to its NATO-led allies. Despite the reduction of US-transferred TNWs to a few NATO allies, there are still about 200 TNWs stationed that could be readied and deployed in the event of major conventional war with its adversary.[37] The NPT is silent on this issue.

Second, the NPT provisions seem blurred and create contradictions for the future survival of the NPT. For example, Article I of the NPT directs the nuclear weapons states party to the NPT to 'undertake not to transfer to any recipient whatsoever nuclear weapons or other nuclear explosive devices or control over such weapons of explosive devices directly or indirectly'.[38] Similarly, in accordance with Article II of the NPT, 'the non-nuclear weapon states party to the treaty undertakes not to receive the transfer from any transferor whatsoever of nuclear weapons or other nuclear explosive devices or of control over such weapons or explosive devices directly or indirectly'.[39] The US transfer and its NATO-led allies being the recipient of TNWs violate the provisions of the NPT.[40] In addition, the recent US-Indian nuclear deal includes the provisions of nuclear technology to India, which encouraged Russia and Australia to strike similar nuclear deals with India, is also viewed as a violation of the NPT. This in turn provides incentives for other established nuclear weapon states of the NPT to assist states outside the treaty.[41]

Third, Article X of the NPT provides a provision of withdrawal. This indicates: 1 the NPT member state can withdraw from the treaty any time it considers necessary; 2 there is no clause of punishment in relation to its withdrawal; 3 the withdrawn state can develop and acquire nuclear weapons because of an 'extra-ordinary event' that damages the 'supreme interest' of this state; and 4 any withdrawal from the NPT for protecting the national interests and security, thus, building nuclear weapons is not considered a violation of the NPT. For example, North Korea withdrew from the NPT in 2003 and developed nuclear weapon technology in 2006. Despite NPT membership, Iran developed nuclear weapons for security purposes and could withdraw from the NPT enjoying the benefits of Article X of the NPT. Iran could go nuclear, unpunished.[42]

Last, but hardly least, the NPT creates discrimination between the nuclear 'haves' and 'have nots'. It permits all the established nuclear weapon states such as the USA, Russia, the UK, France and China to be legitimate nuclear weapon states, but denies this legitimacy to non-NPT nuclear states. It is one of the major obstacles for the non-NPT nuclear states to sign the treaty. It is a loophole within the treaty that could allow other states to develop nuclear weapons capability.[43]

The continuous salience of nuclear weapons at the global level

Although it is considered that the established nuclear weapon states have helped to create and participate in arms control and disarmament treaties including the formation of the NPT, they have not played an effective role yet in terms of reducing their nuclear weapons to an acceptable minimum level, which in turn failed to win them the confidence of the minor nuclear weapon states in the process of complete disarmament of nuclear weapons. The established nuclear weapon states have undertaken, in accordance with Article VI of the NPT, that they would work together both to 'cease the nuclear arms race' and endeavour for a 'general and complete disarmament under strict and effective international control'.[44] Although it is urged that the established nuclear weapon states take the first initiative as a moral obligation to reduce their nuclear weapons, the established nuclear weapon states, particularly the USA and Russia, might expect China, India and Pakistan to join the collective disarmament process.

The consistent modernization of US conventional forces, keeping the options of a BMD system and reliance on the mix of missile and strategic weapons, provides incentive to others. James Acton, a Carnegie-based nuclear policy expert, states that 'The problem is not simple – as it is sometimes portrayed to be – that by pursuing ballistic missile defence and long range high precision conventional weapons, the United States is threatening Russia's and China's nuclear forces and undermining their security'.[45] Thus, many in Russia suggest TNWs as a counterweight to the USA.[46] The logic is applicable to the South Asian region, albeit the environment is different. These practices are observed between nuclear rivals India and Pakistan. For example, India prepares for the CSD whilst Pakistan, as part of a strategic action-reaction phenomenon, responds by building TNWs as a counter-weight.[47] These strategic policy options between the established nuclear weapons states and the minor nuclear weapon states provide incentives for increasing arms competition and consequent dangers of military escalation. As a result, these developments become hurdles to the peaceful creation of an ACR.

According to James Acton, 'During the Cold War, nuclear reductions were essentially a US-Russia bilateral issue. This will change in the not-too-distant future when the downward trajectory of the American and Russian arsenals risks colliding with the upward trajectory in China, India, and Pakistan'.[48] Nevertheless, hundreds and thousands of nuclear weapons are still in US and Russian possession, which makes the case for the NPT's Article VI weak.[49] In this scenario, neither India nor Pakistan would sign the NPT, nor could this encourage them to establish an ACR in South Asia. India holds responsible the established nuclear weapon states nuclear proliferation and the discrimination within the NPT. The policy options of both India and Pakistan converge on this point, that unless they are declared legitimate nuclear weapon states and other nuclear weapons states disarm themselves first, both South Asian nuclear rivals may not become part of the NPT.[50] Besides the USA and Russia, other established nuclear weapon states such as France, the UK and China are in possession of hundreds, if not thousands, of nuclear weapons with sophisticated delivery systems, although they have kept their deterrent forces at a modest level. For example, the UK was recently thought to have reduced the salience of nuclear weapons, but with the changed strategic environment, particularly North Korea's intention of building more nuclear forces including inter-continental ballistic missiles, this has threatened the deterrent capability of the UK. The minor nuclear weapon states urge the established nuclear weapon states to play a meaningful role in complete and verified non-proliferation, thus providing incentives to smaller nuclear weapon states to be part of the process of a non-proliferation regime. So long as the established nuclear weapons states keep and plan to upgrade and modernize their deterrence forces, it is difficult for minor nuclear weapon states to forego nuclear weapons and sign the NPT.[51]

The external factor

The external factor becomes an outstanding hurdle in defining not only the parameters for a true minimum deterrence, but also creating difficulties for Pakistan to sign the NPT. Each state's policy affects the strategic calculus of other states, which in turn becomes the barrier for the creation of an ACR. An action-reaction phenomenon reflects in the South Asian region that if India has its concerns about the Pakistan-China strategic nexus, then Pakistan equally has serious concerns over the India-USA nuclear deal, including India's recent deals with other developed states in terms of seeking leverage in relation to fissile enriched materials. Pakistan considers that these strategic developments have implications for the region. Given these realities, Muhammad Khurshid Khan recommended to Islamabad that 'the current delicate strategic equilibrium between India and Pakistan may not hold well over the next five to ten years if appropriate measures by Pakistan are not taken because a substantial anti-missile capability with India will make the difference. Pakistan would, therefore, be forced to review its strategic policies'.[52]

The external factor affects the South Asian strategic environment and Pakistan is pulled into these strategic developments. It is interesting to observe that there is no establishment of an ACR at the regional level, say, between India and China. The absence of this keeps the two nuclear rivals active in their arms build-up, which in turn puts strategic pressure on Pakistan to uphold its deterrent forces. Therefore, the salience of nuclear weapons between the USA and Russia affects China, and China's modernization of its deterrent forces affects the South Asian strategic environment. India is observed to strike an arms deal with the USA and seeks an NSG special arms treatment, and Pakistan responds at the proportionate level to maintain its credibility of deterrent forces, hence remaining defiant of the non-proliferation regimes. The complex strategic environment from the top to bottom trajectory is not conducive to Islamabad and New Delhi building a framework for a regional ACR.

Conclusion

This chapter analysed Pakistan's policy towards the NPT, the CTBT and the FMCT, with special reference to its policy of minimum credible deterrence. It traced out the variables that explain Pakistan's changing approaches towards the non-proliferation regimes from a normative to a strategic dimension. The analysis shows that the 'India factor' played an important role in judging Pakistan's non-adherence to the non-proliferation regimes, including an FMCT negotiation. However, the deeper look at Pakistan's approach to these treaties indicates that the India factor cannot be the *only* factor as conceptualized by many. Although the India factor remains a part of Pakistan's policy of arms control and disarmament and 'Indian-centricity' exists in its nuclear policy, the immediate aftermath of its nuclear tests show that Pakistan's stance on non-proliferation regimes goes beyond India. Islamabad developed what Chakma calls a 'nuclear nationalism', demanding nuclear legitimacy.[53] In other words, Pakistan would sign the NPT only as a recognized nuclear weapons state, which goes against the NPT's Article IX. Therefore, Pakistan did not sign the NPT and the CTBT, and 'nuclear nationalism' was played out in Pakistani domestic nuclear politics. It can be assumed that the domestic political dynamics played a key role in dissuading successive Pakistani governments from capitulating to the non-proliferation regimes. Hence, Pakistan does not only want India to sign first, but it also expects the NPT regime to accept its demand to be a recognized nuclear weapon state before signing the treaty.

On the FMCT, Pakistan's policy is more or less similar to that of the NPT and the CTBT. Pakistan demands that the FMCT should be crafted on an internationally verifiable non-discriminatory platform for a successful disarmament process. Particularly, Islamabad demands that the issue of 'existing stockpiles' of fissile material needs to be addressed on a non-discriminatory and verifiable basis. The US-Indian nuclear deal, India's motives for BMD development, the NSG's special waiver on India, the development of a CSD and India's pursuit of acquiring fissile material are the emerging factors that Islamabad calculates strategically. Islamabad remains defiant of the FMCT against the backdrop of these developments in the South Asian strategic environment. It would, perhaps, remain reluctant in the future to withdraw its veto for a successful FMCT negotiation unless these issues were addressed.

The domestic, regional and international factors in relation to Pakistan's policy towards the NPT, the CTBT and the FMCT make Islamabad not only defiant to the norms of these non-proliferation regimes, but also encourage it to accelerate production of its stockpile of fissile material. This is to offset its conventional vulnerabilities and enhance the credibility of its deterrent forces. Does the minimum remain sustainable for Pakistan in such a fast-changing South Asian strategic environment? Perhaps the minimum remains unsustainable and the chances for the establishment of an ACR remain dim, given the weaknesses of the NPT, salience of nuclear weapons and external factors in the South Asian strategic account. This in turn undermines the struggle for potential change: a call for an actual minimum.

Notes

1 Sarwar K. Hassan, *Pakistan and the United Nations*, New York: Manhattan Publishing Company, 1960, 257.
2 The UN General Assembly Official Records (GAOR), 4th Session, *Ad Hoc* Political Committee, 34th Meeting (11 November 1949), 196.
3 The GAOR, 6th Session, Agenda Items 16 and 66, (1951/1959): ST/LIB/SER.B/ A. 2.
4 For details, see 'United States Disarmament Commission', www.un.org/disarmament/HomePage/DisarmamentCommission/UNDiscom.shtml (accessed 2 August 2012).
5 For details, see 'Selected Documents of the Bandung Conference: Texts of Selected Speeches and Final Communiqué of the Asian-African Conference, Bandung, Indonesia', 18–24 April 1955.
6 Bhumitra Chakma, *Strategic Dynamics and Nuclear Weapons Proliferation in South Asia: A Historical Analysis*, New York: Peter Lang, 2004, 225.
7 See 'Disarmament Problems: Convocation Address, Sindh University', 30 March 1962, quoted in *Zulfiqar Ali Bhutto Speeches – Interviews 1948–1966*, bhutto.org/Acrobat/Bhutto_Speeches_1948-66.pdf (accessed 8 May 2012), 170–77.
8 Although Pakistan signed the PTBT in 1963, despite being critical of this as reflected in both Ayub's and Bhutto's addresses to the UNGA on arms control and disarmament, Pakistan ratified this treaty in 1988.
9 Chakma, *Strategic Dynamics*, 227–28.

10 See the US Arms Control and Disarmament Agency, *Documents on Disarmament, 1974*, Washington, DC: Government Printing Office Series, 1975, 166.
11 The General Assembly Official Record, 22nd Session, First Committee, 1566th Meeting (13 May 1968), 19–20.
12 Ansar Abbasi, 'Pakistan May Sign NPT if Declared Nuclear Power', *The News*, 13 February 2004.
13 Ghulam A. Malik, 'Nuclear Non-Proliferation and the NPT Review Conference: The Pakistani Perspective', in *Nuclear Disarmament and Non-Proliferation: The Role of the Nuclear Non-Proliferation Treaty*, 2000, www.kas.de/wf/doc/kas_5077-1522-2-30.pdf?040722104256 (accessed 7 May 2012), 44.
14 Rumsfeld stated this in a press conference in Finland in June 2001. See 'Washington Shifts its South Asia Nuclear Policy', *Arms Control Today*, July–August 2001: 30.
15 Bhumitra Chakma, 'The NPT, the CTBT and Pakistan: Explaining the Non-adherence Posture of a de facto Nuclear State', *Asian Security* 1(3), 2005: 267–84.
16 Ibid., 277.
17 Pakistan's prime minister to the 53rd Session of the UNGA, 23 September 1998, www.bu.edu/globalbeat/southasia/sharif092398.html (accessed 22 March 2013).
18 Andrew Koch, 'South Asia, Public Opinion, and the Comprehensive Test Ban Treaty', *Weekly Defence Monitor* 2(37), 17 September 1998.
19 Zia Mian, 'Why Pakistan Should Sign the CTBT', *The News*, 5 August 1996; Zafar Nawaz Jaspal, 'A Case for Signing the CTBT', *Strategic Issues* 3, 2000, Islamabad: Institute of Strategic Studies; Pervez Hoodbhoy, 'Pakistan's Nuclear Future', in Samina Ahmed and David Cortright (eds) *Pakistan and the Bomb: Public Opinion and Nuclear Options*, Indiana: University of Notre Dame Press, 1998.
20 Moonis Ahmar, *The CTBT Debate in Pakistan*, New Delhi: Har Anand, 2001.
21 Chakma, 'The NPT, the CTBT and Pakistan', 279–80.
22 Andreea Berger, 'Finding the Right Home for FMCT Talks', *Arms Control Today*, October Issue, 2012.
23 See UN Security Council Resolution 1172, 6 June 1998, www.un.org/ga/search/view_doc.asp?symbol=S/RES/1172 (accessed 24 March 2013), emphasis added.
24 Munir Akram, ambassador of Pakistan, 'Fissile Material Treaty', Statement at the Conference on Disarmament, 11 August 1998.
25 A Canadian ambassador, Gerald Shannon, who helped secure a mandate for an Ad Hoc Committee of the CD to negotiate an FMCT, which was later named the 'Shannon Mandate'. The Shannon Mandate called for an 'internationally and effectively verifiable treaty'. For details, see Robert J. Einhorn, 'Controlling Fissile Materials World Wide: A Fissile Material Cut-off Treaty and Beyond', media.hoover.org/sites/default/files/documents/9780817949211_ch8.pdf (accessed 24 March 2013).
26 The Pakistani ambassador to the UN's statement on the FMCT, 11 August 1998, www.acronym.org.uk/articles-and-analyses/fmt-breakthrough-last-cd?page=show (accessed 24 March 2013).
27 Quoted in Mahmood Afzal, 'Pakistan's Stance on FMCT', *Dawn*, 12 January 1999.
28 Quoted in Rifaat Hussain, 'Prospects for Peace between India and Pakistan', *National Development and Security* IX(3), Serial No. 35, 2001: 14.
29 Maleeha Lodhi, 'FMCT and Strategic Stability', *The News International*, 26 January 2010.
30 Tariq Osman Hyder, 'FMCT: Facts and Fiction', *The News*, 28 March 2012; Adil Sultan, *Fissile Material Treaty: Prospects and Challenges*, Research Paper No. 49, 2011, www.isn.ethz.ch/isn/Digital-Library/Publications/Detail/?lng=en&id=151243 (accessed 24 March 2013).
31 See NCA concluding statements on the FMCT, 'NCA Rules Out Signing of Treaty on N-materials', *Dawn*, 15 December 2010, dawn.com/2010/12/15/nca-rules-out-signing-of-treaty-on-n-material-2/ (accessed 24 March 2013).

32 Berger, 'Finding the Right Home for FMCT Talks'.
33 A Pakistani representative stated at the February 2010 Conference on Disarmament that, 'along with the commitments to build up its [India's] strategic and conventional capabilities has encouraged its hegemonic ambitions, which are aimed at charting a course of dangerous adventurism whose consequences can both be unintended and uncontrollable ... Pakistan would not move forward with negotiations on the FMCT, and by extension, it would continue to expand its stockpiling of fissile material': Andrew Bast, 'Pakistan's Nuclear Calculus', *Washington Quarterly* 34(4), 2011: 79.
34 Zafar Nawaz Jaspal, 'Future of FMCT: Assessing the Prospects and Constraints', Institute of Strategic Studies Islamabad, 2010, www.issi.org.pk/publication-files/1299560158_80128402.pdf (accessed 11 May 2012).
35 See 'The South Asian Nuclear Balance: An Interview with Pakistani Ambassador to the CD Zamir Akram', *Arms Control Today*, December 2011.
36 Malik, 'Nuclear Non-Proliferation and the NPT Review Conference', 43.
37 For details, see Hans M. Kristensen, 'US Nuclear Weapons in Europe: A Review of Post-Cold War Policy, Force Levels, and War Planning', 2005, www.nrdc.org/nuclear/euro/contents.asp (accessed 15 May 2012); Tom Saur and Bob van der Zwaan, 'US Tactical Nuclear Weapons in Europe After NATO's Lisbon Summit: Why their Withdrawal is Desirable and Feasible', 2011, belfercenter.ksg.harvard.edu/publication/21074/us_tactical_nuclear_weapons_in_europe_after_natos_lisbon_summit.html (accessed 15 May 2012); and 'Global Zero NATO-Russia Commission Report: Removing US and Russian Tactical Nuclear Weapons from European Combat Bases', February 2012, www.globalzero.org/en/nato-russia-commission-report (accessed 15 May 2012). These findings show that the estimated presence of TNWs in Europe is about 200: Belgium, Germany and the Netherlands each have 20 TNWs, Italy is in possession of 50, and Turkey is estimated to have 50 to 90 US TNWs.
38 See NPT, Article I, 'Treaty on the Non-Proliferation of Nuclear Weapons', IAEA, 22 April 1970, www.iaea.org/Publications/Documents/Infcircs/Others/infcirc140.pdf (accessed 14 May 2012).
39 See NPT, Article II, ibid.
40 The Iranian ambassador to the IAEA, Ali Asghar Soltanieh, stated during the first session of the NPT Preparatory Committee in Vienna that 'The deployment of hundreds of the US tactical nuclear weapons in EU states is a blatant violation of the NPT by the US and the host countries': 'US, EU Worst Nuclear Proliferators, NPT Violators, Iran Says', 7 May 2012, www.presstv.com/detail/240046.html (accessed 3 August 2012).
41 Many in Pakistan accuse the USA of violating not only the NPT, but also UN Security Council resolution 1172, which was adopted after the South Asian nuclear adversary tested nuclear weapons in May 1998, to deter them from carrying out more tests. See Bast, 'Pakistan's Nuclear Calculus', 79. For useful studies on the Indo-US nuclear deal, see Jayshree Bajoria, 'The US-India Nuclear Deal', 2010, www.cfr.org/india/us-india-nuclear-deal/p9663 (accessed 7 August 2012); Nasrullah Mirza and M. Sadiq, 'Indo-US 123 Agreement: Impacts on Deterrence Stability in South Asia', 2008, www.sassu.org.uk/pdfs/Research_Report_7.pdf (accessed 7 August 2012); V.M. Ramana, 'The Impact of the Indo-US Nuclear Deal on the NPT and the Global Climate Regime', 8 December 2009, www.boell.de/intlpolitics/security/foreign-affairs-security-7983.html (accessed 7 August 2012).
42 See NPT, Article X, 'Treaty on the Non-Proliferation of Nuclear Weapons'; 'Iran Threat to Quit Atomic Treaty', BBC News, 7 May 2006, news.bbc.co.uk/1/hi/4981940.stm (accessed 3 August 2012).
43 It is stated in the NPT's Article IX that, 'for the purposes of this Treaty, a nuclear weapon state is one which has manufactured and exploded a nuclear weapon or

other nuclear explosive device prior to January 01, 1967': 'Treaty on the Non-Proliferation of Nuclear Weapons'. States that have or will have acquired nuclear weapons are not nuclear weapon states in light of Article IX of the NPT, despite their nuclear weapon acquisition; when they join the treaty, they will join with no status of a nuclear weapon state.
44 See NPT, Article VI, 'Treaty on the Non-Proliferation of Nuclear Weapons'.
45 James M. Acton, 'Bombs Away? Being Realistic about Deep Nuclear Reduction', *Washington Quarterly* 35(2), 2012: 49.
46 Sergei M. Rogov, Viktor Esin, Paval S. Zolotarev and Valerity Yarynich, 'Sood'ba Stratyegichyeskih Voyennoye Obozryeniy Poslye Pragi' [The Fate of Strategic Arms after Prague], 2010, www.ng.ru/concepts/2010-08-27/1_strategic.html (accessed 23 October 2012).
47 Zafar Khan, 'Cold Start Doctrine: The Conventional Challenge to South Asian Stability', *Contemporary Security Policy* 33(3), 2012: 577–94.
48 Acton, 'Bombs Away?' 38.
49 Mario E. Carranza, 'Can the NPT Survive? The Theory and Practice of US Nuclear Non-Proliferation Policy after September 11', *Contemporary Security Policy* 27(3), December 2006: 489–525; George Perkovich and James M. Acton (eds), *Abolishing Nuclear Weapons: A Debate*, Carnegie Endowment for International Peace, 2009.
50 Chakma, *Strategic Dynamics*.
51 Carranza, 'Can the NPT Survive?'
52 Muhammad Khurshid Khan, 'Fissile Material Cut-off Treaty: An Overview from Pakistan', Institute of Strategic Studies Islamabad, 2011, www.issi.org.pk/publication-files/1315811133_20447390.pdf (accessed 11 May 2012).
53 Chakma 'The NPT, the CTBT and Pakistan'.

8 Conclusion
A call for an actual minimum

Introduction: revisiting minimum deterrence

The primary aim of this book is to sketch a broader picture of Pakistan's policy of minimum deterrence after the 1998 nuclear weapon tests. It mainly analyses Pakistan's declared nuclear policy of 'minimum credible deterrence' (MCD). It examines why 'minimum' and if the minimum is workable at the theoretical level and sustainable at the operational level. It critically evaluates Pakistan's MCD in light of theoretical and conceptual essentials of minimum deterrence. There appears to be an interesting dichotomy as Pakistan's nuclear policy evolves. On the one hand, Pakistan claims to follow minimum deterrence to meet strategic challenges, but on the other hand, the Pakistani nuclear weapons programme, as various reliable sources indicate, is rapidly expanding. The two views seem to contrast and add more ambiguity. The radical changes in Pakistan's nuclear policy can be observed. Why, when, how and what made this policy shift is a primary focus of this book. Put simply, this study evaluates why Pakistan could not sustain the minimum deterrence it conceived initially after its May 1998 nuclear tests.

Although minimum deterrence has been a declaratory policy option for the country, the practice of a true minimum deterrence does not seem to exist in the case of Pakistan. Indeed the idea of a minimum can be conceptually critiqued, and is perhaps valid if one closely examines Pakistan's nuclear behaviour. The minimum has been criticized as it confronts the definitional issue. For Pakistani security planners and nuclear experts alike, the term minimum cannot concretely be defined, but rather needs to be seen as a flexible term. Whilst looking at the rapid expansion of the South Asian nuclear arsenal, the idea of a minimum needs to be reconceptualized. Indeed, Pakistani officials insist that the term minimum does not remain static but rather keeps changing in accordance with the region's strategic developments. This study has analysed this in the context of minimum deterrence.

Given this context, Pakistan's rationale of minimum deterrence, the sustainability of a minimum, its nuclear force-building posture, the usability of nuclear forces and the policy of arms control and disarmament are all discussed in this study. Before analysing what Pakistani officials and nuclear experts think of minimum deterrence and how Pakistan can be located within the essentials of minimum deterrence, it is important to revisit the basics of minimum deterrence.

The basics of minimum deterrence

Chapter 1 set out the essentials of minimum deterrence. The concept of minimum deterrence was developed during the Cold War period when the USA and the Soviet Union were rapidly expanding their deterrent forces to inflict unacceptable damage on each other, at the same time as world critics established an idea of a minimum which revolves around a few survivable nuclear forces. This small stock of nuclear forces could inflict unacceptable damage. A few went further to note that the use of *one* nuclear weapon could be unacceptable to an adversary. The minimum provided the idea that an adversary's attacks could be prevented with the fewest number of nuclear weapons possible. In other words, the minimum could deter and there was absolutely no need for building more. Indeed, force structure build-ups, the operationalization and declaratory policy orientation of deterrent forces are required at the minimum level. Minimum deterrence is a complex conceptual phenomenon. The minimum based on 'the lowest level of damage ... with the fewest number of nuclear weapons'[1] permits a number of interpretations regarding the precise nature of that particular level of damage and/or number of warheads. A long-forgotten concept of minimum deterrence existed in the USA during the early stages of the Cold War when the US Navy claimed it could destroy 'all of Russia' with 45 submarines and 720 warheads,[2] and this may still be interpreted as the minimum compared with the hundreds and thousands built in the later phases of the Cold War. British, French and Chinese notions of minimum deterrence remain modest.[3] Both Pakistan and India follow minimum deterrence, but they are reluctant to define what they mean by a minimum. Despite the complexity, how best can the basics of a minimum explain minimum deterrence?

First, after the use of nuclear weapons in Hiroshima and Nagasaki, nuclear weapon states learnt a lesson about the military use of nuclear weapons. Given the destructive characteristics of nuclear weapons, it was decided that these are another type of weapons and must never be used militarily in the event of a crisis. Therefore, the political aspect was prioritized which supports the minimalist nature of deterrence to achieve the political objectives. The political aspect entails: the minimum the deterrent forces, the least we rely on them, the better.

Second, the idea behind a political priority of deterrent forces was that these forces can cause unacceptable destruction. Risk is the starting point in elaborating the basics of minimum deterrence, which remains central to nuclear deterrence. The fear and risk of nuclear weapons use deter the adversary from starting a war. At the minimalist level, risk centrally focuses that there is no 'probability of victory', and adversaries may confront the 'possibility of annihilation'. A minimum highlights that risk is associated with the use of nuclear weapons and it would cause more damage than create benefit. Central to the fear and risk of nuclear weapons use, states are deterred from waging a war. The risk and fear associated with nuclear weapons use have a close link with 'existential deterrence', whereby the mere existence of nuclear weapons could deter the adversary from waging a war in the first place.

Third, if risk is the starting point to elaborate the basics of minimum deterrence, then fewer, not more, are enough to deter. Powerful nuclear weapon states with larger numbers of more sophisticated weapons have been deterred by smaller nuclear weapon states with fewer, less sophisticated deterrent forces. The USA in the Cuban Missile Crisis in 1962 and the Soviet Union in the Sino–Soviet border conflict were deterred by small nuclear forces.[4] Similarly, the smaller numbers of nuclear forces of Pakistan and India deterred each other from waging a full-scale war during both the Kargil Crisis in 1999 and the 2001–02 border confrontation.[5]

Fourth, although the Cold War-style deterrence was based on more, larger and more technically sophisticated forces, these are discouraged at the minimalist level. Since it is viewed that nuclear weapons are not used for warfighting purposes and, therefore, should not be militarily prioritized, larger, more expensive and sophisticated arms are discouraged. They matter little at the minimalist level, and the survivability of a small number of forces can be a deterrent, which may help build a second-strike capability in exchange for a triad. Larger, more sophisticated and greater numbered nuclear forces encourage arms competition between two adversaries and create difficulty in the command and control posture. The smaller the nuclear weapons, the easier they can be hidden, and the quicker they can be assembled if absolutely needed to ensure the credibility of nuclear deterrence. The larger the deterrent forces, the harder the command and control system becomes, and the more difficult the concealment and dispersion.

Fifth, minimum deterrence requires, to recall the always/never taxonomy, that deterrent forces should never be used when they are not needed and should always be under the command and instructions of the political leaders when absolutely needed in order to induce the credibility and survivability of nuclear weapons from accidental use. However, the essence of minimum deterrence prioritizes the political aspect of nuclear deterrence. It encourages the dispersal and concealment of nuclear forces. The deployment at the forward position is discouraged, which permits the risk of pre-delegation and force protection. Delegation of launch authority is criticized. Minimum deterrence encourages centralized command and control to avoid these worries of deterrent forces.

Sixth, the essence of minimum deterrence urges an arms control and disarmament process to reduce the danger of an arms race and the possibility of nuclear weapons use. At the minimalist level, the process of arms control and disarmament discourages the salience of nuclear weapons and helps reduce the risk of military escalation to the nuclear level.

In summary, minimum deterrence requires little to deter. A few survivable forces deterred states with more, larger and more sophisticated weapons during the Cold War period. There is no reason why this could not deter in the present era. The mere existence and centrality of the risk and fear associated with nuclear weapons use induces the credibility and prioritizes the political prospect of deterrent forces.

The rationale of minimum deterrence

Chapter 2 gave a brief historical analysis of Pakistan's development of its nuclear programme. It examined how the Pakistani nuclear programme evolved and why Pakistan chose to embark on developing nuclear weapons. It showed that Pakistan's nuclear programme is Indian-centric, driven by security concerns. In the immediate aftermath of nuclear weapons tests, Pakistan opted for a policy of minimum deterrence. Against the backdrop of the basics of the minimum, as discussed in this study, it is interesting to note that the concept of a minimum existed even before Pakistan tested nuclear weapons. The Pakistani elites and policy experts viewed that a few nuclear weapons would suffice to deter the adversary and a small number of nuclear weapons could meet Pakistan's security requirements. The study helped trace the rationale of Pakistan's minimum deterrence in Chapter 3.

A smaller number and state security

In the immediate aftermath of tests, it was widely held in Pakistan that a small number of nuclear weapons would be enough to deter and there was no need to waste time and money on producing more. The rationale for maintaining a smaller number was that these could protect the state's sovereignty and territorial integrity. The minimalist views existed in the Pakistani elite. Niaz Naik, then foreign secretary of Pakistan, expressed a minimalist view in May 1999 that the capacity to drop one bomb on one Indian city would be sufficient to deter India.[6] General Pervaiz Musharraf stated in March 2003 that a large number did not matter 'beyond a point', and that Pakistan had a sufficient deterrent capability.[7] Pakistan's Major-General Durrani expressed that the government had quantified the nuclear deterrent forces (although the number is not revealed): 'If a few can do the job, why more?'[8] In a similar vein, Pakistani leading nuclear scientist Samar Mubarakmand, former SPD Director Naeem Salik and Pakistani leading nuclear expert Zafar Iqbal Cheema initially stated that a few nuclear weapons would suffice to deter and could meet the state's security needs.

A better command and control system

Chapter 3 demonstrated that one rationale of Pakistan keeping a small number of forces helped Pakistan build a less complex, but effective command

and control system. Pakistan was able to establish an NCA and SPD within a few years of nuclear tests. The concept exists that a small number of nuclear forces can have better, more effective command and control. In other words, these deterrent forces can easily be centralized to avoid the worries of unwanted and accidental nuclear weapons use. The minimum deterrence highlights that a smaller number of nuclear forces may not only have effective command and control, but can also easily be protected and dispersed.

Concealment and dispersal

Theorists conceptually developed an idea that new nuclear weapons states would not opt for larger sizes and numbers of forces, as did the USA and Soviet Union during the Cold War. They explained that new nuclear weapon states could have better command and control of their nuclear forces if these forces were kept small and properly concealed and dispersed. It is widely believed that Pakistani nuclear forces are dispersed and concealed to avoid accidental nuclear weapon use and to avert the adversary's pre-emptive strikes. The dispersal and concealment of the deterrent forces are consistent with the minimum deterrence that is central to stability. On various occasions, Pakistani security planners have expressed views that Pakistani deterrent forces are under an effective command and control system and they are concealed and dispersed in various unknown locations. The concealment and dispersal of deterrent forces mean that they are kept away from the delivery systems and are not on hair-trigger alert. The Pakistani deterrent forces, if properly concealed and dispersed, appear to meet the basics of minimum deterrence on this rationale aspect which induces stability.

Cost effectiveness and easing external pressure

This study examined the way in which a smaller number of nuclear forces could be cost effective for Pakistan and would also ease external pressure. Given the weak economic condition of Pakistan, Islamabad may not sustain a large number of deterrent forces. The rationale behind maintaining minimum deterrence is to make Pakistan's nuclear programme cost effective. A 'minimum-cost deterrent' was the initial conceptualization of minimum deterrence, which could prevent Islamabad from the vicious cycle of an arms race against New Delhi. The elite thought that Pakistan had a poor economic base and would suffer more if it were to be pulled into an arms competition with its adversary.[9] Although it is not clear how much Pakistan spends on its deterrent forces, it has been revealed very recently that Pakistan has an increasing defence budget to meet the requirements of minimum deterrence. It is interesting to note that Pakistan still spends less on its deterrent forces because of its poor economy, compared to India which spends seven times more. According to reliable sources, Pakistan is currently upgrading and expanding its deterrent forces and Islamabad plans to spend more on its deterrence force capability. These sources also reveal that Pakistan has become one of the fastest growing nuclear weapon states. Pakistani elites deny this and express their views that Pakistan still maintains a minimum deterrence. It can be assumed that the rationale behind this is to ease external pressure. The study helped unpack those variables analysing why the minimum is not minimal – in other words, why Pakistan could not sustain a minimum deterrence as conceptualized in the immediate aftermath of the nuclear tests.

The sustainability of minimum deterrence

It was widely held that it was not necessary or desirable for Pakistan to match the Indian nuclear warheads; the country does not require a bomb-for-bomb ratio in relation to its adversary.[10] In a similar vein, the Pakistani elites, as examined in Chapter 3, viewed that minimum deterrence could meet Pakistan's security needs. Later, Islamabad found that the minimum could not be sustained as a minimum. It cannot be quantified as a fixed term. It remains dynamic and will change in accordance with the region's altered strategic environment. Islamabad confronted the issues of credibility, survivability and invulnerability of its deterrent forces against the adversary's security threats. This subtle policy shift in Pakistan's nuclear policy orientation turned the earlier conceptualized version of minimum deterrence into minimum *credible* deterrence. However, the term minimum and the addition of credibility remain indeterminate in Pakistan's nuclear policy. Chapter 4 analysed the sustainability of minimum deterrence.

The addition of credibility and the practice of ambiguity

The Pakistani elites, policy makers and policy experts later deemed that the credibility of minimum forces is important in order to make deterrence more effective in the changed South Asian security environment. In other words, Islamabad would maintain the credibility of its deterrent forces against the adversary. Pakistan's elites view that a minimum cannot be defined and the minimum in 2000 may not necessarily be the same today; it remains dynamic. What this shows is that Pakistan would increase and upgrade its deterrent forces against the rising threats that Islamabad perceives. Although Pakistanis do not feel that Islamabad should get into a vicious cycle of arms competition in the South Asian region, they believe that the country may increase at the proportionate level to enhance the credibility of Pakistan's deterrent forces. Chapter 4 examined how Pakistan's NCA, SPD and Foreign Ministry from time to time issued policy statements on maintaining the credibility of its minimum deterrence. The Pakistani ambassador to the UN Security Council stated in April 2004 that the country would 'continue to develop its nuclear missiles and related strategic capability to maintain the minimum credible deterrence against our eastern neighbour which has embarked on major programs for nuclear weapons, missiles, anti-missiles, and conventional

136 Conclusion

arms acquisitions and development'.[11] Chapter 4 also examines how Pakistan's minimum deterrence with the addition of credibility remains viable, flexible and dynamic. The Pakistani policy statements in relation to minimum credible deterrence show that the minimum is unsustainable for Pakistan. This further indicates that the minimum remains a complex and ambiguous phenomenon.

Islamabad also practices ambiguity. Chapter 2 examined how the practice of nuclear ambiguity was generated during the Zia military regime in the 1980s, when he turned Pakistan's nuclear programme clandestine in order to avert external pressure. General Zia ul-Haq stated: 'With respect to ... nuclear capabilities, if they create ambiguity, that ambiguity is the essence of deterrence.'[12] Nuclear ambiguity has become the central theme of Pakistan's nuclear policy. Although some hold that Pakistan's policy orientation should be 'unambiguous'[13] and that nuclear ambiguity can be written,[14] the Pakistani policy makers argue that ambiguity works. The study examined that nuclear ambiguity, which is intentional, has prevented Pakistan from officially announcing its nuclear policy. Pakistan seems to keep its adversary guessing about its operational and declaratory policy options. As long as nuclear policies remain ambiguous and complex, it is difficult, if not impossible, to define minimum deterrence. This study traces out the various obstacles that hamper sustaining the minimum as a minimum in Pakistan.

Policy shifts

In addition to nuclear ambiguity and credibility, the minimum may not be sustained by Pakistan because Pakistani security planners view that the region's quickly changing security environment affects Pakistan's nuclear policy approach. Islamabad observes New Delhi's rapid upgrade of deterrence forces through striking deals with the USA and other developed states, its pursuit of a BMD, development of a war-fighting doctrine – the CSD, march towards multiple independently target able reentry vehicles (MIRVs) technology, and its plans for increasing its stockpile of fissile material, all of which tempts Pakistan to maintain the credibility of its deterrent forces. Islamabad thinks that it is threatened by these developments. The policy shifts between India and Pakistan make the minimum unsustainable for Pakistan and the South Asian region. It can be argued that it is India who triggers the arms race in the South Asian region.

The absence of CBMs for an ACR

The absence of an ACR is one of the obstacles before Pakistan to sustain minimum deterrence. Although both India and Pakistan have talked about the establishment of a strategic regime, these talks were unproductive. The study examined that although there are various types of CBMs between the two South Asian adversaries, these talks usually do not comprise nuclear or military CBMs. Even where there are talks at the military and nuclear levels, these talks are not productive.

The formative phases of arms build-up

The absence of an ACR and regular nuclear and military CBMs indicate that both the South Asian nuclear rivals are in the formative phase of a nuclear force build-up. Unless they are pulled out of this phase of arms competition, both Pakistan and India will continue to build their deterrent forces, even if they opt for a triad in order to achieve second-strike capability.

Trust deficit

The policy shifts on both sides of the border, as mentioned above, become yet another obstacle to sustaining minimum deterrence. They also create a trust deficit in South Asia. Even though both India and Pakistan hold talks, these talks remain immature most of the time and fail to result in productive outcomes. The trust deficit is an issue that affects not only the talks between the two sides, but also the urge to maintain minimum deterrence.

External factors

External factors also affect the principle of a sustained minimum deterrence. For example, the US modernization of both nuclear and conventional forces affects the policy of China, China affects India as its adversary, and India in turn affects Pakistan's nuclear policy. The book examined how the chain reaction affects policy options. Islamabad calculates all these tangible and intangible factors into the changed South Asian strategic environment, which affects the credibility of Pakistan's deterrent forces. These factors show that Pakistan may not sustain minimum deterrence in the foreseeable future. Currently, Pakistan is viewed as one of the fastest growing nuclear weapon states. Against the backdrop of these factors, Pakistan upgrades and expands its deterrent forces in order to sustain the credibility of its deterrent forces.

Nuclear force building

Chapter 5 examines how Pakistan upgrades not only its delivery systems (i.e. missile systems and aircraft), but also its plans for a triad – that is, developing a nuclear submarine. Although the minimum highlighted that a few survivable nuclear forces could replace a triad, Pakistan seems to be developing a nuclear submarine. If Pakistan plans the development of a triad, then it may not meet the basics of minimum deterrence. Islamabad seems consistent with the policy of upgrading its Hatf series of missile systems. The country has recently developed the Nasr missile system, which is a TNW, in reaction to India's development of its CSD. Pakistan also has the modernized F-16 aircraft, which can be used as a delivery system for its deterrent forces. Pakistani policy makers claim that Islamabad has acquired the full spectrum of deterrence ensuring the credibility of its deterrent forces. Islamabad expresses that the country maintains the credibility of its deterrence against the evolving strategic environment of South Asia. In addition, Pakistan is also building-up its nuclear reactor to produce more fissile material, which could help develop more sophisticated, lethal and miniaturized nuclear forces. Islamabad believes that these would enhance the credibility of its deterrent forces. Apparently, Pakistan's attempt to build more indigenous nuclear reactors to produce more fissile material is in reaction to the US-Indian nuclear deal and the NSG's special treatment of India. Islamabad believes that these developments undermine the deterrence stability in South Asia and in turn affect Pakistan's security. Therefore, its strategic enclave notes that these developments cause Pakistan to upgrade, preserve and expand its deterrent forces. General Aslam Beg stated in an interview in July 2000 that Pakistan estimated that its 50–60 nuclear weapons would increase if India increased its nuclear warheads.[15] This contradicts what Beg earlier conceptualized. On building a triad, Durrani stated in 2004 that although Pakistan had not provided a serious thrust in building a nuclear submarine, it would work on its development of a triad deterrent force.[16] Against the recent development of India's nuclear submarines, Pakistan's navy chief expressed concern and maintained that it would develop a nuclear submarine system in the near future. Pakistan's leading nuclear expert, Jaspal, stated: 'Possession of several systems greatly reduces India's ability to destroy all Pakistan's retaliatory forces.'[17] The basic idea of the development of nuclear submarines in the American and Soviet discourses was to make their triads hard to track in vast waters. This has limitations in the context of South Asia, where the distances are not akin to those of the USA and former Soviet Union. Nuclear submarines may be tracked down, undermining the credibility of a triad. In contrast, few Pakistani security experts note that the survivable, concealed and dispersed deterrent forces could provide a triad to replace the nuclear submarine system.

The FU option

Pakistan develops a defensive approach to its nuclear weapons use, which is to deter both conventional and nuclear attacks. Islamabad rejects New Delhi's offer of an NFU on the stance that Pakistan is conventionally weaker than its adversary. Pakistani policy makers and various nuclear experts view that it makes sense for Pakistan to maintain the FU option because it confronts a huge adversary with greater conventional power capability. Therefore, Pakistan cannot rescind the FU option. Chapter 6 examines where, when, how and why Pakistan would use its nuclear weapons, critiquing the discussion between the FU and a last resort option. On the one hand Islamabad says that it would be the first to use nuclear weapons, but on the other hand it says that it would use nuclear weapons only as a last resort. Thus, it is not clear when, where and how Pakistan would use its nuclear weapons, creating more ambiguity. Some Pakistani elites express that Pakistan does not subscribe to the FU option, but rather that it has a no first use option, blurring the debate between the FU and NFU. Moreover, the Pakistani policy makers pinpoint that Pakistan would use its nuclear weapons under 'extreme conditions'. Others state that if a large part of Pakistan were occupied, its economy strangled and a large portion of its land and air forces destroyed, then the country would consider using nuclear weapons. These points are subject to various interpretations. Others visualize the last resort scenario which depicts Pakistan using all other options before resorting to nuclear weapons.

Minimum deterrence discourages nuclear states to use nuclear weapons in the event of a crisis. The 1999 Kargil Crisis and the 2001–02 border confrontation between India and Pakistan show that nuclear weapons were not deployed, although the danger existed. The minimum highlights that the mere nuclear shadow was sufficient in these crises to deter both nuclear rivals from escalating into major military actions. The risk of nuclear weapons use deterred the adversaries. The non-deployed posture of minimum deterrence becomes central to deterrence stability in South Asia.

Targeting options and the danger of escalation

Chapter 6 examines the nuclear weapons use options for both scenarios: counter-value and counter-force targeting. It is unclear whether Pakistan would opt for a counter-value or counter-force targeting strategy. Some sections of Pakistan prefer counter-value, others suggest counter-force targeting options. There are a few who consider that both need to be brought into its targeting calculations. Matinuddin recommends both options: 'While giving primacy to counter-value targets, the enemy's concentration of armoured formations in the rear should also be considered as target for a nuclear strike.'[18] With the recent development of TNWs, the use of either option can be critiqued. This study examines how the use of TNWs increases the Cold War-style worries of pre-delegation, command and control, and force protection. Besides, the use of TNWs against the adversary's armed forces could also hit nearby populated cities. The limited war could escalate to the nuclear level and might blur the 'academic' distinctions between the two targeting options. Pakistani Brigadier A.R. Siddiqi (rtd), editor of *Defence Journal*, makes the point that 'the virtual disappearance of the dividing line between cities and the cantonments' make the distinction between the two targeting options 'wholly academic'.[19] Since Pakistan developed TNWs to counter the adversary's development of CSD, and CSD is meant to wage a limited war in the presence of nuclear weapons, this study examines the danger that a limited war could spin out of control into a major military escalation to the nuclear level. If minimum deterrence worked in the mere non-weaponized posture in the 1980s and the 1990s and if it did deter the adversary in the

Kargil 1999 and 2001–02 crises at the very low level of threat, then the basics of minimum deterrence impart that it should also work in possible future crises. The minimum minimizes the danger of military escalation. In the meantime, Pakistan remains consistent in its policy of minimum credible deterrence, which allows the country to preserve, upgrade and expand its deterrent forces against the emerging threats that it perceives. It appears that the policy prospects for arms control and disarmament are dim – Pakistan is unlikely to lift its non-adherence policy approaches to the NPT, the CTBT and the FMCT in the very near future.

The policy option of arms control and disarmament

Since US President Eisenhower's speech on 'atom for peace' in December 1953, Pakistan has remained supportive of arms control and the disarmament process. In the 1950s and the 1960s, Pakistan had a normative approach towards the PTBT and establishment of the NPT. On various occasions, Pakistani policy makers urged the international community to work for a non-proliferation regime on a non-discriminatory and internationally verifiable basis. Chapter 7 examines how Pakistan supported the establishment of a non-proliferation regime in the form of the NPT and why it later changed its normative policy approach to a strategic one. From the 1970s to May 1998, Pakistan's policy towards non-proliferation regimes was based on Indian-centricity, which was largely driven by security concerns in the South Asian region. Pakistan would not sign the NPT unless India did so first.

The post-1998 nuclear tests saw a dramatic policy shift in Pakistan's approach towards the CTBT and the NPT: Pakistan would sign the NPT only if it were recognized as a nuclear weapon state, which goes against Article IX of the NPT. Pakistan's policy towards the FMCT was also driven by the non-adherence principle. These factors include the US-Indian nuclear deal, India's pursuit of a BMD programme, the development of CSD, and Pakistan's security concerns in the South Asian region regarding its adversary. On the FMCT, Pakistan still remains reluctant to withdraw its veto for holding a successful FMCT negotiation. Pakistan's policy makers and security analysts contend that Islamabad would join the FMCT negotiation, thus ending the 17-year deadlock, only if it were provided with Indian-style treatment by both the USA and the NSG. This study also examines Pakistan's defiance towards the FMCT – that is, Islamabad views that the treaty should bring the 'existing stockpile' of fissile material into account and it should be based on non-discriminatory and internationally verifiable approaches. The Pakistani elite and policy experts have stated that the FMCT negotiation is unacceptable and Islamabad will remain defiant to the FMCT as long as these issues are not addressed on an equitable basis. A call for an ACR remains a pipe dream as long as Pakistan remains defiant of the non-proliferation regime and the outstanding issues linked to the Pakistani policy approach towards the FMCT remain unresolved.

Future scholarship

This study has shown that Pakistan's nuclear policy orientation is India-specific – that is, Pakistan develops a 'reactive posture' to what India does. The minimum remains indeterminate. Notwithstanding, there are some aspects of Pakistan's nuclear policy that may conform to the tenets of minimum deterrence. Pakistan's non-deployed posture, centralized command and control system, absence of more nuclear tests, dispersal and concealment tactics of its deterrent forces, and its policy towards arms control and disarmament (although not post-1998 policy approaches) are evident in relation to the basics of minimum deterrence. They may change depending on how the strategic environment of South Asia evolves. On the other hand, Pakistan's rapid build-up of its deterrent forces, upgrade of its missile systems, plans for a triad, a road towards an 'offensive deterrence posture', and the construction of nuclear reactors all may remain inconsistent with the essentials of minimum deterrence. Apparently, inconsistencies became the focal point of Pakistan's nuclear policy post-1998, which could have implications for Pakistan's future efficacy of nuclear deterrence. To be sure, inconsistencies remain parts of the nuclear doctrinal posture of other established nuclear weapon states as well. Perhaps the actuality of minimum deterrence does not exist amongst the nuclear weapons states either emerging or established. The fully fledged practice of the actuality of a minimum would require thorough and transparent structuring of nuclear doctrinal posture both at the regional and international levels.

First, the apparent policy shift within Pakistan's minimum deterrence, moving towards a 'sufficient' or 'offensive deterrence posture', and its implications for the deterrence stability in South Asia, is not covered by this study. The future scholarship could look at this emerging issue substantially. Currently, it is unclear whether Pakistan could maintain a minimalist approach towards its nuclear policy orientation. As this study shows that Pakistan could not sustain the minimum deterrence that Islamabad thought could be fixed and quantified, Pakistan would possibly work for the future efficacy of its minimum credible deterrence. The region's changing strategic environment could force Islamabad to be more sufficient in its deterrent capability. What challenges Pakistan might confront in shaping such an expansive deterrent policy and how this will impact the deterrence stability of South Asia are changing dynamics that the future scholarship would need to explore.

Second, if Islamabad plans for an 'offensive deterrence policy' and frames a more sufficient deterrent policy, then the country could find lots of pressure on the command and control mechanism of its deterrent forces. Given the weak economic base and lack of resources, how Islamabad would chalk out and how sufficiency would affect Pakistan's nuclear command and control system would need to be examined. Future studies could cover the impact of the changing contours of Pakistan's deterrent policy on its command and control system.

Conclusion

Third, since the minimum remains a sketchy and unwieldy concept, it would be difficult for smaller nuclear weapon states to judge how much and how little would be enough for deterrence. This could lead them to expand and upgrade their deterrent capability without realizing the cost of the security and safety of a sufficient number of nuclear forces. Pakistan, a minor nuclear weapon state, is preserving and upgrading its deterrent forces. Islamabad is also constructing nuclear reactors which could provide Pakistan with more capability of producing plutonium-based deterrent forces. What could the economic repercussions be of sufficient deterrent capability, and how could Islamabad ensure the safety and security of sufficient deterrent forces given the worldwide concerns of terrorism and extremism in Pakistan?

Last but not least, Islamabad is reluctant to withdraw its veto to commence the FMCT negotiations. It has also not yet joined the NPT for various reasons, as explored in this study. Recently, Islamabad categorically stated that it would adhere to the principles of the non-proliferation regimes if it were recognized as a nuclear weapon state and its security needs were addressed. How would Islamabad's emerging policy shift towards arms control and disarmament impact the non-proliferation regimes and the establishment of an ACR in South Asia? While not covered in this study of the country's nuclear policy post-1998, could Pakistan, a smaller nuclear weapon state, possibly become part of a wider multilateral disarmament process towards Global Zero, given its contemporary defiance of non-proliferation regimes?

Notes

1 Peter Gizewski, *Minimum Nuclear Deterrence in a New World Order*, Aurora Papers 24, Ottawa: Canadian Centre for Global Security, 1994, 2.
2 Ibid., 2–3.
3 Avery Goldstein, *Deterrence and Security in the 21st Century: China, Britain, France, and the Enduring Legacy of the Nuclear Revolution*, California: Stanford University Press, 2000; John C. Hopkins and Weixing Hu (eds), *Strategic Views from the Second Tier: The Nuclear Weapons Policies of France, Britain, and China*, London: New Brunswick, 1995.
4 Rajesh Rajagopalan, *Second Strike: Arguments about Nuclear War in South Asia*, New Delhi: Viking, 2005, 89–106.
5 M.R. Basrur, *Minimum Deterrence and India's Nuclear Security*, California: Stanford University Press, 2006; M.R. Basrur, 'Nuclear Deterrence Thinking in Pakistan', in E. Sridharan (ed.) *International Relations Theory and South Asia, Volume II*, New Delhi: Oxford University Press, 2011, 107.
6 Quoted in Ayesha Siddiqa, *Pakistan's Arms Procurement and Military Build-up, 1979–99: In Search of a Policy*, New York: Palgrave, 2001, 179–80.
7 B. Reddy Muralidhar, 'Pak. Has Sufficient Deterrence', *The Hindu*, 7 March 2003.
8 Mahmud Ali Durrani, 'Pakistan's Strategic Thinking and the Role of Nuclear Weapons', 2004, www.cmc.sandia.gov/cmc-papers/sand2004-3375p.pdf (accessed 18 June 2012), 31–32.
9 Munir Ahmed Khan, 'Nuclearisation of South Asia and its Regional and Global Implications', *Regional Studies* 26(4), 1998: 3–58.

10 Kamal Matinuddin, *The Nuclearisation of South Asia*, Oxford: Oxford University Press, 2002; Rasul Bakhsh Rais, 'Conceptualizing Nuclear Deterrence: Pakistan's Posture', *India Review* 4(2), 2005: 144–72.
11 See 'Pak Charges India with Embarking on Major Nukes Program', *The Times of India*, 30 April 2004.
12 Quoted in Gregory F. Giles and James E. Doyle, 'Indian and Pakistan Views on Nuclear Deterrence', *Comparative Strategy* 15, April–June 1996: 147.
13 Shireen M. Mizari, 'Understanding Pakistan's Nuclear Doctrine', *Strategic Studies* XXIV(3), 2004: 1–20.
14 Zafar Iqbal Cheema, 'Pakistan's Posture of Minimum Credible Deterrence: Current Challenges and Future Efficacy', in Zulfqar Khan (ed.) *Nuclear Pakistan: Strategic Dimensions*, London: Oxford University Press, 2011, 43–84.
15 Quoted in Rodney W. Jones, *Minimum Nuclear Deterrence Postures in South Asia: An Overview*, USA: Defence Threat Reduction Agency Advanced Systems and Concepts Office, 2001, 204.
16 Durrani, 'Pakistan's Strategic Thinking'.
17 Zafar Nawaz Jaspal, 'India's Missile Capabilities: Regional Implications', *Pakistan's Horizon* 54(1), 2001: 60.
18 Matinuddin, *The Nuclearisation of South Asia*, 243.
19 Quoted in Giles and Doyle, 'Indian and Pakistan Views on Nuclear Deterrence', 149.

Bibliography

Abbasi, Ansar (2004) 'Pakistan May Sign NPT if Declared Nuclear Power', *The News*, 13 February.
Abbasi, Rizwana (2012) '*Pakistan and the New Nuclear Taboo: Regional Deterrence and International Arms Control Regime*', Oxford and New York: Peter Lang.
Abdullah, Sannia (2012) 'Cold Start in Strategic Calculus', *IPRI Journal* XII(1), Winter Issue: 1–27.
Abida, Syeda Hussein (1995) 'Don't Give Up! What is yours and the World will Come Around', in Tariq Jan (ed.) *Pakistan's Security and the Nuclear Option*, Islamabad: Institute of Policy Studies, 107–20.
Acton, M. James (2012) 'Bombs Away? Being Realistic about Deep Nuclear Reduction', *Washington Quarterly* 35(2): 37–53.
Ahmar, Moonis (2001) *The CTBT Debate in Pakistan*, New Delhi: Har Anand.
Ahmed, Khalid (1994a) 'Pakistan's America Problem: Crisis of Defiance', *The Friday Times* (Lahore), 24–30 March.
——(1994b) 'NPT: More Troubles Ahead for Pakistan', *The Friday Times* (Lahore), 1–7 December.
——(1995) 'After Hiroshima: Why Do We Still Love the Bomb?' *The Friday Times* (Lahore), 17–23 August.
Ahmed, Khurshid (1995) 'Summation: Capping the Nation', in Tariq Jan (ed.) *Pakistan's Security and the Nuclear Option*, Islamabad: Institute of Policy Studies, 145–58.
Ahmed, Mansoor (2011a) 'Understanding Pakistan's Plutonium Option', *Weekly Pulse* (Islamabad), 3 June, weeklypulse.org/details.aspx?contentID=706&storylist=2 (accessed 29 November 2012).
——(2011b) 'Why Pakistan Needs Tactical Nuclear Weapons', *Weekly Pulse* (Islamabad), weeklypulse.org/details.aspx?contentID=563&storylist=9 (accessed 29 November 2012).
——(2012) 'Security Doctrines, Technologies and Escalation Ladders: A Pakistani Perspective', www.nps.edu/Academics/Centers/CCC/PASCC/Publications/2012/2012_002_Ahmed.pdf (accessed 29 November 2012).
Ahmed, Nazir (1958) 'The Pakistan Atomic Energy Commission', *Pakistan Quarterly* 8(3).
Ahmed, Samina (1999) 'Pakistan Nuclear Weapons Program: Turning Points and Nuclear Choices', *International Security* 23(4): 178–204.
——(2000) 'Security Dilemma of Nuclear-Armed Pakistan', *Third World Quarterly* 21(5): 781–93.

—— (2005) 'Nuclear Weapons and the Kargil Crisis: How and What Have Pakistani Learned?' in Dittmer Lowell (ed.) *South Asia's Nuclear Security Dilemma: India, Pakistan, and China*, New York: East Gate.

Ahmed, Samina and Cortright, David (eds) (1998) *Pakistan and the Bomb: Public Opinion and Nuclear Option*, Indiana: Notre Dame Publications.

Ahmedullah, Muhammad (2001) 'India Air Force Advocates First Strike Capability', *Defence Week*.

Akhtar, Rabia (2009) 'Pakistan's Nuclear Assets: Safe and Secure', June, www.ipcs.org/cbrn-brief/pakistan/pakistans-nuclear-assets-safe-and-secure-13.html (accessed 28 June 2011).

Albright, David (2001) 'Securing Pakistan's Nuclear Weapons Complex', www.isis-online.org/publications/terrorism/stanleypaper.html (accessed 28 June 2011).

Albright, David and Avagyan, Robert (2012) 'Construction Progressing Rapidly on the Fourth Heavy Water Reactor at the Khushab Nuclear Site', Institute for Science and International Security, isis-online.org/isis-reports/detail/construction-progressing-rapidly-on-the-fourth-heavy-water-reactor-at-the-k/ (accessed 22 June 2012).

Alexei Arbatov, Alexi, Dyorkin, Vladimir and Oznobishchev, Sergey (eds) (2012) *Russia and the Dilemmas of Nuclear Disarmament*, Institute of World Economy and International Relations, Russia Academy of Sciences, www.imemo.ru/en/publ/2012/12009a.pdf (accessed 23 October 2012).

Ali, Akhtar (1984) *Pakistan's Nuclear Dilemma: Energy & Security Dimensions*, Karachi: Economic and Research Unit.

Ali, Choudhary Rehmat (1978) *Complete Works of Rehmat Ali*, Pakistan: National Commission on Historical and Cultural Research.

Ali, Mehrunisa (1974) 'Implications of Indian Nuclear Blast', *Dawn*, 24 June.

Ali, Zafar (2007) 'Pakistan's Nuclear Assets and Threats of Terrorism: How Grave is the Danger?' www.stimson.org/books-reports/pakistans-nuclear-assets-and-HGHthreats-of-terrorism-how-grave-is-the-danger/ (accessed 28 June 2011).

Almeida, Cyril (2010a) 'Uncontested Dominance', www.dawn.com/wps/wcm/connect/dawn-content-library/dawn/the-newspaper/columnist (accessed 2 September 2010).

—— (2010b) 'Kayani Spells out Threat Posed by India', pakistankakhudahafiz.wordpress.com/2010/02/04/kayani-spells-out-threat-posed-by-indian-doctrine/ (accessed 6 April 2012).

Amin, Tahir (1995) 'The Paradox of Civil-Military-US Triangle and Pakistan's Security', in Tariq Jan (ed.) *Pakistan's Security and the Nuclear Option*, Islamabad: Institute of Policy Studies, 99–106.

Ansari, Shaukatullah (1944) *Pakistan: The Problem of India*, Lahore: Minerva Books Shop.

Arif, M.K (1993) 'Expanding Indo-Israel Nexus', *Dawn*, 17 June.

—— (1995) 'Retaining the Nuclear Option', in Tariq Jan (ed.) *Pakistan's Security and the Nuclear Option*, Islamabad: Institute of Policy Studies, 121–29.

Armstrong, David and Trento, J. Joseph (2007) '*America and the Islamic Bomb: The Deadly Compromise*', New Hampshire: Steerforth Press.

Aron, Raymond (1966) '*Peace and War' A Theory of International Relations*, trans. R. Howard and A. Baker, Garden City: Doubleday Publications.

Ashraf, M. Tariq (2003) '*Aero-Space Power: The Emerging Strategic Dimension*', Peshawar: PAF Book Club, 148.

—— (2004a) 'Doctrinal Reawakening of the Indian Armed Forces', *Military Review*, tamilnation.co/intframe/indian_ocean/ashraf_on_indian_maritime_doctrine.pdf (accessed 15 September 2010).

——(2004b) *A Nuclear Pakistan: The Way Ahead*, unpublished manuscript, Islamabad, 38.
Asian-African Conference (1955) 'Selected Documents of the Bandung Conference: Texts of Selected Speeches and Final Communiqué of the Asian-African Conference, Bandung, Indonesia', 18–24 April.
Aziz, Khurshed Kamal (1987) *Rehmat Ali: A Biography*, Lahore: Vanguard.
Bailey, C.K. (1991) *Doomsday Weapons in the Hands of Many*, Chicago: University of Illinois Press.
——(1993) *Strengthening Nuclear Non-Proliferation*, Colorado: West View Press.
Bajoria, Jayshree (2010) 'The US-India Nuclear Deal', www.cfr.org/india/us-india-nuclear-deal/p9663 (accessed 7 August 2012).
——(2012) 'The US-India Nuclear Deal', www.cfr.org/india/us-india-nuclear-deal/p9663#p7 (accessed 9 February 2012).
Bajpai, Kanti (2000) 'India's Nuclear Posture after Pokhran II', *International Studies* (New Delhi) 37(4): 1–31.
——(2009) 'To War or Not to War: The India-Pakistan Crisis of 2001–2', in S. Ganguly and P. Kapur (eds) *Nuclear Proliferation in South Asia: Crisis Behaviour and the Bomb*, London: Routledge, 162–82.
Bajpai, Kanti, Chari, P.R., Chemma, Iqbal Pervez, Cohen, Philip Stephen and Ganguly, Sumit (1995) *Brasstacks and Beyond: Perception and Management of Crisis in South Asia*, New Delhi: Manohar Publications.
Ball, Desmond (1974) *Déjà Vu: The Return to Counterforce in the Nixon Administration*, California: Seminar on Arms Control and Foreign Policy.
——(1981) 'Counterforce Targeting: How New? How Viable?' *Arms Control Today*.
——(1986) 'The Development of the SIOP, 1960–83', in Desmond Ball and Jeffrey Richelson (eds) *Strategic Nuclear Targeting*, New York: Cornell University Press.
Baloch, Qadar Bakhsh (2008) 'Beyond Nuclear Deterrence: The Transformation of Indo-Pak Equation', *Defence Journal* (Pakistan): 26–37.
Basrur, M. Rajesh (2001) 'Nuclear Weapons and Indian Strategic Culture', *Journal of Peace Research* 38(2): 181–98.
——(2003) 'Nuclear India at the Crossroads', *Arms Control Today*, www.armscontrol.org/act/2003_09/Basrur (accessed 25 February 2012).
——(2005) 'Nuclear Command and Control and Strategic Politics in South Asia', *Contemporary South Asia* 14(2): 155–61.
——(2006) *Minimum Deterrence and India's Nuclear Security*, California: Stanford University Press.
——(2011a) 'South Asia: Tactical Nuclear Weapons and Strategic Risk', www.rsis.edu.sg/publications/Perspective/RSIS0652011.pdf (accessed 9 April 2012).
——(2011b) 'Nuclear Deterrence Thinking in Pakistan', in E. Sridharan (ed.) *International Relations Theory and South Asia, Volume II*, New Delhi: Oxford University Press.
Bast, Andrew (2011) 'Pakistan's Nuclear Calculus', *Washington Quarterly* 34(4): 73–86.
Baylis, John and Booth, Ken (eds) (1987) *Contemporary Strategy: Theories and Policies*, New York: Holmes & Meier.
Beg, Aslam Muhammad (1994a) 'Who Will Press the Button?' *The News*, 23 April.
——(1994b) *Development and Security: Thoughts and Reflections*, Rawalpindi: Foundation for Research on National Development and Security Press.
——(1996) 'Pakistan's Nuclear Program', in John Gjelstad and Olav Njolstad (eds) *Nuclear Rivalry and International Order*, Oslo: International Peace Research Institute.

——(2005) 'Responding to Indo-US Defence Pact', archives.dawn.com/2005/08/11/op. htm (accessed 9 February 2012).
Behera, K. Laxman (2012) 'India's Defence Budget 2012–13', *IDSA Comment*, www. idsa.in/idsacomments/IndiasDefenceBudget2012-13_LaxmanBehera_200312 (accessed 15 June 2012).
Bennett, Andrew (2010) 'Process Tracing and Casual Inference', in H.E. Brady and D. Collier (eds) *Rethinking Social Inquiry: Diverse Tools Shared Standard*, 2nd edn, Lanham, MD: Rowman and Littlefield Publishers, 207–20.
Berger, Andrea (2012) 'Finding the Right Home for FMCT Talks', *Arms Control Today*, October Issue.
Berry, Ken (2009) 'The Security of Pakistan Nuclear Facilities', icnnd.org/Documents/Berry_Pakistan_Nuclear_Security.pdf (accessed 22 June 2012).
Besser, Linton (2009) 'At the Precipice: Is Pakistan About to Fail?' spaces.brad.ac. uk:8080/pages/viewpage.action?pageId=984 (accessed 25 December 2010).
Bhambri, P.C. and Nair, M. Bhaskaran (1995) 'Corruption in Pakistan Civil Service: An Analytical Survey', in Verinder Grover and Ranjana Arora (eds) *Political System in Pakistan*, New Delhi: Deep and Deep Publications.
Bhola, L.P (1994) *Pakistan's Nuclear Policy*, New Delhi: Sterling Publishers.
Bhutto, Zulfiqar Ali (1962) 'Address on Disarmament Problems: Convocation Address', Sindh University, 30 March, in *Zulfiqar Ali Bhutto Speeches – Interviews 1948–1966*, bhutto.org/Acrobat/Bhutto_Speeches_1948-66.pdf (accessed 8 May 2012).
——(1963) 'Address to the UN General Assembly's 1220th Plenary Meeting on its 18th Session', 30 September, in *Speeches Delivered by Zulfiqar Ali Bhutto (1957–1965)*, www.scribd.com/doc/14560791/Speeches-Delivered-by-Zulfiqar-Ali-Bhutto (accessed 9 May 2012), 73–74.
——(1965) 'Declaration to the UN General Assembly', in A. Jala and H. Khan (eds) *Reshaping Foreign Policy: Articles, Statements, and Speeches, Vol. 1 1948–66*, Karachi: Pakistan Publications.
——(1969) *The Myth of Independence*, London: Oxford University Press.
——(1979) *If I am Assassinated ...* , New Delhi: Vikas Publishers.
——(1993 [1966]) 'Bhutto's Larkana Declaration December 29, 1966 on Pakistan and Nuclear Proliferation', in S. Wolpert (ed.) *Zulfi Bhutto of Pakistan: His Life and Times*, Oxford: Oxford University Press, 113.
Blackett, P.M.S. (1961) 'A Critique of Defence Thinking', *Survival* 3(3), April: 126–34.
——(1962) *Studies of War: Nuclear and Conventional*, London: Oliver & Boyd Publications.
Blair, Bruce (1985) *Strategic Command and Control: Redefining the Nuclear Threat*, Washington, DC: The Brookings Institution.
——(1993) *The Logic of Accidental Nuclear War*, Washington, DC: The Brookings Institution.
Blair, Bruce and Brewer, D.G. (1977) 'The Terrorists Threat to World Nuclear Program', *Journal of Conflict Resolution* 21(3): 379–403.
Blair, Bruce and Kendall, Henry (1990) 'Accidental Nuclear War', *Scientific American* 263(6): 53–58.
Bracken, Paul (1983) *The Command and Control of Nuclear Forces*, New Haven, CT: Yale University Press.
Bradley, Oman (1948) 'Armistice Day 1948 Address: General Omar N. Bradley', www. opinionbug.com/2109/armistice-day-1948-address-general-omar-n-bradley/ (accessed 24 April 2012).

Braun, Chaim (2008) 'Security Issues Related to Pakistan's Future Nuclear Program', in H. Sokolski (ed.) *Pakistan's Nuclear Future: Worries beyond War*, Pennsylvania: Strategic Studies Institute, 277–346.

Brodie, Bernard (1954) 'Nuclear Weapons: Strategic or Tactical', *Foreign Affairs* 32(1/4): 217–22.

——(1966) *Escalation and the Nuclear Option*, New Jersey: Princeton University Press.

——(1978) 'The Development of Nuclear Strategy', *International Security* 2(4): 65–83.

Brodie, Bernard, Dunn, S. Frederick, Wolfers, Arnold, Corbett, E. Percy and Fox, T. R. William (1946) *The Absolute Weapon: Atomic Power and World Order*, New York: Harcourt, Brace and Co.

Bull, Hedley (1961) *The Control of the Arms Race*, London: Weidenfeld & Nicolson.

Bundy, McGeorge (1969) 'To Cap the Volcano', *Foreign Affairs* 48(1): 1–20.

——(1983) 'The Bishops and the Bomb', *The New York Review of Books*, 16 June.

——(1984) 'Existential Deterrence and its Consequences', in Douglas MacLean (ed.) *The Security Gamble: Deterrence Dilemmas in Nuclear Age*, Totowa, NJ: Rowman & Allanheld.

Bundy, McGeorge, Kennan, F. George, McNamara, S. Robert and Smith, Gerard (1982) 'Nuclear Weapons and Atlantic Alliance', *Foreign Affairs*: 753–86.

Bunn, George (2005) 'The World's Non-Proliferation Regime in Time', *IAEA Bulletin* 46(2), www.iaea.org/Publications/Magazines/Bulletin/Bull462/46203590809.pdf (accessed 9 May 2012).

Butt, Tariq (1998) 'Only Gohar, Mushahid Allowed to Speak on Foreign Policy', *The Nation*, 19 May.

Buzan, Barry (1987) *An Introduction to Strategic Studies*, Macmillan Press.

Buzzard, Anthony (1956) 'Massive Retaliation and Graduated Deterrence', *World Politics* 8(2): 228–37.

——(1961) 'Defence, Disarmament and Christian Decision', *Survival* 3(5): 207–19.

Buzzard, Anthony, Slessor, John and Lowenthal, Richard (1956) 'The H-Bomb: Massive Retaliation or Graduated Deterrence?' *International Affairs* 32(2): 148–65.

Canby, L. Steven (1984) *The Conventional Defence of Europe: The Operational Limits of Emerging Technology*, Wilson Centre Working Paper No. 55, Washington, DC.

Carnegie Endowment (2011) *Report on Nuclear Policy: 2011 Carnegie International Nuclear Policy Conference*, carnegieendowment.org/2011/03/29/two-triads-india-pakistan-china-and-china-u.s.-russia/2t0t (accessed 11 February 2012).

Carranza, E. Mario (2006) 'Can the NPT Survive? The Theory and Practice of US Nuclear Non-Proliferation Policy after September 11', *Contemporary Security Policy* 27(3), December: 489–525.

——(2009) *South Asian Security and International Nuclear Order: Creating a Robust Indo-Pakistani Nuclear Arms Control Regime*, London: Ashgate.

Central Intelligence Agency (2010) 'Pakistan Nuclear Study', 26 April 1978, top secret, declassified, excised copy at www.gwu.edu/~nsarchiv/nukevault/ebb333/index.htm#1 (accessed 1 January 2012).

Chakma, Bhumitra (2002) 'Road to Chagai: Pakistan's Nuclear Programme: Its Sources and Motivations', *Modern Asian Studies* 36(4): 871–912.

——(2004) *'Strategic Dynamics and Nuclear Weapons Proliferation in South Asia: A Historical Analysis'*, Oxford and New York: Peter Lang.

——(2005) 'The NPT, the CTBT and Pakistan: Explaining the Non-adherence Posture of a de facto Nuclear State', *Asian Security* 1(3): 267–84.

—— (2006) 'Pakistan's Nuclear Doctrine and Command and Control System: Dilemmas of Small Nuclear Forces in the Second Atomic Age', *Security Challenges* 2(2), July: 115–33.

—— (2009) *Pakistan's Nuclear Weapons*, London: Routledge.

—— (2010) 'Nuclear Arms Control Challenges in South Asia', *Indian Review* 9(3): 364–84.

—— (2011a) 'Pakistan's Post-Test Nuclear Use Doctrine', in B. Chakma (ed.) *The Politics of Nuclear Weapons in South Asia*, London: Ashgate, 75–89.

—— (ed.) (2011b) *The Politics of Nuclear Weapons in South Asia*, London: Ashgate.

Chari, P.R. (2001) 'Nuclear Restraint, Nuclear Risk Reduction, and Security-Insecurity Paradox in South Asia', in M. Krepon and C. Gagne (eds) *The Stability-Instability Paradox: Nuclear Weapons and Brinkmanship in South Asia*, Washington, DC: Henry L. Stimson Center.

—— (2003) '*Nuclear Crisis, Escalation Control, and Deterrence in South Asia*', Stimson Working Paper, Washington, DC: Henry L. Stimson Center.

Chari, P.R., Cheema, Iqbal Pervez and Cohen, P. Stephen (2003) *Perception, Politics, and Security in South Asia: The Compound Crisis of 1990*, London: Routledge Curzon.

Chari, P.R., Gupta, Sonika and Rajain, Arpit (2003) *Nuclear Stability in Southern Asia*, New Delhi: Manohar.

Checkel, Jeffery T. (2008) 'Tracing Causal Mechanism', *International Studies Review* 8 (2): 362–70.

Cheema, Zafar Iqbal (1996) 'Pakistan's Nuclear Policies: Attitudes and Posture', in P. R. Chari, I. Cheema and Iftekharuzzaman (eds) *Nuclear Non-Proliferation in India and Pakistan: South Asian Perspective*, New Delhi: Manohar Publications, 103–30.

—— (2000) 'Pakistan's Nuclear Use Doctrine and Command and Control', in S.D. Sagan, J.J. Wirtz, J. James and L.R. Peter (eds) *Planning the Unthinkable: How New Powers will Use Nuclear, Biological, and Chemical Weapons*, London: Cornell University, 158–81.

—— (2004) 'The Role of Nuclear Weapons in Pakistan's Defence Strategy', *IPRI* 4(2): 72–87.

—— (2007) 'The Role of Nuclear Weapons in Pakistan's Defence Strategy', in M.B. Alam (ed.) *Constructing Nuclear Strategic Discourse: The South Asian Scene*, New Delhi: India Research Press.

—— (2011) 'Pakistan's Posture of Minimum Credible Deterrence: Current Challenges and Future Efficacy', in Zulfqar Khan (ed.) *Nuclear Pakistan: Strategic Dimensions*, London: Oxford University Press, 43–84.

Cheema, Pervaiz Iqbal (1980) 'Pakistan's Quest for Nuclear Technology', *Australian Journal of International Affairs* 34(2): 188–96.

Chengappa, M. Bindanda (1995) 'Pakistan: Military Role in Civil Administration', www.idsa-india.org/an-may9-9.html (accessed 7 February 2012).

Choudhury, Upendra (2008) *The Indo-USA Nuclear Deal and Its Impact on India's Ballistic Missile Programme*, South Asian Strategic Stability Institute, Research Report 17, 1–25.

Cimbala, J. Stephen (2011) 'Minimum Deterrence and Missile Defences: US and Russia Going Forward', *Comparative Strategy* 30(4): 347–62.

Cirincione, Josef (2005) 'The Declining Ballistic Missiles Threat', www.carnegieendowment.org/pdf/The_Declining_Ballistic_Missile_Threat_2005.pdf (accessed 29 February 2012).

Cloughley, Brian. (1999) *A History of Pakistan Army: Wars and Insurrections*, Karachi: Oxford University Press.
Cohen, Avner (1998) *Israel and the Bomb*, New York: Columbia University Press.
Cohen, Bill (2009) 'Closing Pandora Box: Obama's Pro-Active Nuclear Weapons Initiative Seek to Turn Back the Clock', www.praguepost.com/opinion/1131-closing-pandoras-box.html (accessed 15 May 2012).
Cohen, Craig (2007) 'A Perilous Course: US Strategy and Assistance to Pakistan', csis.org/images/stories/pcr/070727_pakistan.pdf (accessed 28 February 2012).
Cohen, P. Stephen (1984) *The Pakistan Army*, New York: Oxford University Press.
——(2003) 'The Jihadist Threat to Pakistan', *Washington Quarterly* 26(3): 7–25.
——(2010) 'Pakistan and the Cold War', in Chandra Chari (ed.) *Superpower Rivalry and Conflict: The Long Shadow of the Cold War on the Twenty-First Century*, New York: Routledge, 74–87.
Collier, David (2011) 'Understanding Process Tracing', *Political Science and Politics* 44(4): 823–30.
Costanzo, E. Charles (2011) 'South Asia: Danger Ahead?' *Strategic Studies Quarterly*: 92–106.
Crossette, Barbara (1998) 'Nuclear Anxiety: The Rivalry; South Asian Arms Race: Reviving Dormant Fears of Nuclear War', www.nytimes.com/1998/05/29/world/nuclear-anxiety-rivalry-south-asian-arms-race-reviving-dormant-fears-nuclear-war.html (accessed 13 June 2011).
Dawn (2010) 'India to Speed-up Arms Purchase after Plane Deal', www.dawn.com/wps/wcm/connect/dawn-content-library/dawn/news/world/18-india-to-speed-up-arms-purchase-after-scrapping-plane-deal-am-02 (accessed 8 September 2010).
Defence Intelligence Agency (2004) 'The Decade Ahead: 1999–2002, A Premier on the Future Threat', in R. Scarborough, *Rumsfeld's War: the Untold Story of America's Anti-Terrorist Commander*, Washington, DC: Regnery, 194–223.
Delpech, Therese (1999) 'New Stages of Nuclear Disarmament: A European View', in H.A. Feiveson (ed.) *The Nuclear Turning Point*, Washington, DC: The Brookings Institution, 335.
Dikshit, Sandeep (2008) 'Zardari Says he is Against Nuclear Warfare', *The Hindu* (New Delhi), www.hindu.com/2008/11/23/stories/2008112350260100.htm (accessed 16 October 2012).
Dulles, J.F (1954a) 'Policy for Security and Peace', *Foreign Affairs* 32(3): 353–64.
——(1954b) 'The Evolution of Foreign Policy', *Department of State Bulletin*, July: 107–10.
Dunne, A. Lewis (1977) 'Nuclear Proliferation and World Politics', *Annals of the American Academy of Political and Social Sciences* 430: 96–109.
——(2009) 'The NPT', *The Non-Proliferation Review* 16(2): 143–72.
Durrani, Mahmud Ali (2004) 'Pakistan's Strategic Thinking and the Role of Nuclear Weapons', www.cmc.sandia.gov/cmc-papers/sand2004-3375p.pdf (accessed 18 June 2012).
Dutta, Sujan (2003) 'Rethink on No-First-Use Doctrine', *Telegraph*, www.telegraphindia.com/1030114/asp/nation/story_1571767.asp (accessed 8 November 2010).
Eirabi, Ghani (1993) 'Blackmailing Can Backfire', *Dawn*, 18 April.
Eisenhower, D. (1953) 'President Eisenhower's Atom for Peace Speech', www.atomicarchive.com/Docs/Deterrence/Atomsforpeace.shtml (accessed 7 August 2010).
Ellsberg, D. (1993) 'Manhattan Project II: Anti-Nuclear Initiative', findarticles.com/p/articles/mi_m1295/is_n8_v57/ai_13201819/ (accessed 12 July 2010).

Evangelista, Matthew A. (1983) 'Offense or Defence: A Tale of Two Commissions', *World Policy Journal* 1(1): 45–69.

Evera, V. Stephen (1997) *Guide to Methods for Students of Political Science*, New York: Cornell University Press.

——(1998) 'Offense, Defence, and the Causes of War', *International Security* 22(4): 5–43.

——(1999) *Causes of War: Power and the Roots of Conflict*, New York: Cornell University Press.

Ezdi, Asif (2012) 'India's Military Spending', *The News*, www.thenews.com.pk/Todays-News-9-99572-Indias-military-spending (accessed 15 June 2012).

Fair, Christine (2009) 'Pakistan's Relations with Central Asia', in R. Jelty (ed.) *Pakistan in Regional and Global Politics*, London: Routledge, 125–49.

——(2011a) 'The Militants Challenge in Pakistan', *Asia Policy* 11, Washington.

——(2011b) 'The US-Pakistan F-16 Fiasco', afpak.foreignpolicy.com/posts/2011/02/03/the_f_16_fiasco (accessed 28 February 2012).

Feaver, D. Peter (1990) 'The Evolution of American Nuclear Doctrine', in G.T. Allision, Jr, R.D. Blackwill, A. Carnesale, J.S. Nye, Jr and R.P. Beschel, Jr (eds) *A Primer for the Nuclear Age*, CSIA Occasional Paper Series, 30–34, belfercenter.ksg.harvard.edu/publication/3034/primer_for_the_nuclear_age.html (accessed 18 April 2012).

——(1992a) 'Command and Control in Emerging Nuclear Nations', *International Security* 17(3): 160–87.

——(1992b) *Guarding the Guardians: Civilian Control of Nuclear Weapons in United States*, Ithaca, NY: Cornell University Press.

——(1993) 'Proliferation Optimism and Theories of Nuclear Operations', *Security Studies* 2(3/4): 172–73.

Federation of American Scientists (1992) 'The Pressler Amendment and Pakistan's Nuclear Weapons Program', Senate, 31 July, www.fas.org/news/pakistan/1992/920731.htm (accessed 28 February 2012).

——(1998) 'Pakistani Foreign Minister's Statement in Response to India's 11 May 1998 Nuclear Test', www.fas.org/news/pakistan/1998/05/index.html (accessed 14 June 2011).

——(2000) 'Hatf-II-Pakistan Missile Special Weapons Delivery Systems', www.fas.org/nuke/guide/pakistan/missile/hatf-2.htm (accessed 29 February 2012).

——(2012) *Status of World Nuclear Forces*, 2 March, www.fas.org/programs/ssp/nukes/nuclearweapons/nukestatus.html (accessed 2 March 2012).

Feiveson, A. Harold and Hogendoorn, J. Ernst (2003) 'No-First Use of Nuclear Weapons', *The Non-Proliferation Review*: 1–9.

Fetter, Steve (1999) 'Nuclear Strategy and Targeting Doctrine', in H.A. Feiveson (ed.) *The Nuclear Turning Point*, Washington, DC: The Brookings Institution Press.

Foote, N. Nelson (1951) 'Identification as the Basis for a Theory of Motivation', *American Sociological Review* 16(1): 14–21.

Forsyth, James Wood Jr, Saltzman, B. Chance and Schaub, Gary Jr (2010a) 'Minimum Deterrence and its Critics', *Security Studies Quarterly*: 3–12.

——(2010b) 'Remembrance of Things Past: The Enduring Value of Nuclear Weapons', *Security Studies Quarterly*: 74–89.

Frantz, Douglas and Collins, Catherine (2008) *The Nuclear Jihadist: The True Story of the Man Who Sold the World's Most Dangerous Secrets*, USA: Grand Central Publishing.

Freedman, Lawrence (2003) *The Evolution of Nuclear Strategy*, New York: Palgrave Macmillan.

Gaddis, John Lewis (1982) *Strategies of Containment: A Critical Appraisal of Post-war American National Security Policy*, London: Oxford University Press.

Gallois, Pierre (1961) *The Balance of Terror: Strategy for the Nuclear Age*, Boston, MA: Houghton Mifflin.

Ganguly, Sumit (2002) *Conflict Unending: India-Pakistan Tensions since 1947*, New York: Columbia University Press.

Ganguly, Sumit and Hagerty, T.D. (2005) *Fearful of Symmetry: India-Pakistan Crises in the Shadow of Nuclear Weapons*, New Delhi: Oxford University Press.

Ganguly, Sumit and Howenstein, Nicholas (2009) 'India-Pakistan Rivalry in Afghanistan', *Journal of International Affairs* 63(1): 127–40.

Ganguly, Sumit and Kapur, Paul (eds) (2009) *Nuclear Proliferation in South Asia: Crisis Behaviour and the Bomb*, London: Routledge, 76–99.

——(2010) *India, Pakistan, and the Bomb: Debating Nuclear Security in South Asia*, New York: Columbia University Press.

GAOR (UN General Assembly Official Records) (1949) *4th Session, Ad Hoc Political Committee, 34th Meeting*, 11 November, 196.

——(1951) *6th Session, Agenda Items 16 and 66, (1951/1959): ST/LIB/SER.B/ A. 2.*

Garrett, Geoffrey and Weingast, R. Barry (1993) 'Ideas, Interests, and Institutions: Constructing the European Community's Internal Market', in J. Goldstein and R.O. Keohane (eds) *Ideas and Foreign Policy: Beliefs, Institutions, and Political Change*, Ithaca, NY and London: Cornell University Press, 173–206.

Gartzke, E. and Jo, J. Dong (2007) 'Determinants of Nuclear Weapons Proliferation', *Journal of Conflict Resolution* 51: 167–94.

George, Alexander and Bennett, Andrew (2005) *Case Studies and Theory Development in the Social Sciences*, Cambridge, MA: MIT Press.

George, Nirmala (2010) 'Putin in Deal to Build Nuclear Reactors for India', www.guardian.co.uk/world/2010/mar/12/russia-india-nuclear-reactor-deal (accessed 9 February 2012).

Gerson, S. Michael (2010) 'No First Use: The Next Step for US Nuclear Policy', *International Security* 35(2): 7–47.

Gertz, Bill (2013) 'China, Pakistan Reach Secret Nuclear Deal Reactor Deal for Pakistan', *The Washington Times*, www.washingtontimes.com/news/2013/mar/21/china-pakistan-reach-secret-reactor-deal-pakistan/?page=all (accessed 14 April 2013).

Giles, F. Gregory and Doyle, E. James (1996) 'Indian and Pakistan Views on Nuclear Deterrence', *Comparative Strategy* 15(April–June).

Gill, H. John (2009a) 'Military Operation in the Kargil Conflict', in R.P. Lavoy (ed.) *Asymmetric Warfare in South Asia: The Causes and Consequences of the Kargil Conflict*, New York: Cambridge University Press, 92–129.

——(2009b) 'Brasstacks: Prudently Pessimistic', in S. Ganguly and P. Kapur (eds) *Nuclear Proliferation in South Asia: Crisis Behaviour and the Bomb*, London: Routledge, 36–58.

Giplin, Robert (1975) *US Power and Multinational Corporation: The Principle Economy of Foreign Direct Investment*, New York: Basic Books.

——(1986) 'The Richness of the Tradition of Political Realism', in R.O. Keohane (ed.) *Neo-realism and its Critics*, New York: Columbia University Press, 301–21.

Gizewski, Peter (1994) *Minimum Nuclear Deterrence in a New World Order*, Aurora Papers, 24, Ottawa: Canadian Centre for Global Security.

Glaser, L. Charles (1996) 'Realists as Optimists: Cooperation as Self Help', *Security Studies* 5(3): 122–66.

——(1997) 'Security Dilemma Revisited', *World Politics* 50: 171–201.
Goldstein, Avery (2000) *Deterrence and Security in the 21st Century: China, Britain, France, and the Enduring Legacy of the Nuclear Revolution*, California: Stanford University Press.
Goure, Daniel and Cooper, R. Jeffery (1984) 'Conventional Deep Strikes: A Critical Look', *Comparative Strategy* 4(3): 215–48.
——(2011) 'On Civil Military Relations', www.pakistantoday.com.pk/2011/12/on-civil-military-relations/ (accessed 7 February 2012).
Graham, W. Thomas (1991) 'Winning the Non-Proliferation Battle', *Arms Control Today* 21(7): 8–13.
Grare, Frederic (2006) 'Pakistan-Afghanistan Relations in the Post 9/11 Era', *Carnegie Endowment for International Peace*, South Asia Project No. 72.
Gregory, Shaun (2009) 'The Terrorist Threat to Pakistan's Nuclear Weapons', July, www.ctc.usma.edu/wp-content/uploads/2010/ ... /CTCSentinel-Vol2Iss7.pdf (accessed 28 June 2011), 1–4.
Gregory, Shaun and Fair, Christopher (2008) 'The Cohesion and Stability of Pakistan: An Introduction to the Special Issue', *Contemporary South Asia* 16(1): 3–9.
Grieco, M. Joseph (1993) 'Anarchy and the Limits of Cooperation: A Realist Critique of the Newest Liberal Institutionalism', in A.D. Baldwin (ed.) *Neo-Realism and Neo-Liberalism: The Contemporary Debate*, New York: Columbia University Press, 116–42.
Gupta, Bhabani Sen (1988) *South Asian Perspectives*, New Delhi: B.R. Publishing Co.
Gupta, S. (1994) *India Redefines its Role*, Adelphi Paper, No. 293, London: IISS.
Haas, M. Peter (1989) 'Do Regimes Matter? Epistemic Communities and Mediterranean Pollution Control', *International Organization* 43(3): 377–403.
——(1992) 'Introduction: Epistemic Communities and International Policy Coordination', *International Organization* 46(1): 1–35.
Hagerty, Devin (1995) 'Nuclear Deterrence in South Asia: The 1990 Indo-Pakistani Crisis', *International Security* 20(3): 79–114.
Hali, M. Shafei (2012) 'India Military Expansion 2020: Implications for Pakistan's National Security', *Defence Journal*, April: 66–80.
Halperin, H. Morton (2009) 'Forum: The Case for No First Use: An Exchange', *Survival* 51(5): 17–46.
Hanrieder, F.W. (1979) *Arms Control and Security: Current Issues*, Boulder, CO: Westview Press.
Haq-ul, Zia (2000) 'Declaration to the Nation, August 30, 1979', in K.H. Nizamani (ed.) *The Roots of Rhetoric: Politics of Nuclear Weapons in India and Pakistan*, USA: Praeger, 102.
Harsh, V. Pant (2005) 'India's Nuclear Doctrine and Command Structure: Implications for India and the World', *Comparative Strategy* 24: 277–93.
Hasnat, Syed Farooq (2009) 'Pakistan's Strategic Interests, Afghanistan and the Fluctuating US Strategy', *Journal of International Affairs* 63(1): 141–55.
Hassan, K. Sarwar (1960) *Pakistan and the United Nations*, New York: Manhattan Publishing Company.
Heir, Aidan (2007) 'Is Pakistan a Failed State?' spaces.brad.ac.uk:8080/pages/view page.action?pageId=984 (accessed 25 December 2010).
Hersh, M. Seymour (2009) 'Defending the Arsenal: In an Unstable Pakistan, Can Nuclear Warheads be Kept Safe', www.newyorker.com/reporting/2009/11/16/ 091116fa_fact_hersh (accessed 28 June 2011).

Bibliography

Herz, H. John (1950) 'Idealist Internationalism and the Security Dilemma', *World Politics* 2(2): 157–80.

Hewson, Robert (2005) 'Cruise Missile Technology Proliferation Takes Off', *Jane's Intelligence Review* 17(10): 41–45.

Hibbs, Mark (2010) 'Moving Forward on the US-India Nuclear Deal', www.carnegieendowment.org/2010/04/05/moving-forward-on-u.s.-india-nuclear-deal/5ww (accessed 9 February 2012).

Hibbs, Mark and Rehman, Shahid (2006) 'NSG, US will not Accommodate New Pakistan-China Commerce', *Nucleonics Week*, 2 March, www.pakstop.com/pmforums/f83/nsg-us-wont-accommodate-new-pakistan-china-commerce-21814/ (accessed 28 June 2012).

Hilali, Z.A. (2005) *US-Pakistan Relationship: Soviet Invasion of Afghanistan*, USA: Ashgate.

Hobbes, Thomas (2009) *Leviathan*, USA: Seven Treasures Publications.

Hodes, Cyprus and Sedra, Mark (2007) *The Search for Security in Post-Taliban Afghanistan*, Adelphi Paper, No. 391, London: Routledge.

Hoffmann, Stanley (1965) *The State of War: Essays in the Theory and Practice of International Politics*, New York: Praeger.

Holmes, R. James, Winner, C. Andrew and Yoshihara, Toshi (2009) *Indian Naval Strategy in the Twenty-First Century*, New York: Routledge, 36.

Holmes, R. James and Yoshihara, Toshi (2008) 'Indian's Monroe Doctrine and Asia's Maritime Future', *Strategic Analysis* 32(6): 997–98.

Holsti, J.K. (1985) *The Dividing Discipline*, Boston, MA: Allan & Unwin.

——(1996) *The State, War, and the State of War*, Cambridge and New York: Cambridge University Press.

——(1998) 'International Relations Theory and Domestic War in the Third World', in S.G. Neuman (ed.) *International Relations Theory and the Third World*, London: Macmillan.

Hoodbhoy, Pervez (1995) 'Nuclear Myths and Realities', in Z. Mian (ed.) *Pakistan's Atomic Bomb and the Search for Security*, Lahore: Gautam Publishers, 1–30.

——(1998) 'Pakistan's Nuclear Future', in Samina Ahmed and David Cortright (eds) *Pakistan and the Bomb: Public Opinion and Nuclear Options*, Indiana: University of Notre Dame Press.

——(2007) 'Pakistan: The Threat from Within', spaces.brad.ac.uk:8080/pages/viewpage.action?pageId=984 (accessed 25 December 2010).

Hopkins, C. John and Hu, Weixing (eds) (1995) *Strategic Views from the Second Tier: The Nuclear Weapons Policies of France, Britain, and China*, London: New Brunswick.

Hoyt, D. Timothy (2001) 'Pakistani Nuclear Doctrine and the Dangers of Strategic Myopia', *Asian Survey* XLI(6): 956–77.

——(2005) 'Strategic Myopia: Pakistan's Nuclear Doctrine and Crisis Stability in South Asia', in Lowell Dittmer (ed.) *South Asia's Nuclear Security Dilemma: India, Pakistan, China*, London: M.E. Sharpe.

——(2007) 'Nuclear Rivalry, Nuclear Deterrence', *India Review* 6(2): 116–31.

——(2009) 'Kargil: The Nuclear Dimension', in R.P. Lavoy (ed.) *Asymmetric Warfare in South Asia: The Causes and Consequences of the Kargil Conflict*, New York: Cambridge University Press, 144–70.

Huntington, Samuel (1958) 'Arms Races: Pre-requisites and Results', *Public Policy* VIII: 1–87.

Hussain, Rifaat (2001) 'Prospects for Peace between India and Pakistan', *National Development and Security* IX(3), Serial No. 35.

——(2005) *Nuclear Doctrines in South Asia*, South Asia Strategic Stability Unit, 4.

Hussein, Mushahid (1988) *Pakistan and the Changing Regional Scenario: Reflections of a Journalist*, Lahore: Progressive Publishers.

——(1994a) 'Army and the Nuclear Issue', *The News*, 13 April.

——(1994b) 'The Nuclear Issue and South Asia: Security via Deterrence', *The News*, 14 April.

——(1998) 'Army to the Rescue', *Newsline*, 18–28.

Hussein, Talat Syed (1998) 'Pakistan Hedged on Obvious Bet', *The Nation*, 29 May.

Hyder, Tariq Osman (2012a) 'Concerns over Pakistan's Nuclear Program: Perceptions and Reality', *Policy Perspectives* 9(2): 33–65.

——(2012b) 'FMCT: Facts and Fiction', *The News*, 28 March.

IAEA (International Atomic Energy Agency) (1970) 'Treaty on the Non-Proliferation of Nuclear Weapons', Articles of the NPT, 22 April, www.iaea.org/Publications/Documents/Infcircs/Others/infcirc140.pdf (accessed 14 May 2012).

IISS (International Institute for Strategic Studies) (2007) 'Pakistan's Nuclear Oversight Reforms', in *Nuclear Black Market Dossier: A Net Assessment*, IISS Strategic Dossier, 2 May, www.iiss.org/publications/strategic-dossiers/nbm/nuclear-black-market-dossier-a-net-assesment/ (accessed 11 July 2012).

——(2012) *Military Balance*, March, www.iiss.org/publications/military-balance/the-military-balance-2012/ (accessed 28 February 2012).

Ikenberry, G. John (1993) 'Creating Yesterday's New World Order: Keynesian "New Thinking" and the Anglo-American Post-war Settlement', in J. Goldstein and R.O. Keohane (eds) *Ideas and Foreign Policy: Beliefs, Institutions, and Political Change*, Ithaca, NY and London: Cornell University Press, 57–86.

India Today (1999) 'Minister for External Affairs Shri Jaswant Singh's Interview', *India Today*, 11 January, www.indianembassy.org/inews/February99/feature.html (accessed 25 February 2012).

Inter-Services Public Relations (2012) 'Press Release', 25 April, www.ispr.gov.pk/front/main.asp?o=t-press_release& id=2043#pr_link2043 (accessed 25 April 2012).

Intriligator, D. Michael and Brito, I. Dagoberto (1989) 'On Arms Control', in Edward A. Kolosziej and Patrick M. Morgan (eds) *Security and Arms Control, Vol. 1*, New York: Greenwood Press.

Iqbal, Khalid (2012) 'India Triggers an Arms Race', *The Nation*, www.nation.com.pk/pakistan-news-newspaper-daily-english-online/columns/26-Mar-2012/india-triggers-an-arms-race (accessed 15 June 2012).

ISPR (Inter-Services Public Relations) (2011) 'Press Release', 19 April, www.ispr.gov.pk/front/main.asp?o=t-press_release&id=1721 (accessed 5 April 2012).

——(2012a) 'Press Release', 10 May, www.ispr.gov.pk/front/main.asp?o=t-press_release& latest=1 (accessed 11 May 2012).

——(2012b) *Pakistan Tests Hatf-VIII (RAAD)*, 31 May, www.ispr.gov.pk/front/main.asp?o=t-press_release& id=2080#pr_link2080 (accessed 31 May 2012).

Jansson, Mark (2011) 'The New "Minimum" in Pakistan', csis.org/blog/new-minimum-pakistan (accessed 20 February 2012).

Jaspal, Zafar Nawaz (2000) 'A Case for Signing the CTBT', *Strategic Issues* 3, Islamabad: Institute of Strategic Studies.

——(2001) 'India's Missile Capabilities: Regional Implications', *Pakistan's Horizon* 54 (1): 59–60.

——(2004) *Nuclear Risk Reduction Measures and Restraint Regime in South Asia*, New Delhi: Manohar.
——(2010) 'Future of FMCT: Assessing the Prospects and Constraints', Institute of Strategic Studies Islamabad, www.issi.org.pk/publication-files/1299560158_80128402.pdf (accessed 11 May 2012).
——(2011) 'Tactical Nuclear Weapons and Deterrence Stability in South Asia', 23 September, www.weeklypulse.org/details.aspx?contentID=1252&storylist=9 (accessed 5 April 2012).
——(2012) 'Evolution of Pakistan's Nuclear Programme: Debates in Decision Making', *Regional Studies* XXX(2): 3–38.
Jervis, Robert (1979) 'Why Nuclear Superiority Doesn't Matter', *Political Science Quarterly* 94(4): 617–33.
——(1988) 'The Political Effects of Nuclear Weapons: A Comment', *International Security* 13(2): 80–90.
——(1999) 'Realism, Neo-liberalism, and Cooperation', *International Security* 24(1): 42–63.
——(2009) 'Kargil, Deterrence, and International Relations Theory', in R.P. Lavoy (ed.) *Asymmetric Warfare in South Asia: The Causes and Consequences of the Kargil Conflict*, New York: Cambridge University Press, 377–96.
Joek, Neil (2009) 'The Kargil War and Nuclear Deterrence', in S. Ganguly and P. Kapur (eds) *Nuclear Proliferation in South Asia: Crisis Behaviour and the Bomb*, London: Routledge, 117–43.
Joffe, Josef (1985) 'Nuclear Weapons, No First Use, and European Order', *Ethics* 95 (3): 606–18.
John Paul II, Pope (1981) 'Sayings of Pope John Paul II Address in Hiroshima 1981', www.cdi.org/nuclear/nukequo.html (accessed 24 April 2012).
Johnston, Alastair Iain (1995) 'China's New "Old Thinking": The Concept of Limited Deterrence', *International Security* 20(3): 5–42.
Jones, Owen Bennett (2002) *Pakistan: Eye of the Storm*, New Haven, CT: Yale University Press.
Jones, W. Rodney (1981) *Nuclear Proliferation: Islam, the Bomb, and South Asia*, A Sage Policy Paper: The Center for Strategic and International Studies.
——(1987) 'Pakistan's Nuclear Option', in H. Malik, *Soviet-American Relations with Pakistan, Iran, and Afghanistan*, New York: St Martin Press.
——(1998) 'Pakistan's Nuclear Posture: Arms Race Instabilities in South Asia', *Asian Affairs, an American Review* 25(2): 67–87.
——(2000) 'Pakistan's Nuclear Posture: Quest for Assured Nuclear Deterrence – A Conjecture', *Spotlight* (Regional Studies Islamabad) XIX(1): 1–38.
——(2001) *Minimum Nuclear Deterrence Postures in South Asia: An Overview*, USA: Defence Threat Reduction Agency Advanced Systems and Concepts Office.
——(2005) 'Prospects for Arms Control and Strategic Stability in South Asia', *Contemporary South Asia* 14(2): 191–209.
——(2011) 'Pakistan's Answer to Cold Start', *The Friday Times*, www.thefridaytimes.com/13052011/page7.shtml (accessed 9 April 2012).
Jones, W. Rodney and McDonough, Mark (1998) *Tracking Nuclear Proliferation: A Guide in Maps and Charts*, Washington, DC: Carnegie Endowment for International Peace.
Joshua, Anita (2011) 'Pakistan Tests Short-Range Ballistic Missile', www.thehindu.com/news/international/article1709352.ece (accessed April 2012).

Kahn, Herman (1960) *On Thermonuclear War*, New York: Princeton University Press.

Kaiser, Karl, Leber, George, Mertes, Alois and Schulze, J. Franz (1982) 'Nuclear Weapons and the Preservation of Peace: A Response to an American Proposal for Renouncing the First Use of Nuclear Weapons', *Foreign Affairs* 60(5): 1157–70.

Kak, Kapil (1999) 'Command and Control of Small Nuclear Arsenals', in Jasjit Singh (ed.) *Nuclear India*, New Delhi: Institute for Defence Studies and Analysis.

Kanwal, Gurmeet (2001) 'Nuclear Defence – Shaping the Arsenal', New Delhi: IDSA, 110–11.

——(2006) 'Cold Start and Battle Groups for Offensive Operations', *Strategic Trends* 4(18).

Kapur, Ashok (1976) *India's Nuclear Option: Atomic Diplomacy and Decision Making*, London and New York: Praeger.

——(1987) *Pakistan's Nuclear Development*, New York: Croom Helm.

Kapur, S. Paul (2003) 'Nuclear Proliferation, the Kargil Conflict, and South Asian Security', *Security Studies* 13(1): 79–105.

——(2005) 'India and Pakistan's Unstable Peace: Why Nuclear South Asia is Not like Cold War Europe', *International Security* 30(2): 127–52.

——(2007) *Dangerous Deterrent: Nuclear Weapons Proliferation and Conflict in South Asia*, California: Stanford University Press.

——(2008) 'Ten Years of Instability in Nuclear South Asia', *International Security* 33(2): 71–92.

Katzenstein, J. Peter (ed.) (1996) *The Culture of National Security: Norms and Identity in World Politics*, New York: Columbia University Press.

——(1998) *Cultural Norms and National Security: Police and Military in Post-War Japan*, New York: Cornell University Press.

Kazi, Reshmi (2007) 'Pakistan's Nuclear Doctrine and Strategy', www.ipcs.org/article_details.php?articleNo=2361 (accessed 19 June 2012).

Kerr, K. Paul and Nikitin, Mary Beth (2011) *Pakistan's Nuclear Weapons: Proliferation and Security Issues*, Congressional Research Service, www.fas.org/sgp/crs/nuke/RL34248.pdf (accessed 28 February 2012).

Khalilzad, Zalamay (1976) 'Pakistan: The Making of a Nuclear Power', *Asian Survey* 16(6): 580–92.

——(1978) *Nuclear Power and Economic Development: Seven Cases; Brazil, India, Iran, Korea, Philippines, Pakistan and Turkey*, Los Angeles: Pan Heuristics.

——(1979) 'Pakistan and the Bomb', *Survival* 21(6): 224–50.

——(1985) 'Pakistan', in J. Goldblat (ed.) *Non-Proliferation: The Way and Wherefore*, London: Taylor & Francis, 131–38.

——(1999) 'Congage China', RAND Issue Paper, www.rand.org/pubs/issue_papers/2006/IP187.pdf (accessed 23 May 2012).

——(2012) 'A Strategy of "Congagement" Toward Pakistan', *The Washington Quarterly* 35(2), Spring: 107–19.

Khan, Abdul Qadeer (1984) 'Interview', *Nawa-i-Waqt* (in Urdu); English version reprinted in *Defence Journal* X(4).

——(1987) 'Interview', *The Tribune*, 1 March; reprinted in *Strategic Digest* (New Delhi) XVII(5), May: 7–8.

Khan, Ali Zulfiqar (1995) 'Pakistan's Security and Nuclear Option', in Tariq Jan (ed.) *Pakistan's Security and the Nuclear Option*, Islamabad: Institute of Policy Studies, 137–44.

Khan, Ayub (1960) 'Pakistan Perspective', *Foreign Affairs* 38(1/4): 547–56.

—— (1962) 'Address to the 17th Session of UN General Assembly's 1133rd Plenary Meeting', 26 September, in *Speeches Delivered by Zulfiqar Ali Bhutto (1957–1965)*, www.scribd.com/doc/14560791/Speeches-Delivered-by-Zulfiqar-Ali-Bhutto (accessed 9 May 2012), 75.

—— (1964) 'The Pakistan-American Alliance: Stresses and Strains', *Foreign Affairs* 42 (2): 195–209.

—— (1967) *Friends, Not Masters: A Political Autobiography*, London: Oxford University Press.

Khan, Azam Muhammad (2010) 'The Indian Undersea Nuclear Deterrence and Pakistan Navy', *IPRI Journal* X(2): 89–110.

Khan, Faisal (2007) 'Corruption and the Decline of the State in Pakistan', *Asian Journal of Political Science* 15(2): 219–47.

Khan, Gohar Ayub (1998) 'Interview', 12 May, *The News International*.

Khan, Hassan Feroz (2003a) 'Challenges to Nuclear Stability in South Asia', *The Non-Proliferation Review* 10(1): 59–74.

—— (2003b) 'The Independence-Dependence Paradox: Stability Dilemmas in South', www.armscontrol.org/act/2003_10/Khan_10 (accessed 15 March 2011).

—— (2005) 'Nuclear Command and Control in South Asia During Peace, Crisis and War', *Contemporary South Asia* 14(2): 163–74.

—— (2006) 'Nuclear Proliferation Motivations', *The Non-Proliferation Review* 13(3): 501–17.

—— (2009) 'Nuclear Security in Pakistan: Separating Myth from Reality', *Arms Control Today*: 12–20.

—— (2010) 'Prospects for Indian and Pakistani Arms Control and Confidence-Building Measures', *Naval War College Review* 63(3): 105–21.

—— (2011) 'Minimum Deterrence: Pakistan's Dilemma', *RUSI Journal* 156(5): 44–51.

—— (2012) *Eating Grass: The Making of Pakistani Bomb*, California: Stanford University Press.

Khan, Hassan Feroz, Lavoy, R. Peter and Clary, Christopher (2009) 'Pakistan's Motivations and Calculations for the Kargil Conflict', in R.P. Lavoy (ed.) *Asymmetric Warfare in South Asia: The Causes and Consequences of the Kargil Conflict*, New York: Cambridge University Press.

Khan, Hassan Feroz and Masellis, M. Nick (2012) 'US-Pakistan Strategic Partnership: a Track II Dialogue', www.dtic.mil/cgi-bin/GetTRDoc?AD=ADA555421 (accessed 9 April 2012), 26.

Khan, Muhammad Khurshid (2011) 'Fissile Material Cut-off Treaty: An Overview from Pakistan', Institute of Strategic Studies Islamabad, www.issi.org.pk/publication-files/1315811133_20447390.pdf (accessed 11 May 2012), 195–223.

Khan, Munir Ahmed (1998) 'Nuclearisation of South Asia and its Regional and Global Implications', *Regional Studies* 26(4): 3–58.

—— (1999) 'Speech on Pakistan's Nuclear Weapons', 20 March, www.pakdef.info/nuclear&missile/speech_munirahmed.html (accessed 28 January 2013).

Khan, Saira (2001) 'A Nuclear South Asia: Resolving or Protracting the Protracted Conflict?' *International Relations* 15(4): 61–77.

—— (2002) *Nuclear Proliferation in Protracted Conflict Regions: A Comparative Study of South Asia and the Middle East*, Sydney: Ashgate.

—— (2005) 'Nuclear Weapons and the Prolongation of the India-Pakistan Rivalry', in V.T. Paul (ed.) *The India-Pakistan Conflict: An Enduring Rivalry*, Cambridge: Cambridge University Press.

—— (2009) *Nuclear Weapons and Conflict Transformation: The Case of India-Pakistan*, New York: Routledge.
Khan, Zafar (2010) 'Makers of the US Nuclear Strategy: From Policy of Massive Retaliation to Nuclear Stability', *IPRI Journal* X(2): 69–80.
—— (2012a) 'Pakistan's Nuclear Weapons Testing May 1998: External and Internal Pressures', *IPRI Journal* 12(1): 28–45.
—— (2012b) 'Cold Start Doctrine: The Conventional Challenge to South Asian Stability', *Contemporary Security Policy* 33(3): 577–94.
—— (2013a) 'Pakistan and the NPT: Commitments and Concerns', *Journal of National Defence University*, Pakistan (March–April).
—— (2013b) 'Pakistan's Policy of Minimum Deterrence: Why Minimum is not the Minimum' *Defence and Security Analysis* 29(1): 30–41.
—— (2013c) 'Pakistan's Policy of Arms Control and Disarmament: A Call for Arms Control Regime in South Asia', *Defence Studies* 1 (May–June).
Khan, Zulfqar (2005) 'The Politics of Nuclear Non-Proliferation with Particular Reference to South Asia', *IPRI Journal*: 1–16, ipripak.org/journal/winter2005/the politics.shtml (accessed 14 May 2012).
—— (ed.) (2011) *Nuclear Pakistan: Strategic Dimensions*, London: Oxford University Press.
Kidwai, Khalid (2002) 'An Interview with the Italian Research Group Landau Network', in C.P. Ramusino and M. Martellini, *Nuclear Safety, Nuclear Stability and Nuclear Strategy in Pakistan*, www.pugwash.org/september11/pakistan-nuclear.htm (accessed 13 September 2010), 7.
King, E. James (1956) 'Nuclear Plenty and Limited War', *Foreign Affairs* 34(1/4): 238–56.
Kissinger, Henry (1957) *Nuclear Weapons and Foreign Policy*, New York: Harpers and Brothers.
—— (1979) 'Kissinger's Critique', *The Economist*, 3 February.
Kissinger, Henry, Nunn, Sam, Perry, William and Shultz, George (2008) 'Towards a Nuclear Free World', *Wall Street Journal*, 15 January.
Knopf, W. Jeffrey (2012) 'The Concept of Nuclear Learning', *The Non-Proliferation Review* 19(1): 79–93.
Knorr, K. (1962) 'Limited Strategic War', in K. Knorr and T. Read (eds) *Limited Strategic War: Essays in Nuclear Strategy*, New York: Pall Mall Press, 3–31.
Kober, Stanley, Jones, C. David, Ravenal, C. Easl, Anderson, N. Carl and Hafner, L. Donald (1982) 'The Debate over No First Use', *Foreign Affairs* 60(5): 1171–80.
Koch, Andrew (1998) 'South Asia, Public Opinion, and the Comprehensive Test Ban Treaty', *Weekly Defence Monitor* 2(37), 17 September.
Koreshi, S.M. (1995) 'The Method in American Duplicity', in Tariq Jan (ed.) *Pakistan's Security and the Nuclear Option*, Islamabad: Institute of Policy Studies, 131–36.
Kothari, Smitu and Mian, Zia (eds) (2001) *Out of Nuclear Shadow*, London: Zed Books.
Krepon, Michael (2011) 'The Limits of Influence', *The Non-Proliferation Review* 18 (1): 96.
Krepon, Michael, Haider, Ziad and Thornton, Charles (2004) 'Are Tactical Nuclear Weapons Needed in South Asia', in M. Krepon, R.W. Jones and Z. Haider (eds) *Escalation Control and the Nuclear Options in South Asia*, www.stimson.org/books-reports/escalation-control-and-the-nuclear-option-in-south-asia-/ (accessed 10 April 2012), 129.
Krieger, David (2008) 'NATO Nuclear First Use Option', www.wagingpeace.org/articles/2008/01/23_krieger_nato_first.php (accessed 29 January 2012).

Krieger, David and Ong, Carah (2002) 'No First Use', www.wagingpeace.org/articles/2002/04/00_krieger_no-first-use.htm (accessed 1 February 2012).

Krishnan, Ananth (2013) 'Pak, not China, Likely Source of N-Korea n-Plan, says Kerry', *The Hindu*, www.thehindu.com/news/international/world/pak-not-china-likely-source-of-n-korea-nplan-says-kerry/article4613550.ece (accessed 14 April 2013).

Kristensen, M. Hans (2005) 'US Nuclear Weapons in Europe: A Review of Post-Cold War Policy, Force Levels, and War Planning', www.nrdc.org/nuclear/euro/contents.asp (accessed 15 May 2012).

Kristensen, M. Hans and Norris, S. Robert (2011) 'Nuclear Notebook: Pakistan's Nuclear Forces, 2011', *Bulletin of the Atomic Scientists* 67(4): 91–99.

Kristensen, M. Hans, Norris, S. Robert and Oelrich, Ivan (2009) *From Counterforce to Minimal Deterrence: A New Nuclear Policy on the Path Toward Eliminating Nuclear Weapons*, Federation of American Scientists & the Natural Resources Defence Council, Occasional Paper No. 7, 1–57.

Kux, D. (2001) *The United States and Pakistan, 1947–2000: Disenchanted Allies*, Washington, DC: Woodrow Wilson Center Press.

Ladwig, C. Walter (2008) 'A Cold Start for Hot Wars? The Indian Army's New Limited War Doctrine', *International Security* 32(2): 158–90.

Larssen, M. Rolf (2009) 'Nuclear Security in Pakistan: Reducing the Risks of Nuclear Terrorism', *Arms Control Today*, July–August: 6–11.

Lavoy, R. Peter (1993) 'Nuclear Myths and the Causes of Nuclear Proliferation', *Security Studies* 2(3) 192–212.

——(1994) 'Civil-Military Relations, Strategic Conduct, and the Stability of Nuclear Deterrence in South Asia', in S.D. Sagan (ed.) *Civil-Military Relations and Nuclear Weapons*, Stanford, CA: Centre for International Security and Arms Control, 79–109.

——(1995) 'The Strategic Consequences of Nuclear Proliferation: A Review Essay', *Security Studies* 4(4): 695–753.

——(1996) 'Arms Control in South Asia', in A.J. Larsen and J.G. Rattray (eds) *Arms Control Toward the 21st Century*, Boulder, CO: Lynne Rienner, 272–82.

——(2006a) 'Nuclear Proliferation over the Next Decade', *The Non-Proliferation Review* 13(3): 433–54.

——(2006b) 'Learning to Live with the Bomb? India and Nuclear Weapons, 1947–74', in B. O'Neil, *Nuclear Weapons and National Prestige*, Cowles Foundation, Yale University, 1–44.

——(2007) 'Pakistan's Nuclear Posture: Security and Survivability', www.npolicy.org/Essays/20070121-Lavoy-PakistanNuclearPosture.pdf (accessed 1 September 2010).

——(ed.) (2009) *Asymmetric Warfare in South Asia: The Causes and Consequences of the Kargil Conflict*, New York: Cambridge University Press.

Lavoy, R. Peter and Meyers, D.G (2004) 'Dissuasion in US Defence Strategy', www.nps.edu/Academics/centers/ccc/conferences/recent/dissOct04_rpt.pdf (accessed 11 July 2010).

Levy, Adrian and Clark, Catherine Scott (2007) *Deception: Pakistan, the United States, and the Secret Trade in Nuclear Weapons*, New York: Walker & Company.

Lieber, A. Kier and Press, G. Daryl (2006) 'The End of MAD: The Nuclear Dimension of US Primacy', *International Security* 30(4): 7–44.

Liska, George (1965) 'Nuclear Diffusion: Domestic, Regional, and Global Perspectives', in *Political Problems of Nth Country Arms Choices 1966–1980*, Mershon Centre for Education in National Security, Ohio: Ohio State University, 86–119.

Lodgaard, Sverre (2002) 'Obstacles to No First Use', Pugwash Meeting No. 279, www.pugwash.org/reports/nw/lodgaard.htm (accessed 5 March 2013).
Lodhi, Maleeha (2010) 'FMCT and Strategic Stability', *The News International*, 26 January.
Lodi, F. Sardar (1999) 'Pakistan's Nuclear Doctrine', www.defencejournal.com/apr99/pak-nuclear-doctrine.htm (accessed 13 March 2012).
Luongo, N. Kenneth and Salik, Naeem (2007) 'Building Confidence in Pakistan's Nuclear Security', *Arms Control Today*, www.armscontrol.org/act/2007_12/Luongo (accessed 14 June 2012).
Mahmood, Afzal (1988) 'Priorities in Foreign Policy', *Dawn*, 14 December.
——(1999) 'Pakistan's Stance on FMCT', *Dawn*, 12 January.
Malik, A. Ghulam (2000) 'Nuclear Non-Proliferation and the NPT Review Conference: The Pakistani Perspective', in *Nuclear Disarmament and Non-Proliferation: The Role of the Nuclear Non-Proliferation Treaty*, www.kas.de/wf/doc/kas_5077-1522-2-30.pdf?040722104256 (accessed 7 May 2012), 43–44.
Maoz, Zeev (2003) 'The Mixed Blessing of Israel's Nuclear Policy', *International Security* 28(2): 44–77.
Matinuddin, Kamal (2002) *The Nuclearisation of South Asia*, Oxford: Oxford University Press.
McNamara, S. Robert (1983) 'The Military Role of Nuclear Weapons: Perceptions and Misperceptions', *Foreign Affairs* 62(1): 59–80.
——(1986) *Blundering into Disaster: Surviving the First Century of the Nuclear Age*, New York: Pantheon.
Mearsheimer, J. John (1984) 'Nuclear Weapons and Deterrence in Europe', *International Security* 9(3): 19–46.
——(1993) 'The Case for a Ukrainian Nuclear Deterrent', *Foreign Affairs* 72(3): 51–66.
——(2001) *The Tragedy of Great Power Politics*, New York: W.W. Norton & Co.
——(2009) 'Reckless States and Realism', *International Relations* 23(2): 241–56.
Mecklenbeck, Michale Schulte, Kuehberger, Anton and Ranyard, Rob (2010) *A Handbook of Process Tracing Methods for Decision Research: A Critical Review and User's Guide*, UK: Psychology Press.
Mehdi, Syed Anwer (1994) 'Nuclear Ambivalence Versus a Well-Defined Policy Involving Maximum Political Fallout', *The Citadel* (Pakistan) 2: 55–67.
Mehmood, Saqib (2012) 'Our Nuclear Strategy', *Pakistan Observer*, pakobserver.net/detailnews.asp?id = 119075 (accessed 18 June 2012).
Mehrotra, K. and Mohan, Brij (1980) *Pakistan's Nuclear Bomb*, New Delhi: Sopan Publishing House.
Mesquita, B.B. and Riker, H. William (1982) 'An Assessment of the Merits of Selective Proliferation', *Journal of Conflict Resolution* 26(2): 283–306.
Mian, Zia (ed.) (1995) *Pakistan's Atomic Bomb and the Search for Security*, Lahore: Gautam Publishers.
——(1996) 'Why Pakistan Should Sign the CTBT', *The News*, 5 August.
——(2012) '*Pakistan*', www.princeton.edu/sgs/faculty-staff/zia-mian/Pakistan-nuclear-modernization-2012.pdf (accessed 27 June 2012), 58.
Mian, Zia, Nayyar, H.A. and Ramana, V.M. (2004) 'Making Weapons, Talking Peace: Resolving the Dilemma of Nuclear Negotiations', *Economic and Political Weekly* 39 (29): 3221–24.
——(2006) 'Fissile Materials in South Asia and the Implications of the US-India Nuclear Deal', *International Panel on Fissile Materials*, www.armscontrol.org/pdf/20060711_IPFM-DraftReport-US-India-Deal.pdf (accessed 27 June 2012).

Mian, Zia and Ramana, V.M. (1999) 'Beyond Lahore: From Transparency to Arms Control', *Economic and Political Weekly*, www.epw.in/commentary/beyond-lahore-transparency-arms-control.html (accessed 28 June 2012).

——(2006) 'Wrong Ends, Means, and Needs: Behind the US Nuclear Deal with India', *Arms Control Today* (January–February).

Miller, E. Steven (2002) 'The Utility of Nuclear Weapons and the Strategy of No-First-Use', www.pugwash.org/reports/nw/miller.htm (accessed 31 January 2012).

Mirza, Nasrullah and Sadiq, M. (2008) 'Indo-US 123 Agreement: Impacts on Deterrence Stability in South Asia', www.sassu.org.uk/pdfs/Research_Report_7.pdf (accessed 7 August 2012).

Mizari, M. Shireen (1995) 'NPT: An Unfair Treaty Pakistan Must Not Sign', in Tariq Jan (ed.) *Pakistan's Security and the Nuclear Option*, Islamabad: Institute of Policy Studies, 29–38.

——(1999) *India's Nuclear Doctrine in Perspective and Pakistan's Option*, www.defencejournal.com/oct99/india-doctrine.htm (accessed 4 March 2012).

——(2004) 'Understanding Pakistan's Nuclear Doctrine', *Strategic Studies* XXIV(3): 1–20.

——(2009) 'India's Arihant: Upping the Psychological Ante', pakistankakhudahafiz.wordpress.com/2009/07/30/india%E2%80%99s-arihant-%E2%80%94-upping-the-psychological-ante/ (accessed 21 June 2012).

Morgan, M. Patrick (1999) *Deterrence Now*, Cambridge: Cambridge University Press.

Morgenthau, J.H. (1946) *Scientific Man vs. Power Politics*, Chicago, IL: University of Chicago Press.

——(1978) *Politics Among Nations: The Struggle for Power and Peace*, 5th edn (revised), New York: Knopf.

Moshaver, Ziba (1991) *Nuclear Weapons Proliferation in the Indian Subcontinent*, London: Macmillan.

Muller, J. (1988) 'The Essential Irrelevance of Nuclear Weapons: Stability in the Post War World', *International Security* 13(2): 55–79.

Murphy, Katharine (2011) 'Uranium: Now for a Deal with India', www.theage.com.au/national/uranium-now-for-a-deal-with-india-20111204-1odkn.html (accessed 9 February 2012).

Musharraf, Pervaiz (2000) 'May 28 Address to the Nation', in R. Hussein, *Nuclear Doctrines in South Asia*, SASSU Research Report, No. 4, 12.

——(2005 [2002]) 'An Interview to a German Magazine', in R.P. Lavoy, 'Pakistan's Nuclear Doctrine', in R. Dossani and S.H. Rowen (eds) *Prospects for Peace in South Asia*, California: Stanford University Press, 283.

——(2006) 'Musharraf, Pervaiz's address to the 6th National Security Workshop at National Defence College', 2 March, presidentmusharraf.wordpress.com/2005/01/09/6th-national-security-2006/ (accessed 25 February 2012).

Nadeem, Shehzad (2006) 'The Regional Implications of the US India Nuclear Agreement', www.fpif.org/articles/the_regional_implications_of_the_us-india_nuclear_agreement (accessed 9 February 2012).

Naik, A.J. (1986) *The Pak Bomb and Rajiv's India*, New Delhi: National Publishing House.

Naik, B.B. (1932) *Ideals of Ancient Hindu Politics and the Arthashastra of Kautilya*, Dharwar.

Nair, Vijai (1999) 'The Structure of an Indian Nuclear Deterrent', in Amitabh Mattoo (ed.) *India's Nuclear Deterrent, Pokhran II and Beyond*, India: Har Anand Publications.

Narang, Viping (2009) 'Posturing for Peace? Pakistan's Nuclear Postures and South Asian Stability', *International Security* 34(3): 38–78.

National Security Council (1950) 'A Report to the National Security Council – NSC 68', 12 April, 40, www.trumanlibrary.org/whistlestop/study_collections/coldwar/documents/pdf/10-11.pdf (accessed 3 February 2012).

NATO (North Atlantic Treaty Organization) (2012) 'Deterrence and Defence Posture Review (DDPR)', www.nato.int/cps/en/natolive/official_texts_87597.htm (accessed 22 May 2012).

Nayyar, A.H. and Mian, Zia (2010) 'The Limited Military Utility of Pakistan's Battlefield Use of Nuclear Weapons in Response to Large Scale Indian Conventional Attack', spaces.brad.ac.uk:8080/download/attachments/748/Brief61doc.pdf?version =1&modificationDate=1290273544000 (accessed 11 April 2012).

Nelson, Dean and Farmer, Ben (2011) 'Pakistan Threatens Nuclear Arms Race over India Deal', www.telegraph.co.uk/news/worldnews/asia/pakistan/8286301/Pakistan-threatens-nuclear-arms-race-over-India-deal.html (accessed 9 February 2012).

Nitze, P. (1960) 'The Secretary and the Execution of Foreign Policy', in D. Price (ed.) *Secretary of State*, New Jersey: Prentice Hall.

Nizamani, K. Haider (1999) 'Nuclear Weapons and Kashmir', *Dawn*, 22 February.

——(2000) '*The Roots of Rhetoric: Politics of Nuclear Weapons in India and Pakistan*', USA: Praeger.

——(2008) 'Our Region Their Theories: A Case for Critical Security Studies in South Asia', in N.C. Behera (ed.) *International Relations in South Asia: Search for an Alternative Paradigm*, London: Sage Publications.

——(2009) 'Pakistan Atomic Public: Survey Results', in I. Abraham (ed.) *South Asian Cultures of the Bomb: Atomic Publics and the State in India and Pakistan*, Indiana: Indiana University Press.

Norris, R.S. and Kristensen, H.M. (2007) 'Nuclear Notebook: Pakistan's Nuclear Forces', Bulletin of the Atomic Scientists 63(3): 71–74.

Nunn, Sam (2012) 'Away from a World of Peril', *Survival* 54(1): 234–44.

Nye, S.J. (1981) 'Sustaining Non-Proliferation in the 1980s', *Survival* 23(3): 98–107.

——(1985) 'NPT: The Logic of Inequality', *Foreign Policy* 59: 123–31.

Palit, K.D. and Namboodri, S.K.P. (1979) *Pakistan's Islamic Bomb*, New Delhi: Vikas Publications.

Pande, Aparna (2011) *Explaining Pakistan's Foreign Policy: Escaping India*, New York: Routledge.

Pande, Savita (1991) *Pakistan's Nuclear Policy*, New Delhi: B.R. Publishing Corporation.

Pandit, Rajat (2008) 'Going Ballistic: India Looks to Join Elite Missile Club', *The Times of India*, articles.timesofindia.indiatimes.com/2008-05-13/india/27760252_1_agni-iv-agni-iii-agni-programme-director (accessed 22 June 2012).

——(2012) *Nuclear Weapons Only for Strategic Deterrence: Army Chief*, articles.timesofindia.indiatimes.com/2012-01-16/india/30631202_1_nuclear-arsenal-nuclear-retaliation-nuclear-weapons (accessed 9 April 2012).

Parimoo, N.J. (1984) 'US False Alarm to Pak of Indian Preventive Attack', *Times of India*.

Pathak, K.K. (1980) *Nuclear Policy of India*, New Delhi: Gitajali Prakashan.

Pattnaik, Soumyajit (1998) 'India's "Four-Fold" Nuclear Strategy Noted', *Pioneer*, FBIS-TAC, 98–133.

Payne, B. Keith (2012) 'How Much is Enough? A Goal Driven Approach to Defining Key Principles for Measuring the Adequacy of US Strategic Forces', *Contemporary Strategy* 31(1): 3–17.

Pearlman, Jonathan (2011) 'Julia Gillard Seeks Australia Nuclear Deal with India', www.telegraph.co.uk/earth/energy/nuclearpower/8934139/Australia-ruling-party-backs-plans-to-sell-uranium-to-India.html (accessed 9 February 2012).

Perkovich, George (1993) 'A Nuclear Third Way in South Asia', *Foreign Policy* 91: 84–104.

Perkovich, George and Acton, M. James (eds) (2009) *Abolishing Nuclear Weapons: A Debate*, Carnegie Endowment for International Peace.

Phillips, Andrew (2012) 'Horsemen of the Apocalypse? Jihadist Strategy and Nuclear Instability in South Asia', *International Politics* 49(3): 297–317.

Potter, C. William, Soko, Nikolai, Muller, Harald and Schaper, Annette (2000) 'Tactical Nuclear Weapons: Options for Control', UNIDIR, unidir.org/pdf/ouvrages/pdf-1-92-9045-136-X-en.pdf (accessed 10 April 2012).

Price, M. Richard (1995) *The Chemical Weapons Taboo*, New York: Cornell University Press.

PugWash Council (1995) 'On the No First Use of Nuclear Weapons Towards Global Zero', 10 December, www.pugwash.org/award/Rotblatnobel.htm (accessed February 2012).

Qaiser, Rana (1998) 'Senate Supports Government Against India', *The Nation*, 15 May.

Qayyum, Abdul (1979) 'Nuclear Power and the US Dual Standards', *Dawn*, 26 April.

Quester, G.H. (1973) *The Politics of Nuclear Proliferation*, Baltimore, MD: Johns Hopkins University Press.

——(1991a) 'Conception of Nuclear Threshold Status', in C.R. Karp (ed.) *Security with Nuclear Weapons: Different Perspectives with National Security*, Oxford: Oxford University Press.

——(1991b) 'Knowing and Believing about Nuclear Proliferation', *Security Studies* 1 (2): 270–82.

Rahman, Fazal (2007) 'Pakistan's Evolving Relations with China, Russia, and Central Asia', in I. Akihiro (ed.) *Eager Eyes Fixed on Eurasia: Russia and its Neighbours in Crisis*, Report No. 16-1, The Salvic Research Centre.

Rais, Rasul Bakhsh (2005) 'Conceptualizing Nuclear Deterrence: Pakistan's Posture', *India Review* 4(2): 144–72.

Rajagopalan, Rajesh (2005) *Second Strike: Arguments about Nuclear War in South Asia*, New Delhi: Viking.

Rajaraman, R. (2005a) 'Cap the Nuclear Arsenal Now', www.pugwash.org/reports/nw/rajanews2.htm (accessed 28 June 2012).

——(2005b) 'India-U.S. Deal and the Nuclear Ceiling', *The Hindu*, www.hindu.com/2005/09/10/stories/2005091003921000.htm (accessed 28 June 2012).

Ramana, M.V. (2009) 'The Impact of the Indo-US Nuclear Deal on the NPT and the Global Climate Regime', 8 December, www.boell.de/intlpolitics/security/foreign-affairs-security-7983.html (accessed 7 August 2012).

Rashid, Ahmed (2000) *Taliban. Islam, Oil and the New Great Game in Central Asia*, I. B. Taurus.

Rashid, Haroon (2008) 'Pakistan Reveals Defence Spending', BBC News, 11 June, news.bbc.co.uk/1/hi/world/south_asia/7449179.stm (accessed 15 June 2012).

Ray, Bipasha (2008) 'The Evolving India-US Strategic Relationship: A Compendium of Articles and Analyses', www.comw.org/pda/0603india.html (accessed 9 February 2012).

Reagan, W. Ronald (1983) 'National Address of Ronald Wilson Reagan March 23, 1983', www.presidentialrhetoric.com/historicspeeches/reagan/nationalsecurity.html (accessed 19 February 2012).

Reddy, B. Muralidhar (2003) 'Pak. Has Sufficient Deterrence', *The Hindu*, 7 March.
Riedel, Bruce (2009) 'American Diplomacy and the 1999 Kargil Summit at Blair House', in R.P. Lavoy (ed.) *Asymmetric Warfare in South Asia: The Causes and Consequences of the Kargil Conflict*, New York: Cambridge University Press, 130–43.
Rizvi, Askari Hassan (1993) *Pakistan and the Geostrategic Environment: A Study of Foreign Policy*, New York: St Martin Press.
——(1998a) 'Pakistan in 1998: The Polity Under Pressure', *Asian Survey* 39(1): 177–84.
——(1998b) 'Civil-Military Relations in Contemporary Pakistan', *Survival* 40(2): 96–113.
——(2001) 'Pakistan's Nuclear Testing', *Asian Survey* 41(6): 943–55.
——(2011) 'On Civil-Military Relations', *Pakistan Today*, December, www.pakistantoday.com.pk/2011/12/27/comment/columns/on-civil-military-relations/ (accessed 23 April 2013).
Rogov, Sergei M., Esin, Viktor, Zolotarev, Paval S. and Yarynich, Valerity (2010) 'Sood'ba Stratyegichyeskih Voyennoye Obozryeniy Poslye Pragi' [The Fate of Strategic Arms after Prague], www.ng.ru/concepts/2010-08-27/1_strategic.html (accessed 23 October 2012).
Rosenberg, Mathew and Hussein, Zahid (2009) 'Pakistan's Leader Stirs Fresh Turmoil', *The Wall Street Journal*, online.wsj.com/article/SB123561113179577559.html (accessed 8 November 2010).
Rousseau, J. Jean (1997) 'The State of War', in M.M. Doyle and G.J. Ikenberry (eds) *New Thinking in International Theory*, Boulder, CO: Westview Press.
Saeed, Yousuf (2004) 'Motivation of Nuclear Proliferation in Pakistan: The India Factor', *Journal of South Asia and Middle Eastern Studies* XXVII(4): 34–51.
Sagan, D. Scott (1994) 'The Perils of Proliferation: Organisation Theory, Deterrence Theory, and the Spread of Nuclear Weapons', *Security Studies* 18(4): 66–107.
——(1995) *The Limits of Safety: Organisations, Accidents, and Nuclear Weapons*, New Jersey: Princeton University Press.
——(2000) 'The Origins of Military Doctrine and Command and Control System', in S.D. Sagan, J.J. Wirtz, J. James and L.R. Peter (eds) *Planning the Unthinkable: How New Powers Will Use Nuclear, Biological, and Chemical Weapons*, London: Cornell University, 16–46.
——(2001) 'The Perils of Proliferation in South Asia', *Asian Survey* 41(6): 1064–86.
——(2009a) *Inside Nuclear South Asia*, California: Stanford University Press.
——(2009b) 'The Case for No First Use', *Survival* 51(3): 175–76.
Sagan, D. Scott and Waltz, Kenneth (2003) *The Spread of Nuclear Weapons: A Debate Renewed*, New York: W.W Norton & Co.
Sahni, Varun (2009) 'A Dangerous Exercise: Brasstacks as Non-Nuclear Near War', in S. Ganguly and P. Kapur (eds) *Nuclear Proliferation in South Asia: Crisis Behaviour and the Bomb*, London: Routledge, 12–35.
Salamat, Zarina (1992) *Pakistan: 1947–58*, Islamabad: National Institute of Historical and Cultural Research.
Salik, Naeem (2006) 'Minimum Deterrence and India-Pakistan Nuclear Dialogue: Case Study on Pakistan', www.centrovolta.it/landau/content/binary/01.%20Naeem%20Salik-Minimum%20deterrence%20and%20India%20Pakistan%20dialogie,%20PAKISTAN.%20Case%20Study%202006.pdf (accessed 18 June 2012).
——(2009) *The Genesis of South Asian Nuclear Deterrence: Pakistan's Perspective*, London: Oxford University Press.
Sasikumar, Karthika (2009) 'Crisis and Opportunity: The 1990 Nuclear Crisis in South Asia', in S. Ganguly and P. Kapur (eds) *Nuclear Proliferation in South Asia: Crisis Behaviour and the Bomb*, London: Routledge, 76–99.

Sattar, Abdul (1995) 'Nuclear Issue in South Asia: A Pakistani Perspective', in Tariq Jan (ed.) *Pakistan's Security and the Nuclear Option*, Islamabad: Institute of Policy Studies, 55–90.
——(2007) *Pakistan's Foreign Policy – 2005: A Concise History*, Karachi: Oxford University Press.
Sattar, Abdul, Khan, Zulfiqar A. and Shahi, Agha (1999) 'Securing the Nuclear Peace', *The News*, 5 October.
Sauer, Tom (2005) *Nuclear Inertia. US Nuclear Weapons Policy after the Cold War*, London: I.B. Tauris.
——(2009) 'A Second Nuclear Revolution: From Nuclear Primacy to Post-Existential Deterrence', *Strategic Studies* 32(5): 745–67.
Sauer, Tom and van der Zwaan, Bob (2011) 'US Tactical Nuclear Weapons in Europe After NATO's Lisbon Summit: Why their Withdrawal is Desirable and Feasible', belfercenter.ksg.harvard.edu/publication/21074/us_tactical_nuclear_weapons_in_eur ope_after_natos_lisbon_summit.html (accessed 15 May 2012).
Schell, J. (1982) *The Fate of the Earth*, New York: Knopf.
——(1984) *The Abolition*, New York: Alfred A. Knopf.
——(2000) 'The Folly of Arms Control', *Foreign Affairs* 79(5): 22–46.
Schelling, Thomas (1962) 'Nuclear Strategy in Europe', *World Politics* 14(3): 421–32.
——(1963) *The Strategy of Conflict*, New York: Oxford University Press, 21–28.
——(1966) *Arms and Influence*, New Haven, CT: Yale University Press, 35–55.
Schemmer, F. Benjamin (1982a) 'NATO's New Strategy: Defend Forward, but Strike Deep', *Armed Forces Journal International*: 50–68.
——(1982b) 'Defend Forward, but Strike Deep: Part II', *Armed Forces Journal International*: 68–73, 92.
——(1983) 'Defend Forward, but Strike Deep: Part III', *Armed Forces Journal International*: 48–54.
Schmidt, R. John (2009) 'The Unravelling of Pakistan', *Survival* 51(3): 29–54.
Schultz, L. Charles, Fried, R. Edward, Rivlin, M.A. and Teeters, H.N. (eds) (1971) *Setting National Priorities: The 1972 Budget*, Washington, DC: The Brookings Institution, 96–99.
Schweller, L. Randall (1996) 'Neo-Realism's Status Quo Bias: What Security Dilemma', *Security Studies* 5(3): 90–121.
Sebastian, Sunny (2011) 'India, Pakistan Should Reduce Military Expenditure: Physicians', *The Hindu*, www.thehindu.com/todays-paper/tp-national/article1485263.ece (accessed 28 June 2012).
Seng, Jordan (1997) 'Less is More: Command and Control Advantages of Minor Nuclear States', *Strategic Studies* 6(4): 50–92.
Shafqat, Saeed (2009) 'The Kargil Conflict's Impact on Pakistani Politics and Society', in R.P. Lavoy (ed.) *Asymmetric Warfare in South Asia: The Causes and Consequences of the Kargil Conflict*, New York: Cambridge University Press, 280–307.
Shahi, Agha (1995) 'Nuclear Non-Proliferation Treaty and the Security Dilemma', in Tariq Jan (ed.) *Pakistan's Security and the Nuclear Option*, Islamabad: Institute of Policy Studies, 39–53.
Shahid, Saleem (2004) 'Musharraf Rules out Rollback of N-Plan', *Gwadar News*, 13 September, www.gwadarnews.com/newsdetail.asp?newsID=341 (accessed 15 June 2012).
Shaikh, Farzana (2002) 'Pakistan's Nuclear Bomb: Beyond the Non-Proliferation Regime', *International Affairs* 78(1): 29–48.

Shamim, Anwar (1988) 'Pakistan's Security Concerns', *Dawn*, 2 November.
Sharif, Nawaz (1999) 'Remarks on Nuclear Policies and the CTBT', National Defence University, Islamabad, 20 May.
Sheean, Vincent (1960) *Nehru: The Years of Power*, London: Gollancz.
Shultz, P.G. (1984) 'Preventing the Proliferation of Nuclear Weapons', *Department of State Bulletin* 84: 1–100.
Shultz, P.G., Perry, J. William, Kissinger, A. Henry and Nunn, Sam (2007) 'A World Free of Nuclear Weapons', January, www.hoover.org/publications/hoover-digest/article/6109 (accessed 15 May 2012).
——(2010) 'How to Protect Our Nuclear Deterrent', *Wall Street Journal*, online.wsj.com/article/SB10001424052748704152804574628344282735008.html (accessed 15 May 2012).
Siddiqa, Ayesha (2001) *Pakistan's Arms Procurement and Military Build-up, 1979–99: In Search of a Policy*, New York: Palgrave.
——(2007) *Military Insurance Inside Pakistan's Military Economy*, London: Pluto Press.
Singh, Abhijit (2011) 'Pakistan: Testing of Tactical Nuclear Weapons', *India Defence Review* 26(3): 1–4, www.indiandefencereview.com/geopolitics/Pakistan-Testing-of-Tactical-Nuclear-Weapons.html (accessed 23 March 2012).
Singh, Jasjit (ed.) (1990) *India and Pakistan: Crisis of Relationship*, New Delhi: Lancer Publications.
——(1993) 'Prospects for Nuclear Proliferation', in Serge Sur (ed.) *Nuclear Deterrence: Problems and Perspectives in the 1990s*, New York: United Nations Institute for Disarmament Research.
——(2000) 'Reducing Defence Expenditure: Issues and Challenges for South Asian Countries', in Jasit Singh and Perviaz Iqbal Cheema (eds) *Defence Expenditure in South Asia: An Overview*, Regional Centre for Strategic Studies, www.rcss.org/publication/policy_paper/RCSS%20Policy%20Studies%2010.pdf (accessed 20 June 2012).
Singh, Madhur (2008) 'US-India Nuclear Deal Goes Through', www.time.com/time/world/article/0,8599,1846460,00.html (accessed 9 February 2012).
Singh, Ranjit (2010) 'Nuclear Weapons as a Deterrent in South Asia: An Analysis', *Asia Pacific Journal of Social Sciences* II(2): 30–53.
Singh, Sampooran (1971) *India and the Nuclear Bomb*, New Delhi: C. Chand.
Singh, Swaran (2011) 'India Nuclear Doctrine: Ten Years Since the Kargil Conflict', in Bhumitra Chakma (ed.) *The Politics of Nuclear Weapons in South Asia*, London: Ashgate, 57–75.
SIPRI (Stockholm International Peace Research Institute) (n.d.) 'Release on Military Expenditure Database', www.sipri.org/databases/milex (accessed 19 March 2012).
Smith, Jeffrey (1996) 'Pakistan's Plans Tit for Tat Test of Nuclear Blast, Officials Say', *The Washington Post*.
Snyder, H. Glenn (1961) *Deterrence and Defence: Towards a Theory of National Security*, Connecticut: Greenwood Press.
——(1965) 'The Balance of Power and the Balance of Terror', in P. Seabury (ed.) *The Balance of Power*, San Francisco: Chandler.
Sokolski, Henry (1994) 'Fighting Proliferation with Intelligence', *Orbis*: 245–26.
——(2008) 'Pakistan's Nuclear Plans: What's Worrisome, What Avertable?' in Henry Sokolski (ed.) *Pakistan's Nuclear Future*, Pennsylvania: Strategic Studies Institute, 1–17.

—— (2010) 'The Nuclear Non-proliferation Treaty's Untapped Potential to Prevent Proliferation', in Henry Sokolaski (ed.) *Reviewing the Nuclear Non-Proliferation Treaty*, USA: Strategic Studies Institute.

Spector, S.L. (1984) *Nuclear Proliferation Today*, Cambridge: Mass Ballinger.

—— (1995) 'Neo-Non-Proliferation', *Survival* 37(1): 66–85.

Spykman, J.N. (1942) *American Strategy in World Politics: The United States and the Balance of Power*, New York: Harcourt Brace and Company.

Squassoni, Sharon (2010) 'The US-Indian Deal and its Impact', *Arms Control Today* (July– August).

State Department (2010a) 'Discussion between Under Secretary Newsom and Pakistan's Minister of State for Foreign Affairs Agha Shahi on the Reprocessing Issue', 14 August 1978, State Department cable 205550 to Embassy Islamabad, declassified, www.gwu.edu/~nsarchiv/nukevault/ebb333/index.htm#1 (accessed 1 January 2012).

—— (2010b) 'Pakistan Reprocessing', 12 August 1978, State Department cable 204785 to Embassy Islamabad, declassified, www.gwu.edu/~nsarchiv/nukevault/ebb333/index.htm#1 (accessed 1 January 2012).

Stout, Mark (2010) *Minimal Deterrence Makes Minimal Sense*, www.au.af.mil/au/awc/awcgate/nssc/op-ed/minimal_deterrence_makes_minimal_sense.pdf (accessed 5 March 2012).

Subrahmanyam, K. (1994) 'Nuclear Force Design and Minimum Deterrence Strategy for India', in Bharat Karnad (ed.) *Future Imperilled*, New Delhi: Viking.

—— (1995) 'The Emerging Environment: Regional Views on WMD Proliferation', in H.W. Lewis and E.S. Johnson (eds) *Weapons of Mass Destruction: New Perspectives on Counter Proliferation*, Washington, DC: National Defence University Press.

—— (1998a) 'Nuclear India in Global Politics', *Strategic Digest* 28(12).

—— (1998b) 'Not a Numbers Game: Minimum Cost of N-Deterrence', *Times of India*.

—— (1999) 'A Credible Deterrent: Logic of the Nuclear Doctrine', *Times of India*.

Sultan, Adil (2011) *Fissile Material Treaty: Prospects and Challenges*, Research Paper No. 49, www.isn.ethz.ch/isn/Digital-Library/Publications/Detail/?lng=en&id=151243 (accessed 24 March 2013).

—— (2012) 'Pakistan's Emerging Nuclear Posture: Impact of Drivers and Technology on Nuclear Doctrine', *Strategic Studies*, www.issi.org.pk/publication-files/1340000409_86108059.pdf (accessed 28 June 2012).

Sundarji, K. (1993) *Blind Men of Hindustan: India-Pak Nuclear War*, New Delhi: UBS Publishers.

—— (1995) 'Proliferation of Weapons of Mass Destruction and the Security Dimensions in South Asia: An Indian View', in H.W. Lewis and E.S. Johnson (eds) *Weapons of Mass Destruction: New Perspectives on Counter Proliferation, National Defence*, Washington, DC: University Press.

Swami, Praveen (2009a) 'A War to End a War: The Causes and Outcomes of the 2001–2 India-Pakistan Crisis', in S. Ganguly and P. Kapur (eds) *Nuclear Proliferation in South Asia: Crisis Behaviour and the Bomb*, London: Routledge, 144–61.

—— (2009b) 'The Impact of Kargil Conflict and Kashmir on Indian Politics and Society', in R.P. Lavoy (ed.) *Asymmetric Warfare in South Asia: The Causes and Consequences of the Kargil Conflict*, New York: Cambridge University Press, 258–79.

Synnott, Hilary (2009) 'What is Happening in Pakistan?' *Survival* 51(1): 61–80.

Taliaferro, W. Jeffrey (2000) 'Security Seeking Under Anarchy: Defensive Realism Revisited', *International Security* 25(3): 128–61.

Tannewald, Nina (1996) *Dogs that Don't Bark: The United States, the Role of Norms, and the Non-Use of Nuclear Weapons*, PhD dissertation, Cornell University, 171.

Tansey, Oisin (2007) 'Process Tracing and Elite Interviewing: A Case for Non-probability Sampling', *Political Science and Politics* 40(4): 1–23.

Tasleem, Sadia (2011) 'Towards an Indo-Pak Nuclear Lexicon-II: Credible Minimum Deterrence', *Nuclear South Asia*, The IPCS Nuclear Security Program Quarterly, www.ipcs.org/Nuke_Quarterly-Jan-Mar_2011.pdf (accessed 18 June 2012).

Thayer, A. Bradley (1995) 'The Causes of Nuclear Proliferation and the Utility of the Nuclear Non-Proliferation Regime', *Security Studies* 4(3): 463–519.

Thee, M. (1986) *Military Technology, Military Strategy and the Arms Race*, London: Croom Helm.

Thucydides (1954) *History of the Peloponnesian War*, trans. Rex Warner, Harmondsworth: Penguin.

Timerbaev, Ronald (2005) 'What Next for the NPT: Facing the Moment of Truth', *IAEA Bulletin* 46(2), March, www.iaea.org/Publications/Magazines/Bulletin/Bull462/46203590407.pdf (accessed 9 May 2012).

Ullman, H. Richard (1972) 'No First Use of Nuclear Weapons', *Foreign Affairs* 50(4): 669–83.

Ullom, Joel (1994) 'Enriched Uranium Versus Plutonium: Proliferant Preferences in the Choice of Fissile Material', *Non-Proliferation Review* (Fall): 1–15.

Umar, Lubna (2010) 'Azm-e-Nau and Renewed Security Trends', *Pakistan Observer*, pakobserver.net/detailnews.asp?id=24748 (accessed 6 April 2012).

United Nations (n.d.) 'United Nations Disarmament Commission', www.un.org/disarmament/HomePage/DisarmamentCommission/UNDiscom.shtml (accessed 2 August 2012).

UN General Assembly (1965) *First Committee, 20th Session*, 22 September–2 December, Political and Security Questions: Summary Records of Meetings, 96–97.

—— (1968) *Official Records, 22nd Session, First Committee, 1580th Meeting*, 6 June, 9.

US Arms Control and Disarmament Agency (1971) *Documents on Disarmament, 1971*, Washington, DC: US Arms Control and Disarmament Agency, 489–90.

—— (1975) *Documents on Disarmament, 1974*, Washington, DC: Government Printing Office Series.

US Government (1965) *Congressional Record III*, 14566, 23 June.

US Senate Committee on Government Affairs (1992) 'Weapons Proliferation in the New World Order', hearing, 102nd Congress, 2nd session, 15 January.

Usmani, Ishrat (1960) 'Atomic Energy in Pakistan', *Pakistan Quarterly* X(2).

Wafa, Jafar (1993) 'Our Security Option', *Dawn*, 3 August.

Waltz, Kenneth (1959) *Man, the State, and War: A Theoretical Analysis*, New York: Columbia University Press.

—— (1979) *Theory of International Politics*, New York: McGraw Hill, Inc.

—— (1981) *The Spread of Nuclear Weapons: More May Be Better*, Adelphi Paper No. 171, London: International Institute for Strategic Studies.

—— (1986) 'Reflection on Theory of International Politics: A Response to My Critic', in R.O. Keohane (ed.) *Neo-realism and its Critics*, New York: Columbia University Press, 322–46.

—— (1989) 'The Origin of War in Neo-Realist Theory', in I.R. Rotberg and K.T. Rabb (eds) *The Origin and Prevention of Major Wars*, Cambridge: Cambridge University Press, 39–52.

—— (1990a) 'Realist Thought and Neorealist Theory', *Journal of International Affairs* 44 (Spring–Summer): 21–37.

—— (1990b) 'Nuclear Myths and Political Realities', *The American Political Science Review* 84(3): 731–45.

—— (1996) 'International Politics is not Foreign Policy', *Security Studies* 6(1): 54–57.

—— (1997) 'Thoughts about Virtual Nuclear Arsenals', *Washington Quarterly* 20(3): 153–61.

Weissman, Steve and Krosney, Herbert (1981) *The Islamic Bomb: The Nuclear Threat to Israel and the Middle East*, New York: Times Books.

Weitz, Richard (2008) 'Pakistan: Analysing Civil-Military Relations in Islamabad', www.eurasianet.org/departments/insight/articles/eav102808.shtml (accessed 7 February 2012).

Wells, F. Samuel (1981) 'The Origin of Massive Retaliation', *Political Science Quarterly* 96(1): 31–52.

Weltman, J. John (1980) 'Nuclear Devolution and World Order', *World Politics* 32(2): 169–93.

—— (1981) 'Managing the Multi-Polarity', *International Security* 6(3): 182–94.

Wilson, Ward (2008) 'The Myth of Nuclear Deterrence', *The Non-Proliferation Review* 15(3): 421–39.

—— (2012) 'Part II: Continuing to Question the Reliability of Nuclear Deterrence', *The Non-Proliferation Review* 19(1): 69–74.

Wirsing, G.R. (1991) *Pakistan's Security under Zia, 1977–1988: The Policy Imperative of a Peripheral Asian State*, New York: St Martin's Press.

Woerner, Manfred and Wurzbach, K. Peter (1982) 'NATO's New Conventional Option', *The Wall Street Journal*, 30.

Wohlstetter, Albert (1958) 'The Delicate Balance of Terror', *Foreign Affairs* 37(1): 211–34.

Wolpert, S. (1993) *Zulfi Bhutto of Pakistan: His Life and Times*, Oxford: Oxford University Press.

Wriggins, Howard W. (1977) 'The Balancing Process in Pakistan's Foreign Policy', in L. Ziring, R. Braibanti and H.W. Wriggins (eds) *Pakistan: The Long Way*, Durham, NC: Duke University Press, 301–39.

Yamin, Tughral (2008) 'Pakistan's Nuclear Policy and Doctrine: Ten Years Hence – Where do We Go from Here?' *Margalla Papers* (Special Issue), Islamabad, Pakistan.

Yasmeen, Samina (1999) 'Pakistan's Nuclear Tests: Domestic Debate and International Determinants', *Australian Journal of International Affairs* 53(1): 43–56.

—— (2001) 'Is Pakistan's Nuclear Bomb an Islamic Bomb?' *Asian Studies Review* 25 (2): 201–15.

Yu, Rong and Guangqian, Peng (2009) 'Nuclear No-First-Use Revisited', *China Security* 5(1): 81–90.

Zahra, Farah (1999) 'Pakistan's Road to a Minimum Nuclear Deterrent', *Arms Control Today* (July–August): 1–8.

—— (2011) 'Comment: Credible Minimum Nuclear Deterrence – II', *Daily Times*, 26 August, www.dailytimes.com.pk/default.asp?page=2011%5C08%5C26%5Cstory_26-8-2011_pg3_2 (accessed 20 February 2012).

—— (2012) 'Credible Minimum Nuclear Deterrence in South Asia', *IPRI* XII(2): 1–14.

Zaman, Ali (2003) 'India's Increased Involvement in Afghanistan and Central Asian: Implications for Pakistan', *IPRI Journal* III(2): 1–20.

Zeb, Rizwan (2006) 'David versus Goliath? Pakistan's Nuclear Doctrine: Motivations, Principles and Future', *Defence & Security Analysis* 22(4): 387–408.

Periodicals

The Balochistan Times (Quetta)
The Daily Times (Lahore)
The Dawn International (Karachi)
Defence Journal (Karachi)
The Economic Times (Mumbai)
The Friday Times (Lahore)
The Frontier Post (Peshawar)
The Guardian (London)
The Hindu (Madras)
The Hindustan Times (New Delhi)
The Indian Express (Mumbai)
The Los Angeles Times (Los Angeles)
The Muslim (Islamabad)
The Nation (Rawalpindi)
The News (Islamabad)
The New York Times (New York)
The New Yorker (New York)
The Observer (London)
The Pakistan Observer (Islamabad)
The Pakistan Times (Islamabad)
The Telegraph (London)
Time Magazine
The Times of India (New Delhi)
The Express Tribune (Pakistan)
The Washington Post (Washington, DC)
Washington Times (Washington, DC)

Useful digital sources

American Academy of Arts and Sciences: www.amacad.org
Arms Control Association, the authoritative source on arms control: www.armscontrol.org/countryresources
Atlantic Council: www.acus.org
Belfer Center for Science and International Affairs: belfercenter.ksg.harvard.edu
Brookings Institute: www.brookings.edu
Carnegie Endowment for International Peace: carnegieendowment.org
Center for Defense Information: www.cdi.org
Center for a New American Security: www.cnas.org
Center for Strategic and International Studies, USA: csis.org
Centre for International Strategic Studies, Islamabad: www.ciss.org.pk
Centre for Security Studies: www.css.ethz.ch/about/index_EN
CIA Directorate of Intelligence: www.cia.gov/offices-of-cia/intelligence-analysis/index.html
Congressional Research Service Report: www.fas.org/sgp/crs/index.html
Cooperative Monitoring Centre: www.cmc.sandia.gov
Council of Foreign Relations: www.cfr.org
European Union Institute for Security Studies: www.iss.europa.eu

Federation of American Scientists: www.fas.org
Foreign Press Centers: fpc.state.gov
Freedom House: www.freedomhouse.org
Gloria Centre: Global Research in International Affairs: www.gloria-center.org
Human Rights Commission of Pakistan: www.hrcp-web.org (articles on overall security apparatus of Pakistan)
Institute for Defence Studies and Analysis, India: www.idsa.in
Institute of Peace and Conflict Studies: www.ipcs.org
Institute of Policy Studies, Islamabad, Pakistan: www.ips.org.pk
Institute for Policy Studies, USA: www.ips-dc.org/nuclear
Institute for Science and International Security: isis-online.org
Institute of Strategic Studies Islamabad, Pakistan: www.issi.org.pk
Institute of World Economy and International Relations: www.imemo.ru/en/
International Atomic Energy Agency: www.iaea.org
International Institute for Strategic Studies, London: www.iiss.org
Inter-Services Public Relations, Pakistan: www.ispr.gov.pk
Islamabad Policy Research Institute, Pakistan: ipripak.org
Kroc Institute for International Peace Studies: kroc.nd.edu
James Martin Center for Nonproliferation Studies: cns.miis.edu
McClatchy – Truth to Power: www.mcclatchydc.com
National Threat Initiative: www.nti.org/index.php
Nonproliferation Policy Education Center: www.npolicy.org
North Atlantic Treaty Organization: www.nato.int/cps/en/natolive/index.htm
Norwegian Institute for Defence Studies: ifs.forsvaret.no
Pakistan Atomic Energy Agency: www.paec.gov.pk
Pakistan Security Research Unit, University of Bradford: spaces.brad.ac.uk:8080/display/ssispsru/Home
Pakistani Parliament (National Assembly and Senate): www.na.gov.pk/library.html and www.senate.gov.pk/library/lib_index.htm
Pew Research Center for the People and Press: people-press.org
RAND, National Security Research Division: www.rand.org/nsrd.html
South Asia Intelligence Review: www.satp.org/satporgtp/sair/
South Asian Strategic Stability Institute, London and Islamabad: www.sassu.org.uk
The Henry L. Stimson Center: www.stimson.org
Stockholm International Peace Research Institute: www.sipri.org
Strategic Studies Institute United States Army War College: www.strategicstudiesinstitute.army.mil
Transnational Institute: www.tni.org
Union of Concerned Scientists: www.ucsusa.org
United Nations Institute for Disarmament Research: www.unidir.org
US Institute of Peace: www.usip.org
US Senate Armed Committee: armed-services.senate.gov
George Washington University, National Security Archives (Electronic Briefings): www.gwu.edu/~nsarchiv/NSAEBB/
Woodrow Wilson Center: www.wilsoncenter.org

Index

abandon 27, 89, 117
abandonment 90, 91
ability 9, 72, 74, 93, 108, 138
abolishing 129, 164, 173
absence 4, 48, 62, 66, 116, 125, 136, 141
absolutely 1, 6, 131, 132
academic 99, 108, 139, 173
accelerated 30, 121
accentuate 60, 116
accommodate 85, 154
accountability 103, 173
achieving 38, 98
acquisition 3, 19, 21, 24, 26, 30, 36, 39, 66, 121, 129
action-reaction 73, 124
adequate 5, 39, 41, 52, 56, 66
administration 28, 36, 77, 90, 108, 110, 117, 146, 149
adopting 14, 38, 91, 115
advantage 24, 31, 41, 44, 46, 71, 98
adversarial 56, 60, 74, 89, 97, 98, 102
aero-space 109, 145
Afghanistan 16, 19, 28, 30, 34, 77, 152, 154, 156, 170
Agni Missile 70
aircraft 30, 54, 61, 74, 77, 78, 81, 84, 88, 111, 137
alliance 23, 90, 107, 115, 148, 158
ambassador 32, 50, 60, 70, 109, 127, 135,
ambiguity 7, 28, 30, 41, 48, 50, 57, 84, 91, 95, 99, 106, 130, 135, 139
ambitions 28, 29, 60, 128
amendment 27, 36, 77, 85, 151
anarchy 153, 168
annihilation 10, 110, 132
apocalypse 16, 71, 164
applicable 4, 44, 55, 62, 123

archives 112, 147, 172
arms control 51, 68, 146, 158, 161
arsenals 3, 7, 11, 17, 39, 44, 46, 55, 63, 87, 124, 157, 170
assembly 23, 35, 120, 126, 147, 152, 169, 172,
assessment 17, 52, 57, 78, 84, 86, 108, 155, 161
asymmetric 152, 154, 156, 158, 160, 165, 166, 168
avoidance 4, 71

backdrop 14, 33, 40, 61, 78, 89, 91, 106, 126, 133, 137
balance 9, 54, 59, 66, 69, 75, 76, 85, 101, 105, 106, 111, 128, 152, 167, 170
ballistic 10, 61, 63, 66, 68, 74, 78, 80, 121, 124, 149, 156, 163
Bandung 114, 126, 146
battlefield 70, 102, 163
behaviour 5, 130, 146, 152, 156, 165, 168
beliefs 152, 155
Bhumitra Chakma 16, 35, 49, 67, 69, 70, 86, 109, 127, 167
bilateral 59, 61, 122, 124
blast 37, 145, 167
blurred 56, 64, 94, 96, 122
Buddha Smile 26
bureaucratic 21, 26, 73, 103

calculated 41, 48, 49, 54, 91
capability 2, 10, 18, 20, 27, 30, 36, 42, 58, 60, 64, 75, 79, 89, 93, 98, 100, 117, 124, 132, 138, 145
catastrophic 8, 92
centralized 11, 12, 132, 134, 141,
challenge 34, 66, 85, 87, 103, 129, 151, 159

changing 2, 5, 13, 39, 117, 125, 130, 136, 141, 155,
changing contour 13
changing strategic 5, 141
charismatic 20
Chinese-made 111
civil-military 17, 70, 103, 104, 111, 112, 160, 165, 170
clandestine 26, 28, 33, 81, 136, 174
classic 4, 28
collaboration 121
comparative 50, 54, 68, 111, 143, 149, 152, 153, 158
competition 2, 5, 12, 42, 44, 64, 73, 104, 124, 132, 137
complexity 44, 54, 57, 131
compromise 57, 145
concealment 11, 44, 132, 141
conceptualization 47, 134, 174
concerned 25, 83, 118, 172
confidence-building 59, 61, 174
conform 102, 113, 141
confrontation 65, 132, 139
consistently 29, 68, 75, 78, 112, 120
constitute 2, 43, 89, 90
containment 16, 28, 152
contentious 84, 93, 96, 107
contingencies 52
contingent 7, 107, 117, 121
contradicts 47, 72, 95, 138
conventional 3, 7, 9, 12, 31, 40, 54, 59, 62, 63, 79, 81, 89, 96, 99, 100, 106, 110, 112, 114, 126, 135, 159, 163
conventional forces 54, 89, 99, 101, 106
conventional vulnerabilities 30, 31, 91
conventional weapons 64
conventional force 92
conventional imbalance 63
conventional weakness 24, 33, 100, 101, 102, 107, 111
counter-force 3, 6, 7, 11, 39, 67, 89, 98, 99, 100, 110, 139, 174
counter-measures 87
counter-value 3, 6, 7, 11, 42, 89, 98, 99, 100, 139, 174
counterforce 11, 98, 99, 110, 146, 160
counterpart 70, 118, 120, 174
credibility 2, 5, 10, 15, 59, 60, 66, 81, 91, 101, 106, 113, 119, 126, 132, 135
critics 4, 11, 39, 49, 50, 55, 68, 89, 131, 151, 152, 169
culture 38, 61, 88, 110, 146, 157

damages 9, 123
dangerous 3, 50, 51, 86, 108, 128, 151, 157, 165
de-emphasis 102, 174
de-escalating 96
de-nuclearization 102
deadlock 119, 121, 140
decades 19, 38, 54, 89, 104
decapitation 11, 174
decision-making 103
declaratory 6, 15, 41, 57, 84, 92, 130, 136
declassified 27, 28, 36, 148, 168
defences 50, 68, 149
defensive 12, 39, 57, 73, 138, 168
defiant 14, 119, 125, 140
deliberately 54, 59, 93, 96
delivery 6, 10, 30, 42, 58, 68, 72, 76, 79, 85, 105, 124, 134, 138, 151
delivery capability 105
delivery missions 77, 78, 85
delivery systems 42, 44, 72, 74, 77, 84, 124, 137, 151
delivery vehicles 10, 68, 74
democracy 29, 30, 99, 103, 105
deployment 7, 11, 38, 50, 54, 56, 63, 73, 79, 103, 105, 111, 128, 132
design 16, 54, 74, 76, 81, 87, 168
destabilizing 41, 50
destroying 3, 56
determinants 20, 37, 152, 170
dilemmas 16, 67, 109, 145, 148, 158
diplomacy 23, 30, 107, 165
disarmament commission 126, 169
discourages 7, 10, 13, 97, 132, 139
dominance 69, 72, 86, 145
dossier 45, 46, 52, 75, 84, 155
dynamic 15, 39, 59, 60, 107, 135, 136

eager 34, 164
early 25, 29, 32, 62, 80, 81, 89, 90, 96, 97, 114, 116, 119, 131
economy 4, 40, 41, 47, 48, 63, 87, 94, 99, 101, 111, 134, 139, 145, 152, 167, 172
emergency 78
emerging 12, 17, 19, 38, 51, 56, 63, 66, 109, 111, 114, 126, 140, 141, 142, 145, 148, 151, 168
equilibrium 60, 66, 125
equitable 114, 140
escalate 11, 139
escalations 9, 106
essence 64, 132, 136

essentials 1, 6, 7, 13, 14, 26, 40, 44, 54, 74, 130, 131, 141
extended 6, 7, 30, 79, 116
extension 30, 31, 128
extra-regional 65, 66
extremism 43, 142

facilitate 2, 61, 85
facilities 20, 21, 23, 24, 25, 43, 44, 46, 61, 78, 98, 100, 122, 147
fast-changing 121, 126
favourable 19, 40, 113
fear 1, 8, 9, 12, 27, 56, 65, 91, 97, 100, 103, 131, 132, 133
fearful 17, 37, 51, 152
first-strike 92
first-use 111, 150, 160, 162, 170
fissile material 66, 75, 76, 77, 84, 119, 120, 121, 126, 129, 136, 138, 140, 158, 168, 169
fledged 42, 141
force-building 14, 60, 72, 73, 130
foreseeable 65, 82, 104, 121, 137
formulated 1, 2
forward-edged 70
Franco-Pakistan 26
fundamental 3, 66, 96, 109

genesis 34, 51, 55, 85, 165
Ghauri 79, 81, 86
Glenn-Symington 27
guardian 152, 171
Gwadar 52, 78, 166

H-bomb 16, 49, 67, 148
Hagerty, Devin 153
hatf missile 80, 81
headquarters 22
heavy-water 22
Herman Kahn 110
horizontal nuclear 26
horsemen 16, 71, 90, 164
hypothetically 12, 58

imbalances 56, 101, 108
imminent 94, 96, 176
imperative 36, 58, 73, 170
indefinite period 30
independence-dependence 158
India-doctrine 110, 162
India-oriented 23
India-specific 65, 141
Indian-centricity 23, 125, 140
indigenous 21, 61, 138

industry 20, 21, 22
influential 31, 90, 91, 107
inspection 12, 23, 115
installations 11, 61, 78, 94, 98
institution 16, 66, 103, 147, 150, 151, 166
intangible 54, 59, 72, 137
intensified 64, 65
inter-mediate-range 80
inter-services 86, 155, 172
internationally 126, 127, 140
invasion 34, 154, 176
Islamabad 1, 4, 5, 13, 29, 30, 50, 64, 69, 72, 77, 81, 83, 85, 88, 108, 111, 120, 126, 134, 140, 144, 145, 157, 166,

Janata 32
Japan 4, 19, 109, 110, 157
Jasjit Singh 15, 17, 157
Jervis, Robert 156
Jihadist 16, 71, 150, 151, 164
justified 57, 59, 90

Kahuta 27, 29, 94
Kanupp 22, 75
Karachi 19, 22, 25, 26, 35, 51, 111, 145, 147, 150, 166, 171,
Kidwai, Khalid 159
Kissinger, Henry 159

ladder 94
land-based 82
Landau Network 94, 95, 109, 159
large-scale 69, 94, 95
legitimacy 48, 104, 123, 125
lethality 76
limitations 62, 138
long-range 68, 70, 78, 81

Mahmud Ali Durrani 40, 49, 67, 86, 112, 142
maintenance 39, 40, 42, 58, 85
maritime 83, 110, 145, 154
massive 8, 16, 49, 58, 67, 90, 92, 98, 148, 159, 170
maturity 70
maximalist 8, 9
maximum 8, 55, 80, 81, 118, 161
Mearsheimer, John 161
militants 34, 85, 151
military-balance 69, 85, 155
miniaturization 11, 54, 74
minimality 59
minimum deterrence 16, 38, 69

176 *Index*

minimum defensive 57
minimum deterrent 2, 5
miscalculation 63
misperceptions 107, 161
missile-for-missile 56
motorway 78, 86
multidimensional 83
Musharraf, Pervaiz 162

Nagasaki 109, 131, 176
Nasr missile 82, 86, 87, 137
nation-state 101
nationalism 125
negative 6, 119, 121
neo-culturalism 99, 100, 110
nexus 65, 124, 145, 177
no-first-use 111, 150, 160, 162, 170
non-adherence 113, 125, 140, 148
non-conventional 80, 89, 177
non-deployed 6, 12, 13, 44, 63, 97, 139, 141
non-weaponized 1, 3, 5, 139
notwithstanding 10, 141
nuclear doctrinal 109
nuclear forces 70, 85
nuclear proliferation 35
nuclear strategy 17
nuclear taboo 109
nuclear weapons 18, 36, 86
nuclear ambiguity 28
nuclear deterrence 15, 152, 160
nuclear instability 164
nuclear restraint 2, 61
nuclear submarine 82, 138
nuclear-armed 68, 144
nuclear-posture-review 108
nuclear-powered 74, 82, 83, 87
numbers 1, 2, 7, 10, 12, 13, 42, 56, 58, 66, 132, 134, 168

obsessions 59
obstacle 65, 103, 137
occasions 23, 30, 104, 106, 120, 134, 140
operations 16, 43, 55, 78, 82, 86, 151, 157
opportunity 28, 32, 91, 117, 165
optimism 16, 151
organizational 11, 38, 73, 88
outstanding 64, 65, 119, 124, 140
over-ambitious 116

pace 24, 64
pacific 167
Pakistan-Afghanistan 34, 153
Pakistan-China 65, 85, 124, 154
Pakistan-nuclear 109, 159
Pakistan-nuclear-modernization 15, 52, 85
Pakistan-specific 83
paradigm 163
paradox 102, 145, 149, 158
parliament 30, 47, 116, 118, 172
particular 38, 59, 63, 73, 95, 120, 131, 159
payload 79, 80, 81
peaceful 4, 19, 20, 21, 24, 25, 33, 48, 103, 105, 115, 124
penetrability 9, 10, 72
perceived 26, 29, 54, 63
perils 16, 51, 71, 165
Perkovich, George 164
permanent 26, 105
perseveration 42
possession 2, 4, 9, 30, 36, 46, 47, 77, 97, 98, 120, 124, 128, 138
possibility 4, 7, 10, 12, 47, 49, 63, 78, 89, 110, 132
post-existential 16, 166
postures 38, 56, 60, 64, 89, 91, 143, 156, 163
potential 9, 19, 23, 28, 56, 60, 115, 126, 168
powerful 102, 104, 132
pragmatic 5, 64, 97, 114
pre-delegation 11, 132, 139
pre-emption 49, 100, 101
precision 123
priority 7, 8, 13, 19, 25, 131
probability 104, 131
proliferators 17, 128
proponents 31, 89, 91, 108
protection 10, 132, 139
protracted 12, 158
provoke 41, 65
proxies 63
proximity 92, 98, 99, 101
punishment 9, 123
pursuit 13, 20, 31, 33, 47, 48, 63, 121, 126, 136, 140

qualitatively 77
quality 59, 76, 101
quantified 2, 49, 59, 64, 72, 83, 133, 135, 141
quantity 57, 78
quarterly 15, 35, 50, 67, 68, 87, 128, 129, 144, 150, 156, 169, 170
quest 15, 22, 33, 50, 64, 85, 92, 108, 149, 156

radiation 102
radioactive 20, 21
Rajesh Basrur 5, 15, 68
rapid 42, 75, 78, 130, 136, 141
ratified 115, 126
rational 50, 58, 92
rationally 8, 11
reactors 21, 63, 75, 76, 84, 106, 138, 141, 142, 152
realism 99, 152, 156, 161, 168
reappraisal 66, 83
reawakening 110, 145
redefining 16, 147
reduction 13, 62, 64, 70, 122, 129, 143, 144, 149, 156
reflection 10, 169
regimes 103, 113, 116, 118, 122, 126, 140, 142, 153
reliable 11, 17, 55, 75, 103, 130, 134
reluctance 76, 121
reprocessing 24, 26, 27, 36, 75, 168
rescind 89, 91, 92, 100, 106, 138
resolution 17, 64, 115, 120, 127, 147, 152, 161
responsible 21, 43, 48, 50, 58, 113, 120, 124
retaliation 1, 8, 16, 29, 41, 58, 67, 90, 98, 148, 159, 170
risks 6, 9, 58, 124, 160

safeguard 22, 23, 31, 40
salience 107, 123, 124, 125, 126, 138
scenario 32, 58, 60, 65, 83, 99, 102, 113, 116, 124, 139, 155
Schelling, Thomas 166
scholars 39, 91
scientific 76, 147, 162
sea-based 3, 74
security-insecurity 149
self-declared 99
self-deterred 99
self-proclaimed 4, 54, 56
shelters 6, 9, 13, 178
shifts 63, 64, 66, 111, 127, 137
short-range 70, 80, 81, 82, 86, 156
significance 12, 14, 73, 75, 82, 97
Snyder, H. Glenn 167
sophistication 10, 81
sovereignty 29, 40, 95, 96, 99, 133
specific 2, 39, 66, 83
spectrum 55, 83, 138
spiral escalation 78
stability-instability 149
stabilizing 11, 30, 50

stewardship 1, 22
stockpiles 76, 113, 119, 120, 121, 126
strategic-dossiers 45, 46, 52, 84, 155
strengthen 12, 27, 36, 41, 73, 102
strikes 74, 88, 100, 101, 102, 106, 108, 111, 134, 153
sub-conventional 9, 83, 178
submarine 14, 74, 77, 82, 83, 84, 87, 137, 138
submarine-launched 10, 68
submarines 73, 81, 87, 131, 138
substantial 75, 97, 98, 125
superiority 6, 7, 67, 89, 102, 156
superpowers 108
surface-to-surface 74
surveillance 43, 55
survivability 2, 7, 9, 13, 15, 40, 45, 54, 56, 60, 72, 74, 103, 132, 135, 160
survive 105, 129, 148
suspicion 77, 95

taboo 50, 109, 110, 144, 164
tactical 6, 11, 58, 63, 67, 79, 81, 82, 110, 128, 144, 146, 148, 159, 164, 167
tactics 46, 141
Taliban 34, 164
tangible 54, 59, 72, 137
targeting 3, 6, 7, 11, 42, 89, 90, 98, 100, 110, 139, 146, 151
taxonomy 17, 132
technical 3, 4, 21, 29, 42, 46, 47, 80, 111
the-military-balance 85, 155
theoretical 1, 13, 17, 38, 72, 99, 130, 169
thermonuclear 9, 110, 114, 157
traditional 57, 93, 108
trajectory 124, 125
transparent 57, 67, 95, 141
transportation 85, 94
treatment 49, 64, 118, 120, 125, 138, 140

ultimately 28, 33, 70, 94
ultracentrifuge 26
unacceptable 4, 5, 8, 9, 39, 55, 58, 72, 88, 94, 97, 131, 140
unauthorized 6, 12, 17
uncertainty 8, 9, 61, 92, 93
uncontested 69, 86, 145
undersea 87, 158
universal 40, 120
unravelling 166, 179
upgrading 56, 60, 67, 72, 79, 80, 84, 101, 102, 134, 137, 142
useful 16, 34, 49, 67, 85, 94, 109, 128, 171
utility 13, 16, 62, 97, 98, 162, 163, 169

value 68, 83, 93, 151
variety 10, 67, 79, 82
verifiable 119, 120, 126, 127, 140
verified 106, 124
vertical 115
viable 55, 59, 109, 110, 136, 146
vicious 42, 47, 83, 134, 135
victory 8, 12, 90, 131
virtual 3, 4, 15, 18, 139, 170
vis-à-vis 2, 3, 5, 31, 82, 84, 92, 101
vital 8, 94
volume 31, 73, 142, 146
vulnerabilities 30, 45, 46, 91, 126

waiver 120, 126
Waltz, Kenneth 165, 169
Waltzian 10, 179
war-fighting 11, 40, 50, 55, 67, 78, 92, 101, 106, 110, 132, 136
war-like 64, 78

warhead 75, 80, 108
Wassenaar Arrangement 105
weakness 24, 33, 58, 89, 92, 100, 103, 106, 107, 111
weapon-to-weapon 5
weapons-free 121
weapons-grade 76
well-trained 21
Wohlstetter, Albert 170

Yasmeen, Samina 170
yield 75, 76, 108, 110

Zahra, Farah 170
zero-missile 122
Zia 14, 20, 23, 27, 29, 33, 47, 52, 85, 127, 136, 153, 161, 163, 170
zone 121, 122
Zulfiqar Ali Bhutto 147, 158